insight

Elementary Teacher's Book

OXFORD
UNIVERSITY PRESS

Great Clarendon Street, Oxford, OX2 6DP, United Kingdom

Oxford University Press is a department of the University of Oxford.
It furthers the University's objective of excellence in research, scholarship,
and education by publishing worldwide. Oxford is a registered trade
mark of Oxford University Press in the UK and in certain other countries

© Oxford University Press 2013

The moral rights of the author have been asserted

First published in 2013

2017 2016 2015

10 9 8 7 6 5 4 3

No unauthorized photocopying

All rights reserved. No part of this publication may be reproduced, stored
in a retrieval system, or transmitted, in any form or by any means, without
the prior permission in writing of Oxford University Press, or as expressly
permitted by law, by licence or under terms agreed with the appropriate
reprographics rights organization. Enquiries concerning reproduction outside
the scope of the above should be sent to the ELT Rights Department, Oxford
University Press, at the address above

You must not circulate this work in any other form and you must impose
this same condition on any acquirer

Links to third party websites are provided by Oxford in good faith and for
information only. Oxford disclaims any responsibility for the materials
contained in any third party website referenced in this work

ISBN: 978 0 19 401081 8   Teacher's Book
ISBN: 978 0 19 401086 3   Teacher's Resource Disk
ISBN: 978 0 19 401076 4   Teacher's Book pack

Printed in China

This book is printed on paper from certified and well-managed sources

ACKNOWLEDGEMENTS

Illustrations by: Jane Smith pp.55, 53, 136.

Contents

Introducing *insight*	4
Components of the course	6
Student's Book at a glance	8
Workbook at a glance	11
iTools	13

Teaching notes

Welcome Unit	14
Unit 1	24
Unit 2	34
Unit 3	45
Unit 4	55
Unit 5	66
Unit 6	76
Unit 7	87
Unit 8	97
Unit 9	108
Unit 10	118
Workbook answer key	129
Teacher's Resource Disk	156
Communication worksheets	156
insight DVD extra worksheets	158

Introducing *insight*

A note from the author

I'm reading a book called *The Element* by Ken Robinson. On a table nearby, a few teenagers are chatting with their friends after a long day at school. 'Our task is to educate (our students') whole being so they can face the future,' I read. 'We may not see the future, but they will and our job is to help them make something of it.' I look at the kids and think: 'That's quite a big task!'

It's a challenge we all face, whether we're teachers, parents, educational writers or youth workers. Our short-term objectives may be different: we may help teenagers or young adults pass school-leaving exams, understand maths formulae, or take part in community projects. But ultimately our long-term objectives are the same: to help young people develop a passion for and curiosity about life, to give them confidence in their own ideas, to help them become open-minded, global citizens.

When I started writing *insight* I immediately understood that the course was trying to satisfy these two objectives: a rigorous syllabus would help students develop their language skills, but it also had its eye on long-term objectives, too.

Today's students are very sophisticated. They have an amazing ability to multitask, and they often have a broad knowledge of other cultures and countries. They also have a point of view, and in *insight* we value that and seek it out – we also challenge it. We constantly ask students to question, evaluate and make cross-cultural comparisons: What do you think? Do you agree? What would you do? Speaking helps develop their confidence as language learners, but it also develops confidence in their own opinions and beliefs.

In *insight* we've added a special ingredient, too: in many texts and topics there is a fact or point of view students may not have come across before, something surprising or thought-provoking, something they may want to tell their friends in a café after school. The aim of this extra ingredient is to inspire curiosity, and a passion to discover and learn. It might help them think about an issue in a different way, and make a lesson more memorable.

That's what *insight* is all about. It strives to create the right conditions for students to grow, learn and develop their ideas and experience. To become lifelong learners. 'You cannot predict the outcome of human development,' adds Ken Robinson, wisely. 'All you can do is like a farmer create the conditions under which it will begin to flourish.'

Jayne Wildman

Aims of the course

To challenge students to think critically about the world around them

insight has been developed not only to teach students English, but also to increase their awareness of the world around them. Amongst other topics, *insight* addresses social issues, culture, literature, history, social media, science and technology. Students are encouraged to think critically about the issues raised, to evaluate their current point of view, and to share their opinions with others even once they have left the classroom. Texts and recordings include an interesting fact or unexpected opinion which students may want to tell their friends and families about. This will help make the lesson more memorable and help students recall the language and ideas they have learned.

Video documentary clips also cover cultural and historical themes, broadening students' understanding of the customs, traditions and history of English-speaking countries.

Literature insight introduces students to classic works of English literature and offers an alternative way of exploring the culture of English-speaking countries.

To inspire discussion in the classroom

The information-rich and thought-provoking texts and recordings will inspire discussion amongst students. Structured activities encourage students to question their existing opinions and the opinions of others. Activities are designed to stimulate critical thinking and to encourage participation and the exchange of opinions.

The speaking sections also teach the skills needed to be an active participant in discussions, such as interrupting, asking for clarification, disagreeing, and encouraging others to speak.

To give a deeper understanding of vocabulary and build the confidence to use it

insight gives students a deeper understanding of language and goes beyond purely teaching meaning. *insight* explores such areas as collocation, word-building and connotation to provide a fuller understanding of how vocabulary is used. This comprehensive approach allows students to use new language with greater confidence.

Vocabulary is taught in the context of reading or listening texts. All reading and listening texts are accompanied by vocabulary exercises that focus on the meaning of new vocabulary in context. Additionally, the understanding of new vocabulary is reinforced through exercises which practise their use in a new context.

All vocabulary is taught in sets organized by topic, word type or theme. Research has shown that teaching vocabulary in this way makes it easier for students to recall and use.

Vocabulary insight pages in the higher levels of the course not only explore language in more depth, but also build students' study skills, including keeping vocabulary records, ways of recording new vocabulary, and using a dictionary and a thesaurus.

These skills will help students decode, retain and use new vocabulary correctly in the future.

To help students explore the rules of grammar

The guided discovery approach to grammar in *insight* allows students to work out grammar rules for themselves and furnishes them with a better understanding of how grammar works. This approach actively engages students in the learning process, making them more likely to understand and remember the grammar point.

New structures are always presented in the context of a reading or listening text, so that students become familiar with the usage and meaning of the grammar, before manipulating its form. The guided discovery approach means students analyse examples from the texts before they deduce the rules. If necessary, the rules can be checked in the Grammar reference section in the Workbook.

The practice exercises are topic-based, so students are required to understand the usage and meaning of the grammatical structures, as well as the form. The free speaking activities allow students to use the new language in a personalized, productive and creative way.

To encourage students to reflect and take responsibility for their learning

Self-reflection plays a key role in developing active, directed and responsible learners. Learners who are able to look to themselves for solutions to problems rather than always seeking out the help of others will be better equipped for later life in academic or professional environments.

insight encourages students to reflect on their learning in a variety of ways. The Review sections in the Student's Book are an opportunity for them to see what they already know and where more work is needed. Students get marks for completing the Reviews, so they can self-monitor their progress through the book.

The Progress checks in the Workbook help students to identify gaps in their knowledge and skills, and encourage students to rely on themselves when seeking ways of improving.

The self-check feature in the Writing sections teaches students how to evaluate their own work against a set of criteria. The corrected writing assignments can also be a record of their progress.

To encourage autonomous and lifelong learning

insight prepares students for further study and life outside the classroom environment by developing their skills for lifelong learning and encouraging autonomous learning.

Strategy boxes in every unit offer step-by-step guides on how to improve core skills. Students apply the strategy immediately in a series of exercises to allow them to see how the strategy can benefit them. The strategies are relevant to students' studies now and in the future, so they will be able to use the same strategy again and again.

Writing preparation covers extensive practice and development of key skills, such as brainstorming, planning, checking, paraphrasing, avoiding repetition, etc. These skills will also help students beyond the classroom environment.

The use of authentic texts builds students' confidence by showing them that they can tackle these kinds of texts outside the classroom, in real-life situations. The accompanying activities teach students how to think critically – question ideas, analyse, rationalize, synthesize and make reasoned judgements – skills that students will need in all areas of their lives, especially in higher education and the workplace.

Autonomous learning is also encouraged by developing dictionary and thesaurus skills. Students gain a better understanding of how dictionaries and thesauruses look, the information they provide, and how and when to use them. Learning how to use these reference sources will help students with their learning now and in their future life.

These are all skills that teach self-reliance and foster autonomous learning, equipping students for life after school or university.

Components of the course

The **Student's Book** contains:
- a Welcome unit and ten topic-based **units** divided into clear sections that logically follow on from one another.
- ten **Review** pages that test all of the grammar and vocabulary points from the unit.
- five **Cumulative reviews** which review all the language taught up to that point in the Student's Book through a series of skills-based activities.
- a twelve-page **Vocabulary bank** section with twenty-three additional topic-based vocabulary sets.

The **Workbook** contains:
- further practice of everything taught in the Student's Book.
Plus
- **Challenge** exercises for stronger students.
- eleven **Progress check** pages which provide an opportunity for student reflection and self-evaluation.
- five **Literature insight** lessons based on classic works of English literature.
- five **Exam insight** sections with typical exam tasks and strategies to help students become better exam takers.
- a twenty-page **Grammar reference and practice** section containing comprehensive grammar explanations and further practice.
- ten **Pronunciation insight** points with activities to develop students' pronunciation skills.
- a **Wordlist** with dictionary-style entries giving students more information about core vocabulary.

The three **Audio CDs** contain:
- all the listening material for the Student's Book and Workbook.
- the Workbook audio is also available at www.oup.com/elt/insight

The **Teacher's Book** contains:
- **teaching notes** for the Student's Book and **answer keys** for both the Student's Book and Workbook.
- **ideas for optional extra activities** for greater flexibility.
- **background notes**, **cultural information** and **language notes**.
- **suggestions** for teaching **further vocabulary** from reading texts and questions for discussions.
- the **scripts** for the audio from the Student's Book and Workbook.

The **Teacher's Resource Disk** contains:
- additional **communication worksheets** to practise key language from the Student's Book.
- documentary **video clips** linked to each Student's Book unit plus accompanying ready-to-use video worksheets and lesson guides.
- *How to* **guides** which tackle key teaching issues and provide ideas and suggestions for activities to use in the classroom.
- **Functional language bank** – a compilation of key communicative phrases from throughout the Student's Book.
- **Writing bank** – a compilation of the key writing formats practised throughout the course with notes and tips on how to write them.

The **Test Bank MultiROM** contains:
- unit **tests** and mid- and end-of-course tests available as PDFs and editable Word files which you can adapt according to your students' needs.
- A and B versions of each test to help with classroom management.
- **audio** for all the listening tasks. This can be played on a CD player.
- **audio scripts** for all the listening exercises.
- **answers** to all exercises.

iTools contains:
- a **digital version of the Student's Book** and **Workbook** with integrated audio and video.
- interactive class **games** which practise key language from the Student's Book by involving the whole class.
- **answer keys** for all exercises.
- **synched audio scripts** which highlight text as it is played.
- documentary **video clips** with subtitles.
- video clip **worksheets**.
- an unabridged **wordlist**, including definitions for every key word.

Websites
- Student's website (www.oup.com/elt/insight): Workbook audio
- Teacher's website (www.oup.com/elt/teachers/insight): Exam insight answer key

Student's Book at a glance

There are ten main units and a Welcome unit in the Student's Book. Each main unit is divided into five sections (A–E), with a Review. After every two units, there is a Cumulative review. At the back of the book, there is a ten-page Vocabulary bank.

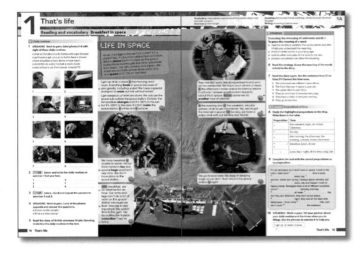

A – Reading and vocabulary

- Students are first presented with a set of key lexis which they practise. Speaking and listening are key skills at this point.
- an information-rich text then establishes the topic of the unit.
- the reading text also contextualizes a vocabulary set which is recycled and practised through the rest of the unit. This is a Vocabulary insight (V insight) set which explores language in greater depth.
- the text previews grammatical structures that students will study in the next section. Students are not expected to engage actively with the new grammar at this point.
- there is a link to the **Vocabulary bank** at the back of the Student's Book where another lexical set is presented and practised.
- the section closes with a speaking activity which allows students to react to the text and demonstrate their understanding of the issues raised or practise target language from the section.

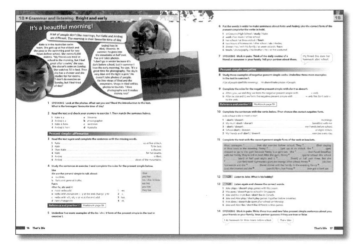

B – Grammar and listening

- section B picks up on the grammatical structures that students met, but may not have recognized, in the reading text in section A.
- the new language is presented in a meaningful context – either a reading or listening text.
- the reading or listening text also establishes a new topic for the section and contextualizes some of the vocabulary from section A.
- the guided discovery approach to grammar ensures that students actively engage with the new language.
- students analyse examples, complete rules or answer questions about the grammar which help them to focus on the new structures, their meaning and use.
- a final speaking activity allows students to use the new language in a personalized and productive way. This happens throughout the Student's Book.
- there is a link to **Grammar reference and practice** in the Workbook where students can find further practice activities and explanations of the grammar for reinforcement.

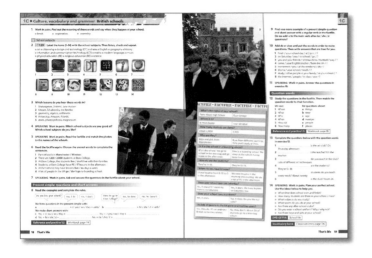

C – Culture, vocabulary and grammar

- section C introduces students to the culture of the English-speaking world through a text on the customs, traditions and history of English-speaking countries or what life is like in those countries.
- there is a cultural comparison element, which encourages students to think about similarities and differences with their own culture.
- the culture text contextualizes the key grammar of the section.
- students learn about the grammar in a guided inductive way.
- there is a link to **Grammar reference and practice** in the Workbook.

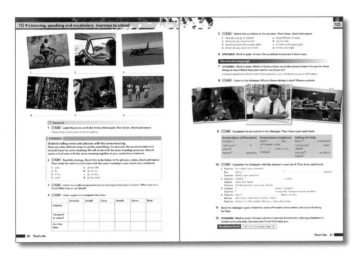

D – Listening, speaking and vocabulary

- a new vocabulary set is presented and practised.
- one or more carefully selected audio recordings and accompanying tasks ensure that students develop their listening skills.
- the section also presents functional language through several model dialogues, as well as controlled and free practice.

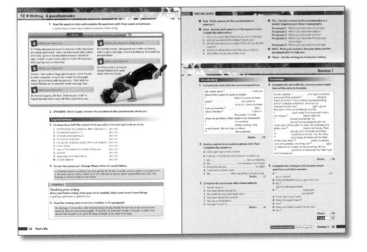

E – Writing

- section E always presents a model text which students analyse for the language, structure and format used.
- a language point illustrates and practises useful writing language and structures.
- a writing strategy develops key elements of the writing process, for example, planning, brainstorming, deciding on register, etc.
- every section includes a step-by-step writing guide which takes students through the process of generating ideas, planning, writing and checking their work.
- the writing task lets students use the language taught throughout the unit in a personalized, productive and creative way.

Review

- the review gives students another opportunity to recycle and check how well they know the vocabulary and grammar they have learned in the unit.
- students get marks for every completed review, so it is easy to monitor progress through the book.
- there is a link to **Pronunciation insight** in the Workbook, which introduces and practises a pronunciation point relevant to the unit.

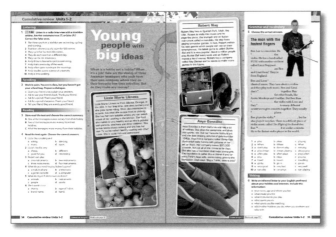

Cumulative review

- there is a two-page cumulative review at the end of every two units. This reviews key language and skills from the Student's Book up to that point through a series of skills-based tasks. Each Cumulative review includes listening, speaking, reading, use of English and writing exercises.
- there is a link to the **Literature insight** and **Exam insight** sections in the Workbook.

Vocabulary bank

- there are three cross-references to the Vocabulary bank from the Welcome unit and two from every other unit.
- each Vocabulary bank presents and practises further vocabulary sets that are topically related to the unit.

Strategies

- in every unit, there is a writing strategy and either a listening or reading strategy.
- each strategy develops students' language skills and helps them to become more confident and autonomous learners.
- the strategies are practised through a number of activities, so that students can immediately apply the skills they have learned.

DVD extra

- there is a link from every unit to a **documentary video clip**.
- each documentary clip builds on a topic of the unit.
- each video is accompanied by a ready-to-use **DVD worksheet** which contains comprehension, language and speaking activities, along with teaching notes.

Workbook at a glance

There are ten main units and a Welcome unit in the Workbook. Each unit has a page to correspond with each Student's Book spread. There is a Progress check at the end of each unit. All Workbook audio can be found on the Class Audio CD, iTools and on the Student's website: www.oup.com/elt/insight.

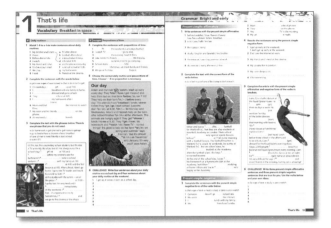

- the Workbook contains grammar, vocabulary and skills activities which practise and reinforce the language covered in the Student's Book.

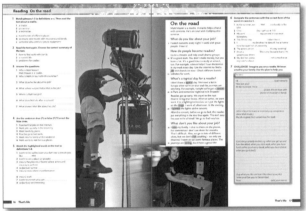

- the reading section presents and practises a new vocabulary set.
- the reading text recycles grammar from the corresponding Student's Book unit.
- new subject matter is introduced in the texts to expand students' knowledge.

- there is a one-page **Progress check** after every unit with short tasks which prompt students to think about how well they understand the grammar, vocabulary and skills taught in the unit. The Progress checks also serve as a record of what has been learned in each unit.
- the **self-evaluation** feature encourages students to reflect on and monitor their own progress.
- the **How can I improve?** feature encourages students to take responsibility for their own learning.

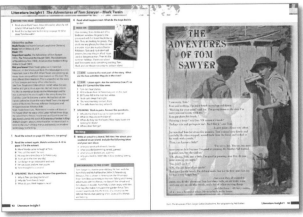

- there are five two-page **Literature insight** lessons in each level of the course.
- **Literature insight** introduces students to classic English literature and encourages reading for pleasure.
- these sections contain shorter reading and listening extracts, but students are encouraged to read the complete works in their own time.
- the literary extracts have been carefully selected to link with the topic and language covered in the Student's Book.
- each lesson presents information about the author, literary extracts to read and listen to, reading and listening comprehension activities, as well as speaking and writing tasks.

11

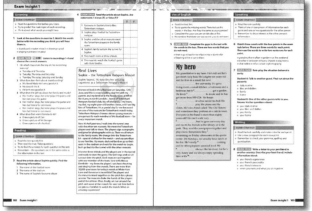

- the five two-page **Exam insight** sections prepare students for common exam tasks.
- there is practice of use of English, reading, listening, speaking and writing.
- through a series of **exam strategies**, students learn how to deal with the most common exam tasks, such as multiple choice, true / false, matching headings to paragraphs, etc.

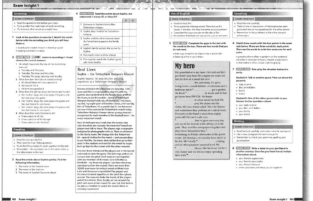

- there is a twenty-page **Grammar reference and practice** section.
- this contains comprehensive explanations of key grammar points from the Student's Book, covering both form and usage.
- each grammar point is accompanied by several exercises to check and consolidate understanding of that point.

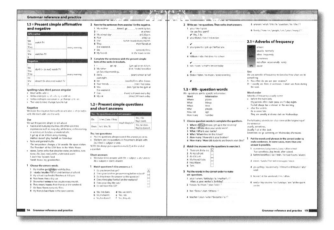

- **Pronunciation insight** focuses on ten pronunciation points – one per main unit.
- points include individual sounds, word stress, sentence stress and intonation.

- a **Wordlist** closes the Workbook.
- the Wordlist features dictionary-style entries, with phonetic transcriptions, definitions and example sentences.
- an extended version can also be found on iTools.

insight iTools

Oxford iTools is software that allows you to present and manipulate course content in an interactive way. *iTools* is designed to be projected in class. To take full advantage of its rich interactive content, it should be used on an interactive whiteboard, but may also be used with a computer connected to a screen or a data projector.

insight iTools contains:

- the complete Student's Book and Workbook.
- interactive games that provide fun whole-class practice of the key vocabulary and grammar.
- video material integrated into the pages, making it easy to access.
- audio tracks integrated into the pages. If you choose to display the script, the words are automatically highlighted as they are spoken, making it easy for students to follow.
- integrated answer keys that make self or peer marking much simpler as students will be able to see the correct answers on screen. You can reveal answers one by one or all at once to suit your students. You can even hide the answers and then reveal them again to see how many they can remember correctly.
- *insight* iTools also comes with built-in teaching tools. These tools open up the content of the course, allowing you to use it in different ways. You can use the hide tool to hide the text on a page and see if your students can predict what it will be about, or work on the vocabulary in a text with the highlighting tool. The spotlight tool lets you focus the whole class on a particular grammar point or exercise.
- the link tool lets you add links to other websites to the Student's Book page, allowing you to access them with a single click during the lesson.

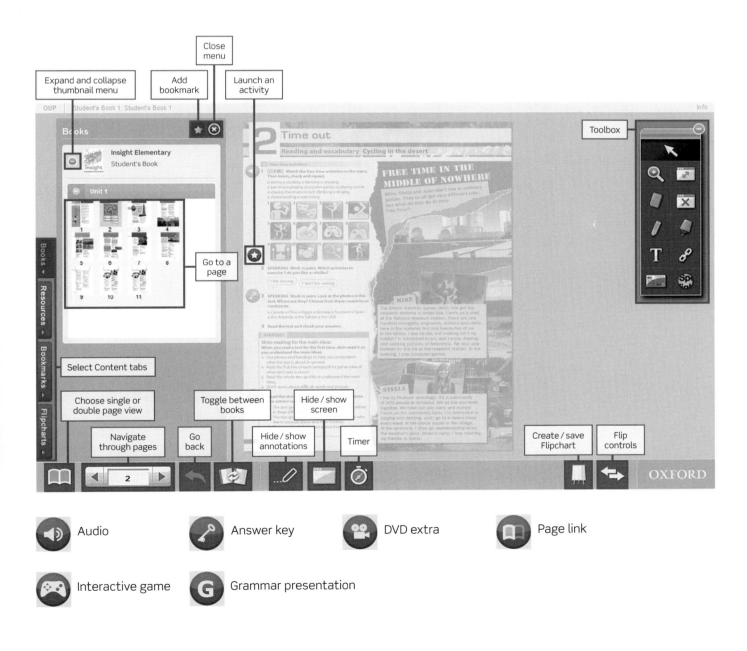

W Welcome

Map of resources

Section A: Student's Book pages 4–5
Workbook page 4
Vocabulary bank, Countries and nationalities page 124

Section B: Student's Book pages 6–7
Workbook page 5
Grammar reference and practice W.1, Workbook page 112

Section C: Student's Book pages 8–9
Workbook page 6
Grammar reference and practice W.2, Workbook page 112
Grammar reference and practice W.3, Workbook page 112

Section D: Student's Book pages 10–11
Workbook page 7
Grammar reference and practice W.4, Workbook page 113
Grammar reference and practice W.5, Workbook page 113
Grammar reference and practice W.6, Workbook page 113
Vocabulary bank, Colours page 125

Section E: Student's Book pages 12–13
Workbook pages 8–9
Vocabulary bank, The time page 125
Progress check Unit W, Workbook page 11

Welcome A

Hello

Lesson summary
Topic: Introductions and interests
Vocabulary: The alphabet; countries and nationalities; interests; numbers 1–30; Vocabulary bank: Countries and nationalities
Reading: A quiz about cultures in different countries
Speaking: Talking about nationality; asking and answering about interests

Lead-in
- Write the following words in a word cloud on the left side of the board: *sixteen*, *football*, *Japan*, *hip hop*. On the right side, write these categories in a word cloud: *country*, *age*, *music*, *sport*.
- In pairs, students match the words on the left with the categories on the right.
- When they have finished, ask students to suggest one more word for each category.

Exercise 1 1·01 page 4
- Play the recording while students read the dialogue.
- Ask questions to check comprehension:
  Where's Daiki from? (Japan)
  Who's fifteen? (Rosie)
  Does Rosie like football? (no)
- Check that students understand the meaning of *be into something* (to like something).
- Before students practise the dialogue, point out the stressed syllables in *fifteen* /ˌfɪfˈtiːn/ and *sixteen* /ˌsɪksˈtiːn/.
- Students practise the dialogue in pairs. When they have finished, ask a few pairs to act out the dialogue for the class.
- With a stronger class, ask students to read dialogue again, but this time substituting their own name, age, country / nationality and interests.

Exercise 2 1·02 page 4
- Students listen to the recording and then repeat the alphabet.
- When students have practised saying the alphabet with the recording, elicit the letters of the alphabet again in the correct order, with each student saying one of the letters. With a **stronger class**, ask students to say the alphabet backwards, starting from Z.

Exercise 3 🔊 1·03 page 4

- Give students time to complete the chart and compare their answers in pairs before you play the recording.
- Ask students to listen to the recording and repeat the letters.
- Check answers as a class.

/eɪ/   A, H, J, K
/iː/   B, C, D, E, G, P, T, V
/e/   F, L, M, N, S, X, Z

Letters which do not have these sounds: I, O, Q, R, U, W, Y

Exercise 4 🔊 1·04 page 4

- Play the recording while students listen.
- Model the dialogue with a student. Then ask students to ask and answer in pairs.
- With a **stronger class**, write only the first letter of each word on the board, with dashes for the missing letters, e.g. a _ _ _ _ (apple). Then ask students to close their books and spell the words from memory.

Exercise 5 page 4

- In pairs, students practise spelling names.
- Circulate and monitor, helping with pronunciation as necessary.

Extra activity: Unusual names

Write some more challenging names on the board as prompts for students to practise unfamiliar letters, e.g. *Xavier, Adeline, Theodore, Henrietta, Willoughby.*

Exercise 6 page 5

- Ask students to look at the pictures and words and match them to the countries. Point out that four of the countries in the list will not be needed.
- Then ask students to suggest words for the remaining countries. They can think of typical food, music, animals or sport.
- Refer students to the answers at the bottom of the quiz.

Culture notes: National symbols

Baseball is also a very popular sport in Japan. Many famous American baseball players continue their careers in Japan after they have retired in the USA.

Pandas are an endangered species. They are threatened by habitat loss and a very low birth rate, especially in captivity. There are now approximately 2,000 pandas living in the wild, and about 300 living in captivity.

The **kangaroo** is a popular unofficial symbol of Australia. The image of the kangaroo is used in Australia's national airline (Qantas), on the Australian coat of arms and on some of its currency.

Cricket is played by two teams of eleven players. The teams take it in turns to bat (hit the ball with a bat) and bowl (throw the ball). The team that is batting tries to score as many runs as possible, while the team that is bowling tries to prevent the batting team from scoring runs. Cricket originated in England, but is also played in other countries, including Australia, India, Pakistan and South Africa.

Karate literally means 'empty hand' in Japanese ('kara' = empty; 'te' = hand).

Samba is a music and dance style which has African roots. It is an important part of Rio de Janeiro's annual carnival in February / March.

Exercise 7 🔊 1·05 page 5

- Give students two minutes to match the nationalities to the countries in the quiz.
- Play the recording for students to listen and check their answers.
- Play the recording again and ask students to repeat the nationalities and the countries.
- Check answers as a class.

the UK British   Brazil Brazilian   Russia Russian
China Chinese   the USA American   Australia Australian
Germany German   India Indian   South Africa South African
Japan Japanese

Vocabulary bank: Countries and nationalities
page 124

1
1 Canada
2 the USA
3 Mexico
4 Brazil
5 Argentina
6 Ireland
7 the UK
8 Belgium
9 the Netherlands
10 Portugal
11 Spain
12 France
13 Germany
14 Poland
15 the Czech Republic

16 Italy
17 Hungary
18 Slovakia
19 Morocco
20 Egypt
21 Kenya
22 South Africa
23 Turkey
24 Russia
25 China
26 India
27 Thailand
28 Japan
29 Australia
30 New Zealand

3
1 Belgian
2 Turkish
3 Canadian
4 Thai
5 Czech
6 Egyptian
7 Polish
8 Argentinian

9 Slovakian
10 Dutch
11 Mexican
12 Kenyan
13 Hungarian
14 (New) Zealander
15 Moroccan

4
1 Northern Ireland
2 Ireland
3 Scotland

4 England
5 Wales

5
1 Irish
2 English

3 Welsh
4 Scottish

Exercise 8 (page 5)

- Ask students to look at the dialogue in exercise 1 again and find the correct question (*Where are you from?*). Elicit that Daiki is Japanese.

Exercise 9 (page 5)

- Ask two students to model the dialogue for the rest of the class. Point out that the nationality is in blue and the country in red.
- If students do not have access to a dictionary, write relevant countries and nationalities on the board.
- Students ask and answer in pairs. Encourage them to use at least three different countries and nationalities.

Exercise 10 (page 5)

- Ask students to look at the dialogue in exercise 1 again and find examples of the phrases: *I love …* , *I like …* , *I'm into …* , *I'm not into …* and *I don't like …* .
- Ask them to look again at the things in exercise 4 and in the quiz and then complete the sentences about them.
- Circulate and monitor, helping with vocabulary if students want to write about other things they like or dislike.

Students' own answers

Exercise 11 1·06 (page 5)

- Play the recording once for students to listen and then again for them to repeat.
- Go round the class and elicit the numbers 1–30 in order, with each student saying one of the numbers.
- With a **stronger class**, go round the class again; this time students say the numbers backwards, starting from 30. You could make this into a timed activity, challenging students to beat their record each time they count up or down.

Exercise 12 1·07 (page 5)

- Focus attention on the table. To check that students understand the different categories, ask them to complete the information about Daiki in exercise 1 (Name: Daiki; Country: Japan; Age: sixteen; Interests: football and karate).
- Play the recording and ask students to complete the chart.
- Students check their answers in pairs.
- Check answers as a class.

Audio script

1
A Hello. What's your name?
B My name's Catherine.
A How do you spell that?
B C-A-T-H-E-R-I-N-E.
A Where are you from, Catherine?
B I'm from the UK.
A How old are you?
B I'm fifteen.
A And what are you into?
B I like music.
2
A Hi. What's your name?
B I'm Gayatri.
A How do you spell your name?
B G-A-Y-A-T-R-I.
A Thanks. And where are you from, Gayatri?
B I'm from Delhi in India.
A How old are you?
B I'm seventeen.
A What are you into, Gayatri?
B I'm into pandas. They're my favourite animal.
3
A Hello. What's your name?
B I'm Hugo.
A How do you spell that?
B H-U-G-O.
A Where are you from, Hugo?
B I'm from Australia.
A And how old are you?
B I'm twenty-four.
A And what are you into?
B I love cricket.

	1	2	3
Name	Catherine	Gayatri	Hugo
Country	the UK	Delhi / India	Australia
Age	15	17	24
Interests	music	pandas	cricket

Exercise 13 (page 5)

- Elicit questions to ask someone's name (*What's your name?*), age (*How old are you?*), nationality (*Where are you from?*) and interests (*What are you into?*).
- Students ask and answer in pairs to complete the *Your partner* column in the table in exercise 12.
- When they have finished, ask a few students to share information about their partner with the class.

Learning outcome

Ask students: *What have you learned today? What can you do now?* and elicit answers: *I can talk about nationalities and interests. I can count from 1–30. I can spell names in English. I can ask and answer questions about personal information.*

Welcome B

Are you in a band?

Lesson summary
Topic: Music and sport
Grammar: *be*: affirmative, negative, questions and short answers
Listening: An interview with a member of a samba band
Reading: A blog
Speaking: Asking and answering about friends and their interests

Lead-in

- If you can find a recording of samba music, bring it to class and play it for students. Ask: *What kind of music is this? Where is it from?*
- Alternatively, write the following on the board:
  MUSIC: *fado*, *flamenco*, *reggae*, *samba*, *tango*
  COUNTRIES: *Argentina*, *Brazil*, *Jamaica*, *Portugal*, *Spain*
  Ask students to match the music to the countries.

16 Welcome

fado Portugal   flamenco Spain   reggae Jamaica
samba Brazil   tango Argentina

Exercise 1 1·08 page 6

- Play the recording while students read the blog post.
- Give students one minute to match the sentence halves. Point out that they do not need to understand every word in order to do the activity.
- Check answers as a class.
- Ask students to find *cosmopolitan* in the blog post. Then ask them to find the phrase that helps to explain the meaning (*from lots of different countries*).
- Check answers as a class.

1 b   2 c   3 a

Exercise 2 page 6

- Check that students understand the difference between the long form of a verb and the contracted form.
- Do the first item together. Read out the blog post and ask students to put up their hands when they hear the form that completes the first gap (*I'm British …*).
- Students then work individually to complete the table.
- Check answers as a class.

1 I'm   2 you're   3 he's   4 it's   5 we're   6 they're

> **Language note: Long and contracted forms**
> In English we often use the contracted, or short form, of a verb when speaking or in informal writing, for example, a blog post. We use the long form in more formal contexts.

> **Reference and practice W.1** Workbook page 112
>
> 1 2 are; aren't   5 is; isn't
>   3 are; aren't   6 'm; 'm not
>   4 is; isn't
>
> 2 2 Is the girl happy?   No, she isn't.
>   3 Are they sixteen?   Yes, they are.
>   4 Are we in London?   No, we aren't.
>   5 Are you my friend?   No, I'm not.
>   6 Is the boy your brother?   Yes, he is.

Exercise 3 1·09 page 6

- Tell students they can use the table in exercise 2 to help them choose the correct words. They then rewrite their sentences using contractions.
- Students compare answers in pairs before they listen to the recording.
- Go round the class, asking individual students to repeat the sentences. Point out any mistakes at the end of the activity.
- Check answers as a class.

1 is   2 am   3 are   4 is   5 is   6 is   7 is

1 My name's Anton.
2 I'm sixteen.
3 You're at my school.
4 He's Chinese.
5 Jim's from the USA.
6 Becca's my friend.
7 She's great.

Exercise 4 page 6

- Write some sentences on the board about yourself and a friend.
- Circulate and monitor as students write their sentences, checking that they are using the correct form of *be* and helping with vocabulary as necessary.
- In pairs, students take it in turns to tell each other about themselves.
- Ask a few students to read their sentences to the class.

Exercise 5 page 6

- Point out that the blog post is by Ryan's friend Leonie.
- Students refer to the blog post to complete the table.
- Check answers as a class.

1 'm not   2 isn't   3 aren't

> **Extra activity: Comprehension**
> Ask students to read the blog post again and find the answers to the following questions:
> *Where's Leonie's home?* (London)
> *What's the name of her football team?* (Hyde Park Girls)
> *Is Leonie good at music?* (no)

Exercise 6 page 7

- Focus attention on the first item and read out the answer. Point out that *Ryan* in the first sentence is replaced by *He* in the second sentence. Tell students to use the correct pronoun for the second sentence in each item. Remind them also to use contracted forms.
- **Fast finishers** can create more prompts. They then swap them with a partner and write sentences.
- Check answers as a class.

2 You aren't into football. You're into tennis.
3 Chelsea and Manchester United aren't Australian teams. They're British teams.
4 We aren't in London. We're in Los Angeles.
5 I'm not good at sport. I'm good at music.
6 Germany isn't in Africa. It's in Europe.

Exercise 7 1·10 page 7

- Ask students to read the interview and predict Bruno's answers before they listen.
- They then listen to the recording and check their answers.
- Ask two students to role play the interview for the class. The rest of the students listen and call out if they think the students have chosen the wrong answer.
- Check answers as a class.

1 Cricket.
2 No, they aren't.
3 Yes, I am.
4 Brazil.
5 Yes, it is.

Exercise 8 page 7

- Students work individually to complete the table.
- Check answers as a class.

1 Are   2 Is   3 Are   4 am   5 are   6 are   7 aren't
8 isn't   9 aren't

Welcome   17

Exercise 9 `page 7`

- Write the following on the board: *your friend / German?* Then elicit or explain how to form the question (*Is your friend German?*).
- Students work individually to write the questions.
- Circulate and monitor as students ask and answer the questions. Encourage them to use rising intonation for their questions.
- Check answers as a class.

1 Are you seventeen?
2 Is your name Richard?
3 Are you at school?
4 Are you good at sport?
5 Are you into tennis?
3 Is your home in a city?
4 Are your friends into music?
5 Are you and your friends American?

Exercise 10 `page 7`

- Model the exercise with a student.
- Give students a few minutes to practise asking and answering the questions in exercise 7. Then ask them to replace the blue words with the words in exercise 10.
- Circulate and monitor, checking students' pronunciation and noting any common errors.

> **Extra activity: Spot the mistake**
>
> Ask students to tell the rest of the class about their partner, but to include one false piece of information. The other students have to spot the deliberate mistake.

Learning outcome

Ask students: *What have you learned today? What can you do now?* and elicit answers: *I can use the affirmative, negative and question form of 'be'. I can read and understand a blog post. I can ask and answer questions about nationality and interests.*

Welcome C

Happy families

> **Lesson summary**
> **Topic:** Families
> **Vocabulary:** Family members; feelings adjectives; plural nouns
> **Grammar:** Possessive adjectives; *this, that, these, those*
> **Reading:** Descriptions of photos
> **Speaking:** Asking and answering about your family

Lead-in

- Draw four stick figures on the board to represent a family: mother, father, daughter and son.
- Ask students to look at the picture and guess what the topic of the lesson will be.
- Elicit the word *family* in the students' own language and ask if any students know what this word is in English.

Exercise 1 1•11 `page 8`

- Focus attention on the diagram and explain the meaning of *family tree*. Point out that this is Max's family tree and ask students to find Max on it. Point out that the family words should all be relevant for him.
- Give students a few minutes to write the family words under the correct names before playing the recording.
- Students listen and repeat the words. Model the pronunciation of *aunt* /ɑːnt/, *grandfather* /ˈɡrænˌfɑːðə/ and *grandmother* /ˈɡrænˌmʌðə/, pointing out that the *d* in the last two words is silent.
- Check answers as a class.

1 grandfather   7 uncle
2 grandmother   8 aunt
3 grandparents   9 brother
4 dad   10 sister
5 mum   11 cousin
6 parents   12 cousin

Exercise 2 1•12 `page 8`

- With a **weaker class**, remind students that they should think about the relationship between the two named people. Do the first item together, eliciting the correct answer.
- Students work individually to do the exercise.
- Play the recording for students to check their answers. Model the pronunciation of *daughter* /ˈdɔːtə/, *husband* /ˈhʌzbənd/ and *niece* /niːs/.
- Check answers as a class.

1 husband   5 son
2 grandson   6 wife
3 niece   7 granddaughter
4 nephew   8 daughter

Exercise 3 `page 8`

- Explain to students that they have to imagine they are one of the people in exercise 1. They then write sentences about their relationships with the people in the family tree.
- Tell students to find Sharon in the family tree and then ask two students to read out the example.
- With a **weaker class**, give another example, e.g. *Clive's my dad*. Then ask students to guess who you are. (Caroline or Mark)
- Students write their sentences and play the guessing game with a partner.

Exercise 4 `page 8`

- Point out that the possessive adjectives in the text are bold.
- Check answers as a class.

1 my   2 his   3 her   4 our   5 their

> **Extra activity**
>
> Ask students to work in pairs. Each student should write four or five names on a piece of paper. The names should be of friends, family members or pets. Students ask and answer to explain who the people are, using possessive adjectives, e.g. *'Who's Enrico?' 'He's my uncle.'*

> **Reference and practice W.2** `Workbook page 112`
> **1** 2 His 3 Their 4 Her 5 Your 6 My

Exercise 5 `page 8`

- Explain to students that they have to read the sentences carefully and decide if the words are subject pronouns or possessive adjectives. Point out that possessive adjectives come before a noun whereas subject pronouns usually come before a verb.
- Students compare answers in pairs.
- Check answers as a class.

1 my; We
2 She; your
3 your; its
4 He; his
5 They; their
6 Her; our

Exercise 6 1·13 `page 9`

- Give students two minutes to look at the pictures and match the adjectives.
- Play the recording for them to check their answers. Model the pronunciation of *angry* /ˈæŋgri/ and *hungry* /ˈhʌŋgri/.
- Check answers as a class.

1 thirsty   2 hungry   3 happy   4 sad   5 angry
6 excited   7 bored   8 tired   9 hot   10 cold

Exercise 7 `page 9`

- Mime *cold* by hugging your arms and shivering. Then ask students to suggest a feeling adjective from exercise 6 to describe how you feel.
- Students do the activity in pairs.

> **Alternative activity**
> You could set up this activity as a team game. Put students into three or four teams. Ask one student from each team to come to the front of the class and mime a word for their team. When their team mates guess the word, a second student mimes another word. The first team to guess six words correctly is the winner.

> **Language note: Plural nouns**
> There are very few irregular plurals in English, so it is a good idea for students to keep a record of them and learn them.
> Other common irregular plurals include: *tooth – teeth*, *foot – feet*, *mouse – mice*, *sheep – sheep*, *deer – deer*.

Exercise 8 1·14 `page 9`

- Focus attention on the table. Elicit that we normally add *s* to the end of a word to make it plural.
- Ask students how *granny* changes when it becomes plural (*-y* changes to *-ies*). Explain that this rule applies to all words that end in a consonant + *-y*. Give an example of a word that ends in a vowel + *-y*, e.g. *day – days*.
- Give students two minutes to rewrite the sentences. Then play the recording for them to check their answers.
- Play the recording again and ask students to listen and repeat. Highlight the pronunciation of *women* /ˈwɪmɪn/.
- Check answers as a class.

1 women; aunts
2 children
3 cousins; friends
4 people; men
5 countries

Exercise 9 `page 9`

- Read out the rules for *this*, *these*, *that* and *those*. Demonstrate by pointing to things in the classroom and use *this* and *these* for things that are close to you and *that* and *those* for things that are further away.
- Ask students to look at the picture of the family group and to identify the people who are in the foreground and those who are in the background.
- They then complete the sentences individually.
- Check answers as a class.

1 These; Those
2 This; that
3 That; this

> **Reference and practice W.3** `Workbook page 112`
> **1** 2 Those 3 this 4 these 5 That 6 Those

Exercise 10 `page 9`

- Draw your own family tree on the board and encourage students to ask you questions about it using *Who is …?*
- Students draw their own family trees. They then work in pairs, asking and answering about the people.
- Some students may need to know the following words in order to describe their family trees: *stepmother*, *stepfather*, *stepbrother*, *stepsister*, *half-brother*, *half-sister*.
- Circulate and monitor, helping where necessary.

Learning outcome

Ask students: *What have you learned today? What can you do now?* and elicit answers: *I can talk about my family. I can use possessive adjectives. I can talk about feelings. I can use plural nouns. I can use 'this', 'that', 'these' and those'.*

Welcome D

Friends

Lesson summary
Topic: Friends
Vocabulary: Appearance adjectives; Vocabulary bank: Colours
Grammar: *have got*; object pronouns; *a/an* and *the*
Speaking: Describing people
Writing: Describing a photo

Lead-in

- Play a game of hangman with the word *friend*: Draw a dash on the board for each letter of the word: _ _ _ _ _ _ .
- Students take it in turns to call out a letter. If the letter is in the word, write it on the corresponding dash. Insist that students say the letters correctly. If a letter is not in the word, write it on the board and then start drawing the hangman.

Exercise 1 1•15 page 10

- Tell students to look at the photos. Ask:
  How many girls are there? (two)
  How many boys are there? (four)
  How many basketballs are there? (two)
  Is there a dog? (no)
  Is there a guitar? (yes)
- Play the recording while students read the dialogue. Then give them a minute to find the people in the photo.
- Students compare answers in pairs.
- Check answers as a class.

A Alice, Dom and Olivia
B Sam
C Josh and Chris

Exercise 2 page 10

- Focus attention on the table and explain that the contracted forms are in brackets. Remind students that we usually use contracted forms in informal written English and when we are speaking.
- Do the first item together. Students then work individually to complete the table.
- Check answers as a class.

1 've got   2 's got   3 Have   4 have   5 Has   6 has

> **Reference and practice W.4** Workbook page 113
>
> 1 3 haven't got
>   4 haven't got
>   5 Has (Anna) got; hasn't
>   6 've got
>   7 has got
>   8 hasn't got
>
> 2 1 d   2 c   3 a   4 e   5 b

Exercise 3 page 10

- Tell students that they can use the table in exercise 2 to help them. Ask them if the text is formal or informal (informal). Remind them that we usually use contracted forms in informal texts.
- Students complete the text individually and then compare answers in pairs.
- Check answers as a class.

1 've got   5 hasn't got
2 haven't got   6 's got
3 've got   7 haven't got
4 's got   8 have got

Exercise 4 1•16 page 10

- Elicit the first question: *Have you got a brother?* Remind students about word order in questions: auxiliary verb + subject + main verb.
- Give students a few minutes to do the exercise. Then play the recording for them to circle Ian's answers.
- Ask students to swap their answers with a partner. Then play the recording again for students to check their partner's answers.
- Check answers as a class.

Audio script

Leah So, Ian, have you got a brother or a sister?
Ian Yes, I have. I've got two brothers, but I haven't got a sister.
Leah Have you got a dog or a cat?
Ian No, I haven't. I love dogs, but I haven't got one.
Leah Have your friends got laptops?
Ian Yes, they have. All the people in my class have got them.
Leah Has your class got nice teachers?
Ian Yes, it has. I like all our teachers this year.
Leah Has your school got a school band?
Ian No, it hasn't, but it's got a guitar club. My brother's in that. I'm in the film club.

1 Have you got a brother? ✓
2 Have you got a sister? ✗
3 Have you got a dog or cat? ✗
4 Have your friends got laptops? ✓
5 Has your class got nice teachers? ✓
6 Has your school got a school band? ✗

Exercise 5 page 10

- Model the activity. Ask: *Have you got a brother?* and elicit a reply from a student.
- Students ask and answer in pairs.
- Circulate and monitor, noting any common errors for a feedback session.

Exercise 6 1•17 page 10

- Give some examples of opposites in the students' own language. Make sure students understand what they have to do.
- Students work individually to do the exercise.
- Play the recording for students to check their answers and repeat the words. Model the pronunciation of *straight* /streɪt/ and *fair* /feə/.
- Check answers as a class.

1 young   2 short   3 curly   4 dark   5 long   6 blue

Exercise 7 page 11

- Write a description of a student on the board, e.g. *He's young. He's tall. He's got short curly hair and brown eyes.* Students ask *yes/no* questions to find out more information about the person you have described.
- Students can do this activity in pairs. Remind them to reply using *Yes, he/she is* or *No, he/she isn't* and *Yes, he/she has* or *No, he/she hasn't*.
- Alternatively, ask different students to come to the front of the class and write their descriptions on the board.

Exercise 8 page 11

- Ask students to look at the dialogue in exercise 1 again and complete the table.
- With a **stronger class**, ask students to cover the dialogue. Play track 1.15 again. Students listen and complete the table.
- Check answers as a class.

1 me   2 him   3 her   4 it   5 them

Welcome

Reference and practice W.5 (Workbook page 113)

1 2 She's got it.
   3 I haven't got them.
   4 Jude likes us.
   5 We are with her.

Exercise 9 (page 11)

- Give students one minute to do the exercise.
- They then compare answers in pairs.
- Check answers as a class.

1 him 2 me 3 it 4 them 5 us 6 you

Language note: Zero article, *the*

- We use **zero article** for countries (with the exception of *the UK* and *the USA*), states, lakes and mountains.
  She lives in France.   *I've got a house near Lake Como.*
- We use *the* for seas and oceans.
  I often swim in the Mediterranean.

Reference and practice W.6 (Workbook page 113)

1 1 The   4 a; a; The
   2 the   5 an; a
   3 a   6 a

Exercise 10 (page 11)

- Focus attention on the rules for *a/an* and *the*.
- Students complete the sentences individually.
- Check answers as a class.

1 an; – ; a   4 a; The; –
2 a; The; – ; –   5 a; the
3 an; The; –

Exercise 11 (page 11)

- Ask students to look at the photo and complete the description. They can use the table in exercise 6 to help them if necessary.
- Check answers as a class.
- Students then write their own description of another photo in the unit.
- Check answers as a class.

1 has got   5 long
2 boys   6 short
3 a   7 has got
4 guitar   8 fair

Extra activity: Photo description

Ask students to bring their own family photos or photos of people from magazines to class. Lay out the photos at the front of the class. Students can choose a photo and write a description of it. Then ask different students to read out the descriptions. Can the other students guess which photo it is?

Vocabulary bank: Colours (page 125)

1 1 green   6 white
   2 red   7 pink
   3 yellow   8 brown
   4 black   9 blue
   5 orange   10 purple

2 1 yellow banana   6 purple dress
   2 blue pen   7 black cat
   3 red bus   8 pink dress
   4 green leaf   9 white horse
   5 orange book   10 brown door

3 Students' own answers

Learning outcome

Ask students: *What have you learned today? What can you do now?* and elicit answers: *I can use 'have got'. I can describe appearance. I can use object pronouns. I can use 'a', 'an' and 'the'. I can describe photos.*

Welcome E

The world is a village

Lesson summary
Topic: Facts and figures
Vocabulary: Days, months and seasons; numbers 31+; ordinals and dates; Vocabulary bank: The time
Reading: Statistics about the world
Speaking: Asking for and giving information

Lead-in

- Write these numbers in a word cloud on the right side of the board: *7,000,000,000; 196; 113; 7; 5*. Then write these words in a word cloud on the left: *seas, continents, people, countries, oceans* If necessary, translate the words into the students' language.
- Ask students to guess the number of people, countries, seas, continents and oceans there are in the world and match the numbers to the words.

7,000,000,000 people   196 countries   113 seas
7 continents   5 oceans

Exercise 1 1·18 (page 12)

- Ask students what day it is in their language. Then ask them to find the corresponding English word in exercise 1.
- Ask students to order the days as quickly as possible. The first student to finish should put their hand up.
- Play the recording for students to check their answers and repeat. Model and drill *Monday* /ˈmʌndeɪ/ and *Wednesday* /ˈwenzdeɪ/.
- Check answers as a class.

Wednesday 3   Friday 5   Sunday 7   Tuesday 2   Saturday 6
Monday 1   Thursday 4

Welcome 21

Exercise 2 1•19 page 12

- Play the recording for students to listen to the endings.
- Play it again so they can repeat and check their answers.
- With a **stronger class**, ask students to close their books. Elicit the months in the correct order, with each student saying one of the months. Then ask them to say the months backwards, starting with *December*.
- Check answers as a class.

January, February, March, April, May, June, July, August, September, October, November, December

Exercise 3 1•20 page 12

- Students match the seasons to the photos.
- Play the recording for students to listen, check and repeat. Ask them if they know which months are in which season in England. (spring: March, April, May; summer: June, July, August; autumn: September, October, November; winter: December, January, February)
- Check answers as a class.

1 spring   2 summer   3 autumn   4 winter

Exercise 4 page 12

- Students ask and answer the questions in pairs.
- Circulate and monitor, checking that students are pronouncing the days of the week and the months correctly.

1 Students' own answers
2 Students' own answers
3a Students' own answers
3b December
4a March, April, May
4b September, October, November

Exercise 5 1•21 page 12

- Give students a minute to put the numbers in the correct order. Then play the recording for them to check their answers and repeat.
- Check answers as a class.

1 thirty   2 sixty   3 seventy   4 a hundred   5 a million

Exercise 6 1•22 page 12

- Play the recording for students to listen and repeat.
- Point out the difference in stress between *sixteen* /ˌsɪksˈtiːn/ and *sixty* /ˈsɪksti/.
- Ask different students to say the numbers and correct any problems with pronunciation or stress.
- Point out the use of hyphens in *thirty-one*, *forty-seven* and *eighty-nine*.
- Students work individually to write the figures in words. Check answers by asking individual students to write the numbers on the board.

1 thirty-five	5 fifty-three
2 two thousand	6 eight million
3 seventy-eight	7 ninety
4 sixty-two	8 nineteen

Extra activity: Numbers

Ask students to work in pairs. One student writes six numbers (higher than 31) on a piece of paper and then dictates them to their partner. Students then swap roles and repeat the activity.

Exercise 7 page 12

- Read out the two example dialogues with a student. Explain that we use *about* when we are not certain of the exact number. Ask students to find another way to express uncertainly in the example dialogues (*I think*).
- If necessary, refer students to exercise 1 on page 8 to remind them of the family words they can use.
- Circulate and monitor, checking that students are pronouncing the numbers correctly.

Exercise 8 1•23 page 13

- Play the recording for students to listen and repeat.
- Write several numbers on the board, e.g. 5, 8, 12, 24. Ask different students to say the number and then the ordinal.

Extra activity: Ordinal numbers

Say *ten* and elicit the ordinal (tenth). Then ask a student to say a different number, e.g. *fifteen*, and to point to another student. That student gives the correct ordinal (fifteenth) and says a different number. Continue round the class, encouraging students to say the numbers and ordinals as quickly as possible.

Exercise 9 1•24 page 13

- Read out the rules. Then ask a student to say today's date and write it on the board.
- Give students two minutes to complete the sentences.
- Play the recording for students to check and repeat.
- Asking different students to say the sentences. Focus on correct pronunciation and stress.
- Check answers as a class.

1 25 December
2 14 February
3 31 December
4 1 January
5 31 October
6–8 Students' own answers

Exercise 10 page 13

- Explain the meaning of *village* (a small town). Read out the first sentence of the text and ask students to answer the question. Do not tell them whether they are correct or not.
- Students read the rest of the text quickly. Check to see if they have changed their minds about the answer to the question.

It is an imaginary village.

Exercise 11 1•25 page 13

- Students work in pairs to choose the correct numbers.
- Circulate and monitor, helping with any difficult vocabulary.
- Play the recording for students to check their answers.

- Check answers as a class.
- Ask students to vote for the most surprising fact in the article.

1 Ten
2 Thirty-four
3 Eighty
4 Two
5 Sixty
6 eleven
7 Seventy-five
8 thirty-three
9 Twenty

Exercise 12 page 13

- Students work individually to match the question halves. They then ask and answer in pairs.
- Ask students to look at the text in exercise 10 again and to compare their answers with the facts in the text.

1 b 2 e 3 a 4 c 5 f 6 h 7 d 8 g

> **Extra activity**
>
> Ask students to carry out a survey of the answers for their class. Then invite one or two students to tell the rest of the class about the results of their survey.

> **Vocabulary bank: The time** page 125
>
> 1 1 six o'clock
>   2 five past six
>   3 ten past six
>   4 quarter past six
>   5 twenty past six
>   6 twenty-five past six
>   7 half past six
>   8 twenty-five to seven
>   9 twenty to seven
>   10 quarter to seven
>   11 ten to seven
>   12 five to seven
>
> 2 1 half past three
>   2 ten past five
>   3 twenty to four
>   4 two o'clock
>   5 quarter past seven
>   6 twenty-five to nine
>   7 five past eleven
>   8 ten to one
>   9 twenty past eight
>   10 quarter to ten
>   11 twenty-five past six
>   12 five to twelve
>
> 3 1 It's two twenty.
>   2 It's six fifty.
>   3 It's ten fifteen.
>   4 It's three thirty-five.
>   5 It's nine oh five.
>   6 It's eight thirty.
>
> 4 Students' own answers

Learning outcome

Ask students: *What have you learned today? What can you do now?* and elicit answers: *I can talk about days, months and seasons. I can use big numbers. I can use ordinal numbers. I can say and write dates. I know some facts and figures about the world.*

1 That's life

Map of resources

Section A: Student's Book pages 14–15
Workbook page 12
Teacher's resource disk, Communication worksheet 1A

Section B: Student's Book pages 16–17
Workbook page 13
Grammar reference and practice 1.1, Workbook page 114

Section C: Student's Book pages 18–19
Workbook page 14
Grammar reference and practice 1.2, Workbook page 114
Grammar reference and practice 1.3, Workbook page 115
Vocabulary bank, Classroom items page 126
Teacher's resource disk, DVD extra + worksheet, School life page 19
Teacher's resource disk, Communication worksheet 1A

Section D: Student's Book pages 20–21
Workbook page 15
Vocabulary bank, Classroom language page 126
Teacher's resource disk, Communication worksheet 1B

Section E: Student's Book pages 22–23
Workbook page 18
Teacher's resource disk, Writing bank
Teacher's resource disk, Functional language bank

Review 1 page 23
Pronunciation insight 1, Workbook page 132
Progress check Unit 1, Workbook page 19
Language and skills tests 1A and 1B, Test Bank

1A Reading and vocabulary

Breakfast in space

Lesson summary
Topic: Daily life
Vocabulary: Daily routines, prepositions of time
Reading: Life in space
Speaking: Talking about daily routines
Communication worksheet 1A: Do you … ?

Lead-in

- To introduce the theme of daily routines and to revise times, write the following words on the board: *breakfast, school, football, dinner, TV*. Tell students that you are going to talk about a typical day in your life. Warn them that they will not understand every word, but they should listen out for the words on the board and try to find out the correct time for each activity.
- Say slowly and clearly: *I have breakfast at half past six. I start school at twenty-five to nine. I play football after school at quarter past four. I have dinner at twenty past eight. I watch TV at nine o'clock.*
- Ask different students to come to the board and write the correct time next to each word.

Exercise 1 page 14

- Focus attention on the photographs. Ask students which of these activities they do every day. Then give them two minutes to label the photos. Remind them that they do not need to use all of the daily routines.
- Tell students that you will not check answers yet – you will do this in exercise 3.

1 read a book
2 get dressed
3 have breakfast
4 do homework
5 use the internet
6 watch TV
7 have lunch
8 go to bed

Exercise 2 1•26 page 14

- Play the recording for students to write the daily routines.
- They then compare answers with a partner.
- Check answers as a class.

Audio script

1 **Callum** Hi, Adam. Hi, Jed.
  Adam Hey, Callum. How are you, mate?
2 [SFX: A football game at an afterschool club: someone kicking a ball, referee's whistle. Then another kick – a free kick that goes straight into goal, and some cheers from a few teenage boys]
3 **Callum** Come on, it's time for class.
4 **Mum** Callum, it's seven o'clock.

24   Unit 1 That's life

5 **Callum** Mum, I'm home.
  Mum Hi, Callum. How was school?'
6 **Callum** Hello.
  Adam Hi, Callum. It's Adam.
  Callum Hi, Adam, what are you …

1 meet friends
2 play football
3 start school
4 get up
5 get home
6 chat on the phone

Exercise 3 1·27 page 14

- Explain to students that they are going to listen to the answers for exercises 1 and 2. Play the recording for students to check their answers.
- Play the recording again for students to repeat the phrases. Draw attention to the /e/ sound of 'ea' in *breakfast* /ˈbrekfəst/.

Exercise 4 page 14

- Ask students to look at the title of the text and the photos. Ask: *Where are the people?* (in space / on a space station)
- Write the following words on the board and ask students to match them to the photos: *exercise, work, eat, sleep*.

Exercise 5 page 14

- Give students a few minutes to read the diary and underline the daily routines. Explain that some of the routines in the text are the same as in exercise 1 but there are also some different daily routines.
- Check answers as a class.

get up, wash, get dressed, have breakfast, do exercise, watch films, start work, do experiments, work on the computers, have lunch, make videos, answer questions, play games, chat, use the internet, have a video chat, go to bed, sleep

Extra activity: Further discussion

Ask students if they are surprised by any of the daily routines on the space station. Then ask: *Would you like to live on a space station? Why / why not?*
You can ask questions, e.g. *What would you miss about life on Earth?* in the students' own language, but encourage them to give their answers in English, e.g. *my family, food from home, nice weather, friends*.

Additional words

The following words are from *Life in space*:

- *star* /stɑː(r)/ (n) one of the small bright lights that you see in the sky at night
- *planet* /ˈplænɪt/ (n) a large round object in space that moves around the sun or another star
- *experiment* /ɪkˈsperɪmənt/ (n) a scientific test that you do to find out what will happen or to see if something is true
- *chat* /tʃæt/ (v) to talk in a friendly, informal way to somebody

Exercise 6 page 15

- Go through the strategy with students.

- With a **weaker class**, give students hints about which strategy to use for each word, e.g. Look at the word in context to understand *speed*. Look at the photo to understand *floats*.
- Ask different students to explain or translate the meanings of the words in bold. Before you say whether they are correct or not, ask the class to vote on whether they agree with the explanation / translation.

Culture note: The International Space Station

The International Space Station is the largest artificial body in orbit around Earth. It has been occupied for over thirteen years by a rotating international crew from sixteen different countries. Students can access live updates from the ISS at spacestationlive.nasa.gov.

Exercise 7 page 15

- Encourage students to read the sentences first and then try to find the relevant information in the diary. Remind them that they do not need to understand every word to decide if the sentences are true or false.
- Check answers as a class.

1 T
2 F: They don't like the food.
3 T
4 F: They do one hour of exercise in the morning and another hour before dinner.
5 F: They have a video chat on Sunday.
6 F: They go to bed early.

Extra activity: Fast finishers

Ask **fast finishers** to work in pairs. Each student writes two more questions about the diary, e.g. *When do they have lunch?* and reads them out to their partner. Their partner tries to answer the questions without looking at the text.

V insight Prepositions of time

Draw the ATONIN time pyramid on the board to help students remember which preposition to use with which time expression. This is useful, but students also have to learn standard expressions, e.g. *at night, at the weekend, in the morning*.

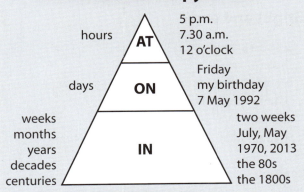

The ATONIN time pyramid

hours — AT — 5 p.m. / 7.30 a.m. / 12 o'clock
days — ON — Friday / my birthday / 7 May 1992
weeks, months, years, decades, centuries — IN — two weeks / July, May / 1970, 2013 / the 80s / the 1800s

Exceptions: at the weekend   at night
in the morning   in the afternoon   in five minutes

Unit 1 That's life 25

Exercise 8 (page 15)
- Give students two minutes to read the diary and complete the table.
- Encourage them to keep a section in their vocabulary notebooks for prepositions of time so that they can add more expressions as they learn them.
- Check answers as a class.

1 at   2 on   3 in   4 before / after

Exercise 9 (page 15)
- Remind students to use the table in exercise 8 to help them with this exercise.
- Circulate and monitor, noting any common errors.
- Check answers as a class.

1 at   2 –   3 In   4 in   5 on   6 –   7 In   8 At   9 –   10 at

Exercise 10 (page 15)
- Give a few example sentences about your own routine.
- Students then work in pairs, taking it in turns to tell their partners about their routines.
- Do not ask students to describe their partner's routines at this point as they have not yet learned the third person form of the verbs.

> **Extra activity: Find the lie!**
> Students work in groups. One student describes their routine to the rest of the group, but they include two lies in their description. The other students listen and call out when they think they have spotted the lie. Demonstrate the activity first, including one obvious lie, e.g. *At half past three I wash my elephant* and one more subtle lie, e.g. *I go to bed at half past six*. Then give students two minutes to prepare their own description before they play the game in groups.

Learning outcome
Ask students: *What have you learned today? What can you do now?* and elicit answers: *I know words for different daily routines. I can understand a text about life in space. I can use prepositions of time. I can talk about my daily routine.*

1B Grammar and listening

Bright and early

Lesson summary
Topic: Interests
Grammar: Present simple: affirmative and negative
Listening: Jake's hobby
Reading: It's a beautiful morning!
Speaking: Describing someone's daily routine

Lead-in
- Write the following questions on the board:
What's your favourite time of day – morning, afternoon or evening? Why? (e.g. *I love the afternoon. I play football after school.*)
What's your favourite hobby?
- Students discuss the questions in pairs.
- Have a class vote on the most popular time of day and the most popular hobbies.

Exercise 1 (page 16)
- Focus attention on the photos. Ask students to guess the girl's hobby (swimming) and the boy's (photography).
- Students then read the introduction to find out what the teenagers' favourite time of day is.
- Check answer as a class.

It's morning.

Exercise 2 (page 16)
- Students read the text quickly to check their answers and then match the sentence halves. Give them a time limit of one minute for this activity so that they focus on finding the answers rather than understanding every word.
- Check answers as a class.

1 c   2 b   3 d   4 a

Exercise 3 (page 16)
- Do the first item together. Read out the first two sentences of the text and ask students to put up their hands when they hear the word that completes the gap (*gets*).
- Students work individually to do the exercise.
- Check answers as a class.

1 gets   4 studies
2 watches   5 lives
3 has   6 likes

> **Language note: Present simple: pronunciation**
> There are three different sounds for the third person present simple ending.
> /s/ e.g. *gets, likes*
> /z/ e.g. *goes, swims, lives*
> /ɪz/ e.g. *watches*

Exercise 4 (page 16)
- Ask students to read the sentences in exercise 3 again.
- Then read out the *Use* part of the rules. You can ask **stronger students** to find an example sentence for each use, e.g. to talk about routines: *She gets up at five o'clock …*; to describe general truths: *Andrej lives in Bled, Slovenia.*
- Give students a few minutes to work out the rules for form.
- Students compare answers in pairs.
- Check answers as a class.

a 2   b 1   c 4   d 3

> **Reference and practice 1.1** (Workbook page 114)
> 1 2 study   3 finishes   4 has   5 writes   6 meet   7 love   8 live

Exercise 5 (page 16)
- Students read the text again to identify more examples of the third person present simple form. Emphasize that they should look only for the affirmative form at this stage.
- Ask a few students to read out their examples and focus on the correct pronunciation.

- Check answers as a class.

She goes to the swimming pool …
She swims 5,000 metres.
… she says.
… he goes into the mountains …
… and takes photos.
… he says.
… it makes money …

> **Extra activity: Present simple**
> Ask students to close their books and work in pairs. Students take it in turns to say a correct sentence about Katie or Andrej. Their partner writes the sentence in their notebook and decides if it is correct or not. Students then open their books and check the sentences together.

Exercise 6 page 17

- Explain to students that these sentences contain extra information about Katie and Andrej.
- Do the first sentence together on the board. Remind students about the spelling rule for verbs ending in consonant + -y.
- Students work individually or in pairs to do the exercise.
- Check answers as a class.

1 Katie studies at Concord High School.
2 Her mum works at her school.
3 Her school finishes at three o'clock. / At three o'clock, her school finishes.
4 Andrej does two hours of homework after school. / After school, Andrej does two hours of homework.
5 He has dinner with his family at seven o'clock. / At seven o'clock, he has dinner with his family.
6 He teaches his brother photography at the weekend. / At the weekend, he teaches his brother photography.

Exercise 7 page 17

- Model the activity for students. Tell them about someone in your family, e.g. *My brother gets up at six in the morning. He goes for a run and then he has breakfast.*
- Students work in pairs to describe the routines.
- When they have finished, ask a few **stronger students** to come to the front of the class and try to remember their partner's friend's / family member's routine. Their partner listens carefully and corrects any mistakes.

Exercise 8 page 17

- Focus attention on the two examples and ask students to find them in the text.
- Students do the exercise individually.
- Check answers as a class.

She doesn't swim on Sunday.
I don't do exercise on Sunday, …
I don't go in winter …

Exercise 9 page 17

- Point out to students that *don't* and *doesn't* are both contracted forms. Elicit or give the full forms (*do not* and *does not*).

- Students complete the rules. Then ask two students to read them out. Model and drill the pronunciation of *doesn't* /ˈdʌzənt/.
- Check answers as a class.

a don't   b doesn't

> **Reference and practice 1.1** Workbook page 114
> 2 2 don't study
>   3 doesn't finish
>   4 doesn't have
>   5 doesn't write
>   6 don't meet
>   7 don't love
>   8 don't live
> 3 2 doesn't make   6 don't go
>   3 starts   7 has
>   4 watch   8 sleeps
>   5 don't like

Exercise 10 page 17

- Students can refer to exercise 9 to do the exercise.
- Individual students read out their sentences. The rest of the class listen and decide if they are correct.
- Check answers as a class.

1 don't like   4 doesn't start
2 doesn't have   5 don't do
3 don't meet

Exercise 11 page 17

- Students work in pairs to complete the text. Point out that they will sometimes need the negative form.
- Circulate and monitor, checking that students are forming the verbs correctly.
- Check answers as a class.

1 don't do   8 finishes
2 like   9 doesn't feel
3 gets up   10 does
4 gets   11 has
5 doesn't have   12 uses
6 goes   13 watches
7 starts   14 doesn't go

Exercise 12 1•28 page 17

- Explain that you are going to play the recording once and students just have to listen to find out Jake's hobby.
- With a **weaker class**, stop the recording after the sentence *We play online games together.* Ask: *What's Jake's hobby?*
- Check answers as a class.

Audio script

Mum Hey, Jake, why are you on the computer? It's time for breakfast.
Jake I know, Mum, but this game's with Mia.
Mum Your cousin Mia, in Singapore?
Jake Yes. She gets home from school in Singapore at this time every day, and we play online games together. It's morning here in Britain, but it's afternoon in Singapore … I play with Alex in Canada, too.
Mum But it's night time in Canada!

Unit 1 That's life   27

Jake Yes, I know. I don't play with Alex before breakfast. I play with him in the evening – at eight o'clock. That's four o'clock in the afternoon in Canada. We only play on Mondays, because on the other days he does sport after school and he gets home late. But on Mondays we play for half an hour.
Mum What's your favourite game?
Jake We haven't got a favourite. We like lots of different games. We like games where you make cities. We all live in different countries, but that's not important.
Mum Well, say hi to Mia from me! But it really is time for breakfast …

playing online games / computer games

Exercise 13 1·28 page 17

- Give students a minute to read the sentences before you play the recording again.
- Play the recording once and then allow students to check their answers in pairs.
- Check answers as a class.

1 plays	4 don't play
2 goes	5 doesn't do
3 don't live	6 like

See exercise 12 for audio script

Exercise 14 page 17

- Model the speaking activity for students.
- They then work in pairs. Circulate and monitor, checking that students are forming the verbs correctly.

Learning outcome

Ask students: *What have you learned today? What can you do now?* and elicit answers: *I can use the affirmative and negative forms of the present simple. I can talk about other people's routines.*

1C Culture, vocabulary and grammar

British schools

Lesson summary
Topic: Different types of schools in Britain
Vocabulary: School subjects; Vocabulary bank: Classroom items
Grammar: Present simple: questions and short answers; question words
Reading: Eton College and Parrs Wood High School
Speaking: Talking about your school
Communication worksheet 1A: Do you … ?

Lead-in

Write BRITISH SCHOOLS in capital letters on the board. Then ask students to discuss what words they associate with British schools, e.g. *school uniform, rules, packed lunch*. Accept suggestions in the students' own language, but write the English translations on the board. Then ask students to open their books and see if any of their words are in the factfile.

Exercise 1 page 18

- Write the following words on the board and model and drill the pronunciation: *break* /breɪk/, *registration* /ˌredʒɪˈstreɪʃn/, *assembly* /əˈsembli/.
- Explain the meanings, or give students time to look them up in a dictionary.
- To check comprehension, ask: *When is break? When is registration? When is assembly?*

Exercise 2 1·29 page 18

- Focus attention on the icons and check that students understand what they represent by asking them to say the subjects in their own language.
- Students match the English words to the icons.
- Ask students to swap their answers with a partner and check their partner's answers as they listen to the recording and repeat.
- Check answers as a class.

1 English
2 information and communication technology (ICT)
3 art
4 design and technology (DT)
5 maths
6 science
7 geography
8 history
9 religious education (RE)
10 citizenship
11 drama
12 physical education (PE)
13 music
14 modern languages

Exercise 3 page 18

- Read out the words and ask students to put up their hands when they are confident they can identify the school subject.
- Check answers as a class.

1 English   2 music   3 maths   4 geography
5 science

Extra activity: Fast finishers

Ask **fast finishers** to write an extra word for each school subject in exercise 3, e.g. *English – Thomas Hardy; music – Beethoven; maths – fractions; geography – volcanoes; science – acid*. Allow them to use a dictionary.

Exercise 4 page 18

- Focus attention on the phrase *be good at* something. Give some examples about yourself, e.g. *I'm good at English. I'm not good at music.*
- Students work in pairs. Circulate and monitor, checking that students are pronouncing the subjects correctly. Pay particular attention to *DT, ICT, PE* and *RE* and refer students to the alphabet phonetics table on page 4 of the Student's Book if necessary.

Exercise 5 page 18

- Give students one minute to read the factfile quickly and match the photos to the names of the schools.

28   Unit 1 That's life

- When they have finished, ask them which information gave them the answers. (Parrs Wood High School is for both boys and girls; Eton College is for boys only.)

Exercise 6 page 18
- Students read the factfile carefully to complete the sentences.
- Check answers as a class.

1 Manchester
2 1,320
3 don't live
4 PE
5 five
6 don't go

Exercise 7 page 18
- Go through the first two questions in the factfile together and point out the falling intonation in Wh- questions.
- Students ask and answer about their own school in pairs.

> **Additional vocabulary**
> The following words are from the factfile:
> - *boarding school* /ˈbɔːdɪŋ skuːl/ (n) a school where students live during term time
> - *uniform* /ˈjuːnɪfɔːm/ (n) the special clothes that everybody in the same job, school, etc. wears
> - *suit* /suːt/ (n) a jacket and trousers or a jacket and skirt, that you wear together and that are made from the same material
> - *ordinary* /ˈɔːdnri/ (adj) not special or unusual

Exercise 8 page 18
- Ask two students to read out the example questions and answers.
- Elicit the correct words to complete the rules.

a Do   b Does   c do, don't   d does, doesn't

> **Reference and practice 1.2** Workbook page 114–115
> 1 2 c 3 f 4 a 5 b 6 d
> 2 2 Does your friend live in London? Yes, he / she does.
>   3 Do your parents get up before you? No, they don't.
>   4 Does William ride his bike to school? Yes, he does.
>   5 Do we have a maths lesson today? No, we don't.
>   6 Does Eloise listen to music every evening? No, she doesn't.

Exercise 9 page 19
- Emphasize that students need to look for a question with a regular verb.
- Check answers as a class.
- Ask two students to read the question and the short answers. Remind them to use rising intonation with *yes/no* questions.
- Elicit that the main verb does not change in present simple questions.

Does your school open on Saturday?
No, it doesn't. Yes, it does.

Exercise 10 page 19
- Do the first sentence together and focus attention on the word order.
- Students work individually to do the exercise.
- Circulate and monitor, noting any common errors.
- Check answers as a class.

1 Does your school day finish at 2 p.m.?
2 Do you go to school on Saturday?
3 Do you and your friends play football at break time?
4 Does your English teacher come from the UK?
5 Do you do homework at the weekend?
6 Does your school teach drama?
7 Do other people in your family study at your school?
8 Do people in class use the internet? / Do people use the internet in class?

Students' own answers

> **Language note: Word order**
> Focus attention on the questions in the factfile again and point out the word order: *do / does* + subject + main verb + object.

Exercise 11 page 19
- Students work in pairs, asking and answering the questions in exercise 10.
- With a **stronger class**, encourage students to give extra information, especially when they answer *no*, e.g. 'Does your school day finish at 2 p.m.?' 'No, it doesn't. It finishes at half past three.'

Exercise 12 page 19
- Ask students to underline or highlight the question words in the factfile.
- With a **weaker class**, give an example for each function word, e.g. *things – tables; time – 1.30; age – seventeen; number – 156; people – Sarah, my father; places – London.*
- Students do the exercise individually or in pairs.
- Check answers as a class.

1 f 2 a 3 e 4 b 5 c 6 d

> **Reference and practice 1.3** Workbook page 115
> 1 2 Where 3 What 4 Who 5 How old
>   6 How many
> 2 2 2 3 1 4 4 5 5 6 3
> 3 2 How old is your house?
>   3 Where does Tessa live?
>   4 Who is your favourite teacher?
>   5 What is the answer to this question?
>   6 How many people are in your family?

Exercise 13 page 19
- Explain that the questions are about an after-school club.
- Tell students to read the answers carefully as they give a clue about the question word that is needed.
- Students compare answers in pairs by reading out the completed questions and answers.
- Check answers as a class.

1 When 2 Who 3 What 4 How old 5 How many
6 Where

Exercise 14 page 19

- Encourage students to be as inventive as possible when planning their perfect school. They can use the ideas in the book as well as their own ideas. Tell them to make notes but not to write full sentences.
- When they have finished, ask a few pairs to come to the front of the class and invite the rest of the class to ask them questions about their perfect school.
- Have a class vote on the best school.

Extra activity: Further discussion

Ask students to discuss these questions in groups:
Do you think school uniforms are a good idea or a bad idea? Why?
Do you think schools with boys and girls together are a good idea or a bad idea? Why?
Think of two advantages and two disadvantages of boarding schools.

DVD extra School life

Vocabulary bank: Classroom items page 126

1
1 poster	15 diary
2 map	16 pen
3 clock	17 exercise book
4 interactive whiteboard	18 dictionary
5 blackboard	19 rubber
6 window	20 ruler
7 chair	21 glue
8 teacher	22 folder
9 bin	23 pencil case
10 door	24 sheet of paper
11 student	25 pencil sharpener
12 school bag	26 scissors
13 desk	27 pencil
14 text book	28 calculator

2 Students' own answers

Learning outcome

Ask students: *What have you learned today? What can you do now?* and elicit answers: *I know words for school subjects. I can understand facts about British schools. I can ask and answer questions using the present simple. I can ask and answer about my own school.*

1D Listening, speaking and vocabulary

Journeys to school

Lesson summary
Topic: Travel and transport
Vocabulary: Transport; Vocabulary bank: Classroom language
Listening: A radio programme about teenagers' journeys to school
Speaking: Classroom language
Communication worksheet 1B: In the classroom

Lead-in

- Write *transport* on the board. Elicit its meaning and then ask students to name, in their own language, all the different forms of transport they can think of, e.g. *train, bus, tram, underground train*. Encourage them to include unusual forms of transport, e.g. *camel, skateboard*. Then ask them to open their books and look for photos of any of the forms of transport they thought of.

Exercise 1 1·30 page 20

- Focus attention on the photos and ask: *Where are the people?* Encourage students to guess the countries and give reasons for their answers.
- Give students one minute to do the matching activity.
- Play the recording for them to check their answers and repeat. Point out the silent L in *walking* /ˈwɔːkɪŋ/.
- Check answers as a class.

1 bike **2** car **3** plane **4** train **5** bus **6** walking

Exercise 2 1·31 page 20

- Read the strategy with the class. Ask students if they can think of any other synonyms, e.g. *like* and *be into*; *great* and *good*.
- Play the recording for students to check their answers.
- Check answers as a class.

1 c **2** d **3** b **4** a

Exercise 3 1·32 page 20

- Tell students that they are going to hear about six different teenagers. Draw their attention to the names of the teenagers in the table in exercise 4.
- Check that students understand *island* and *farm* and remind them that they do not have to understand every word in order to do the task.
- Play the recording.
- Check answers as a class.

Audio script

Speaker Today our programme asks: how do you go to school?
Amanda Hi! I'm Amanda and I live in São Paulo, Brazil. I'm at school from eight in the morning to four in the afternoon. I go to school by train. It takes an hour.

Joseph Hi! I'm Joseph and I'm from Kenya in Africa. One of my friends goes to school on his dad's motorbike. My dad hasn't got a motorbike, so I cycle to school with my sister. It only takes ten minutes.
Claire Hello! I'm Claire and I'm from a small island in Scotland. Only five teenagers live on the island. My friends and I go to school by plane. The journey's fun, and it only takes ninety-six seconds!
Henrik Hello, I'm Henrik and I'm from Norway. I walk to school. It only takes ten minutes, but in winter it's very cold and dark. In my part of Norway, we only see the sun for two or three hours each day in winter.
Salma Hi! I'm Salma and I'm from Morocco in Africa. Lots of my friends walk to school, but it takes thirty minutes. I get the bus to school. I go with my sisters and it only takes fifteen minutes.
Brad Hello, I'm Brad and I'm fifteen. I live on a farm in the USA. Lots of people go to my school on foot or by bus, but the buses don't come to my farm. I drive to school. It takes about twenty minutes.

Brad lives on a farm. Claire lives on an island.

Exercise 4 1·32 page 20

- With a **stronger class**, ask students to try to complete the table before listening to the recording again.
- With a **weaker class**, write the answers in the wrong order on the board and ask students to listen and match the answers to the correct place in the table.
- Play the recording several times if necessary.
- Check answers as a class.

	Country	Transport to school	Journey time
Amanda	Brazil	train	one hour
Joseph	Kenya	bike	ten minutes
Claire	Scotland	plane	ninety-six seconds
Henrik	Norway	walking	ten minutes
Salma	Morocco	bus	fifteen minutes
Brad	USA	car	twenty minutes

See exercise 3 for audio script

Exercise 5 1·33 page 21

- Focus attention on the question words. If necessary, refer **weaker students** to the matching activity in exercise 12 on page 19.
- Give students a minute to match the questions to the answers. They then compare answers in pairs.
- Play the recording again for them to check their answers.
- Check answers as a class.

1 b   2 d   3 a   4 c

Exercise 6 page 21

- Students ask and answer the questions in pairs.
- Circulate and monitor, helping where necessary.

Extra activity: Fast finishers
Write the following prompts on the board:
1 you / like / journey to school?
2 you / travel / with a friend?
3 how / your mum/dad / travel / to work?
Ask students to make questions. They then ask and answer them in pairs.

1 Do you like the / your journey to school?
2 Do you travel with a friend?
3 How does your mum / dad travel to work?

Students' own answers

Exercise 7 page 21

- Read out the six words and phrases and explain any unknown vocabulary.
- Tell students to look at the photos and identify the actions in them.
- Allow students to discuss the questions in their own language. When they have finished, elicit answers in English.

A chat   B use an MP3 player   C throw paper

Exercise 8 1·34 page 21

- Play the recording for students to identify the correct photo. Warn them that there are several different voices in the recording, but they need to listen out for Simon.
- With a **weaker class**, stop the recording after *Simon, don't listen to your MP3 player in class*, and ask students to point to the correct picture.
- Check the answer as a class.

Audio script
Teacher Good morning, class. Sit down, please. OK, please open your book at page 22. Now, what's in this photo?
Joe A bus.
Teacher Yes, very good, Joe. Simon, don't listen to your MP3 player in class. And what else?
Ana Two people. A boy and a girl.
Teacher Yes, well done, Ana.
Boy 2 The bus is … How do you say that in English?
Teacher Yellow. The bus is yellow. Have the students got uniforms, Cara?
Cara Sorry, I don't understand. Can you say that again, please?
Teacher Of course. Have the students got uniforms?
Cara Oh, uniforms! No, they haven't.
Teacher Good, Cara. Now, class, answer the questions in exercise five. But don't write in your textbook. Write in your exercise book. And after that …

photo B

Exercise 9 1·34 page 21

- Ask students to copy the three headings and the gapped sentences into their notebooks. Play the recording again for them to complete the sentences.
- Elicit answers and write them on the board to ensure that students have an accurate copy.

1 please   2 book   3 the   4 listen to   5 Don't
6 don't   7 that   8 you

See exercise 8 for audio script

Unit 1 That's life   31

Exercise 10 1·35 page 21

- Students work in pairs to complete the dialogues.
- When they have finished, ask a few pairs to read out their dialogues.
- Play the recording for students to check their answers.
- Check answers as a class.

1 don't understand
2 Can you say that again
3 don't use your mobile phone
4 How do you say
5 Open your book
6 answer the questions

See Student's Book page 21 for audio script

Exercise 11 page 21

- Ask students to look again at the affirmative instructions and the phrases to ask for help in exercise 9.
- Students look for more examples in the dialogue in exercise 10 and add these to the table.
- Check answers as a class.

Instructions (affirmative) Put the phone in your bag. Guess from the context. Use a dictionary.
Asking for help What does 'journey' mean?

Exercise 12 page 21

- Give students ten minutes to write their dialogues in pairs. Circulate and monitor, helping where necessary and noting any common errors.
- Encourage students to look up new words in a dictionary.
- Invite pairs of students to act out their dialogues.

Vocabulary bank: Classroom language page 126

1 1 read   7 repeat
   2 study   8 open
   3 do   9 listen
   4 look   10 close
   5 write   11 check
   6 work   12 learn

2 A study for the test
   B read the text
   C look at the board
   D do the exercise
   E repeat the words
   F write a sentence
   G open your book
   H work in pairs
   I close the door
   J learn the vocabulary
   K listen to the dialogue
   L check your answers

3 Students' own answers

Learning outcome

Ask students: *What have you learned today? What can you do now?* and elicit answers: *I can talk about different types of transport. I can understand an interview with people describing their journeys to school. I can describe my journey to school. I can use and understand classroom language.*

1E Writing

A questionnaire

Lesson summary
Topic: School questionnaire
Reading: A questionnaire about school
Writing: Capital letters; answering a questionnaire

Lead-in

- Ask students to work in pairs and to think about two things they like best about school. Ask them to think not only about school subjects but also about their classroom, different rooms in the school, after-school activities, etc.
- When they have finished, ask students to share their ideas with the class and write their ideas on the board.
- Have a class vote to find out which are the two most popular things in your school.

Exercise 1 page 22

- Elicit or explain *questionnaire*. Ask students to skim-read the questionnaire and find the main topic.
- Give students one minute to do the exercise.
- Check answers as a class.

1 school day   4 school bag
2 subject   5 time of day
3 teacher

Exercise 2 page 22

- Go through the questionnaire with the class. Point out that the writer has added some extra information for each question. Explain any new vocabulary.
- Circulate and monitor as students ask and answer the questions in pairs. With a **strong class**, encourage students to give extra information.

Exercise 3 page 22

- Explain that the rules concerning the use of capital letters can be different in other languages.
- Ask students to underline the examples in the text and encourage them to keep a page in their vocabulary notebooks for punctuation rules.
- Check answers as a class.

1 yes 2 yes 3 no 4 yes 5 yes 6 no 7 yes
8 no 9 yes 10 no

Exercise 4 page 22

- Write the first sentence on the board and ask students to come up and write capital letters in the correct place.
- Ask students to rewrite the rest of the paragraph using capital letters where necessary.
- Students swap notebooks with a partner and correct each other's work.
- Check answers as a class.

My favourite person is my friend, **M**ax. **H**e's **G**erman, but he lives in **L**ondon and his **E**nglish is very good. **W**e're in the same class at **H**enbury **S**chool. **W**e're very different. **H**e likes **PE** and he plays football every day. **I** like **T**hursday at school because we have drama.

Exercise 5 page 22

- Focus attention on the strategy. Explain that students should always check these things in any piece of writing, whether in their own language or in English.
- Give students five minutes to do the exercise.
- With a **weaker class**, copy the paragraph on the board and underline the mistakes. Then ask students to correct them.

On **S**aturdays, I **don't** see Max in the morning because he **plays** football. He **meets** me **at** two o'clock and we spend the **afternoon** and evening together**.** In **summer**, we meet other friends in the park. In winter, Max doesn't **like** the park, so we go to the shops in Bristol, or he comes to **my** house.

Writing guide page 23

- Read the **task** together. Ask: *What do you have to write?* Elicit that students have to write answers to the questions in the questionnaire.
- Give students five to ten minutes to complete the **ideas** stage and **plan** their answers.
- Circulate and monitor while students **write** their answers, making sure they organize their paragraphs according to their plan and include the information in the ideas section.
- When students have finished, tell them to **check** their work. Refer them to the strategy to make sure they have completed the task as well as they can.

Students' own answers

> **Additional writing task**
>
> Design a questionnaire about students' journeys to school. Write four questions. Then exchange your questionnaire with a partner and write answers to your partner's questionnaire.

Learning outcome

Ask students: *What have you learned today? What can you do now?* and elicit answers: *I can write answers to a questionnaire. I can check my work for grammar, punctuation, spelling and capital letters.*

Review 1 page 23

1 1 at   2 on   3 by   4 at   5 for   6 at   7 In   8 in
    9 On   10 at

2 1 get up
    2 have dinner
    3 go to bed
    4 meet my friends
    5 do homework

3 1 PE   4 geography
    2 history   5 ICT
    3 art   6 drama

4 1 don't go   8 learn
    2 teach   9 read
    3 gets up   10 use
    4 doesn't walk   11 don't stay
    5 start   12 visit
    6 has   13 go
    7 studies   14 watches

5 1 Where do
    2 I don't
    3 How many; do
    4 she does
    5 he doesn't

> **Pronunciation insight 1** Workbook page 132
> **Answer key:** Teacher's book page 154

Unit 1 That's life 33

2 Time out

Map of resources

Section A: Student's Book pages 24–25
Workbook page 20
Vocabulary bank, Sports page 127
Teacher's resource disk, Communication worksheet 2B

Section B: Student's Book pages 26–27
Workbook page 21
Grammar reference and practice 2.1, Workbook page 115
Vocabulary bank, Sports collocations: *play, go, do* page 127
Teacher's resource disk, Communication worksheet 2A

Section C: Student's Book pages 28–29
Workbook page 22
Grammar reference and practice 2.2, Workbook page 116
Teacher's resource disk, DVD extra + worksheet, A famous music school page 29
Teacher's resource disk, Communication worksheet 2B

Section D: Student's Book pages 30–31
Workbook page 23
Grammar reference and practice 2.3, Workbook page 117

Section E: Student's Book pages 32–33
Workbook page 26
Teacher's resource disk, Writing bank
Teacher's resource disk, Functional language bank

Review 2 page 33
Pronunciation insight 2, Workbook page 132
Progress check Unit 2, Workbook page 27
Language and skills tests 2A and 2B, Test Bank

Cumulative review Units 1–2 pages 34–35
Literature insight 1, Workbook page 92
Exam insight 1, Workbook page 102

2A Reading and vocabulary

Cycling in the desert

Lesson summary
Topic: Free-time activities in different places
Vocabulary: Free-time activities; likes and dislikes
Reading: Free time in the middle of nowhere
Speaking: Asking and answering about free-time activities
Communication worksheet 2B: Do you like … ?

Lead-in

- Write the following question on the board: *What do you do at the weekends?* Elicit answers from the class. Accept ideas in the students' own language, but translate them and write the English words on the board.
- When you have at least seven or eight ideas on the board, read out each activity and ask students to raise their hands if they do this particular activity at the weekends. Find out the most and least popular weekend activities.

Exercise 1 1•36 page 24

- Focus attention on the icons. Ask students if they can spot any of the activities they mentioned in the lead-in activity. Give them two minutes to match the words to the icons.
- Students exchange answers with a partner and then listen to the recording to check their partner's answers.
- Check answers as a class. Point out that in single-word free-time activities, the stress is on the first syllable.

1 singing
2 acting
3 dancing
4 swimming
5 rock climbing
6 drawing
7 painting
8 playing computer games
9 cooking
10 playing the drums
11 playing tennis
12 skateboarding

Exercise 2 page 24

- Ask two students to read out the example dialogue. Point out that *don't* needs to be emphasized.
- Students work in pairs and talk about the different activities.

Extra activity: Game
Ask a student to come to the front of the class and mime one of the free-time activities in exercise 1. The rest of the class try to guess the activity. The first student to guess correctly chooses another activity to mime.

Exercise 3 page 24

- Go through the place names with students, checking that they understand all the words. Then tell them to look at the photos and match them to the correct places.
- Ask a few students for their suggestions, but do not say if they are correct or incorrect yet.

Exercise 4 page 24

- Give students one minute to check their answers quickly.
- With a **weaker class**, tell students that they only need to read the first two sentences in each text to find the answer.
- Check answers as a class.

Mike the Antarctic
Stella Scotland
Juan Chile

> **Culture notes: Unusual places to live**
>
> **Rothera Research Station** is based at Rothera Point, Adelaide Island. During the summer, temperatures are 0–5°C, and for several weeks there is sunlight for twenty-four hours a day. During the winter, temperatures range between -5 and -20°C, and for several weeks the sun does not rise above the horizon at all.
>
> **Findhorn** ecovillage's inhabitants are committed to an ecological lifestyle. They do this by focusing on local food production; ecological buildings; renewable energy systems; reducing, reusing and recycling waste; and encouraging cultural and spiritual diversity.
>
> The **Paranal Observatory** is an astronomical observatory operated by the European Southern Observatory. It is the home of several very powerful telescopes. Staff and visitors stay in the ESO Hotel, which is located 200 metres lower and three kilometres away from the telescopes. It is built half into the mountain and contains a restaurant, two gardens, a swimming pool and a gym.

Exercise 5 page 24

- Go through the strategy together. Explain that we often skim-read articles and texts, and give some examples: we skim-read the front page of a newspaper in order to find out which articles we want to read more thoroughly; a book in a library to decide if we want to borrow it; a film review to decide if we want to watch the film.
- Set a strict one-minute time limit for the skim-reading activity to ensure that students do not try to understand every word.
- When they have finished, read out each summary and ask students to put up their hands when you are reading the correct summary. If necessary, explain the meaning of *traditional* and *unusual*.

The correct summary is 2.

Exercise 6 page 25

- Explain to students that they will need to read in more detail to answer these questions. Encourage them to read the questions carefully first and underline the key words. Read out question 1 as an example and elicit the key words (*Mike*, *enjoy*).
- Students work in pairs to answer the questions.
- Check answers as a class.

1 He enjoys drawing and painting pictures of Antarctica.
2 He plays computer games.
3 She works on the community farm.
4 It's at the dance studio in the village.
5 It's difficult because the Atacama desert is 2,400 metres above sea level.
6 He goes rock climbing in the gym.

> **Additional vocabulary**
> The following words are from the article *Free time in the middle of nowhere*:
>
> - *ice* /aɪs/ (n) water that has become hard because it is frozen
> - *community* /kəˈmjuːnəti/ (n) all the people who live in a place
> - *desert* /ˈdezət/ (n) a large dry area of land with very few plants
> - *environment* /ɪnˈvaɪrənmənt/ (n) the air, water, land, animals and plants around us
> - *above sea level* /əˌbʌv ˈsiː levl/ higher than the average height of the sea

V insight Likes and dislikes

The verbs *love*, *like*, *enjoy*, *don't mind* and *hate* can be followed by:

- a noun.
  I love tennis.   She doesn't mind science fiction.
- the *-ing* form of a verb (+ object).
  I love playing tennis. She doesn't mind reading science fiction. I enjoy swimming.

Expressions with prepositions, e.g. *I'm into …* and *I'm interested in …* can also be followed by a noun or the *-ing* form of a verb.
*She's into watching horror films.   We're interested in cooking.
He's into folk music.   I'm interested in fashion.*

- *Be into* is more informal than *like*, *love*, *enjoy* and *be interested in*. It is often used with *really*.
  I'm really into jazz music.

Exercise 7 page 25

- Go through the first example together, pointing out that each dash represents one letter.
- Students read the text again and work in pairs to complete the sentences.
- With a **weaker class**, tell students which text each sentence comes from: 1, 2 and 4 are from Mike's text; 5 is from Stella's text; 3 and 6 are from Juan's text.
- Encourage students to keep a section in their vocabulary notebooks for expressions that take the *-ing* form of a verb.
- Check answers as a class.

1 I like my job.
2 I'm interested in art.
3 I love sport.
4 I enjoy drawing and painting.
5 I'm interested in singing and dancing.
6 I'm into rock climbing.

Exercise 8 page 25

- Go through the strategy together. Elicit a few simple examples of antonyms, e.g. *good – bad*, *cold – hot*, *big – small*.
- Go round the class asking different students to match the phrases in exercise 7 with the antonyms.
- Check answers as a class.

a 4   b 3   c 2,5   d 1   e 6

Unit 2 **Time out** 35

Exercise 9 (page 25)

- Model and drill the stress pattern of the first two questions. Ask a few students to answer the questions.
- Students then work in pairs. Circulate and monitor, checking that they are using the phrases for likes and dislikes correctly.

> **Vocabulary bank: Sports** (page 127)
>
> 1 A basketball B sailing C volleyball D aerobics
>   E canoeing F hockey G archery H running
>   I skiing J athletics K badminton L rugby
>   M cricket N karate O gymnastics
>
> 2 1 hockey 2 basketball 3 volleyball 4 sailing
>   5 rugby 6 skiing 7 cricket
>
> 3 Students' own answers

Extra activity: Further discussion

Ask students to discuss these questions in groups:

You can spend a year in one place: the Paranal Observatory in the Atacama desert, the British Antarctic Survey in Rothera or Findhorn ecovillage in Scotland. Which place do you choose? Why?

Do you prefer very hot places or very cold places to live?

How much free time do you have in the week? How much free time do you have at the weekend?

Learning outcome

Ask students: *What have you learned today? What can you do now?* and elicit answers: *I can talk about free-time activities. I can understand a text about people's hobbies in unusual places. I can skim-read a text to find out its general meaning. I can talk about likes and dislikes.*

2B Grammar and listening

Healthy living

> **Lesson summary**
>
> **Topic:** Sport
>
> **Vocabulary:** Vocabulary bank;: Sports collocations: *play*, *go* and *do*
>
> **Grammar:** Adverbs of frequency
>
> **Listening:** A healthy lifestyle survey
>
> **Reading:** An interview with a sportsperson
>
> **Speaking:** Asking and answering about weekend activities and lifestyle
>
> **Communication worksheet 2A:** How often … ?

Lead-in

- Tell students that you are thinking of a word (e.g. *volleyball*) and that they have to guess what it is. They can ask you questions, but you can only answer *yes* or *no*.
- Start off by writing some categories on the board, e.g. *sports, daily routines, things in the classroom, family, feelings* and elicit the first question, e.g. *Is it a daily routine?* (no)
- Once students have realized that it is a sport, write all their suggestions on the board until someone says *volleyball*. Then ask students to brainstorm more sports words and write them on the board.

Exercise 1 (page 26)

- Remind students that there are words for sports in the Vocabulary bank on page 127. Model the activity by asking students to ask you the questions. Give simple, clear answers.
- Give students three minutes to ask and answer the questions in pairs. Then ask a few students to tell the class about their partner.

Exercise 2 (page 26)

- Focus attention on the photo and ask: *What is the sport?* Check that students understand what a Paralympic sport is. Ask if they can give any examples of other Paralympic sports or famous Paralympic athletes.
- Tell students to read the questions and underline the key words (*play*, *when*, *train*, *watch*) before they read the text. They then do the exercise individually or in pairs.
- Check answers as a class.

1 He plays sitting volleyball, tennis and cricket.
2 He trains before he goes to work, for two hours in the evening and sometimes at the weekend.
3 He watches football.

> **Language note: Adverbs of frequency**
>
> - An *adverb* is a word that adds extra information about the verb. We use adverbs / expressions of frequency to answer the question *How often … ?*
> - Some adverbs / expressions of frequency, e.g. *every day*, *twice a year*, *monthly*, give precise information about frequency. These usually go at the end of a sentence. *He has a music lesson every day.*
> - Other adverbs / expressions of frequency, e.g. *sometimes*, *often*, *never*, give more general information. These usually go before the main verb, or after the verb *be*. *We sometimes meet our friends after school. She's never late.*

Exercise 3 (page 26)

- Focus attention on the diagram and give some examples, using the daily routine vocabulary from Unit 1, page 14: *I always have a shower in the morning. I usually have breakfast at seven o'clock. I never go to bed before half past eleven.*
- Tell students to look at the interview again and underline the adverbs of frequency.
- To check answers, go round the class, with one student asking each question and another answering.

1 Usually
2 sometimes; usually
3 often
4 Sometimes
5 often

Exercise 4 page 26

- Students look at the example sentences in order to understand the rules about word order.
- With a **weaker class**, get students to underline the verbs in each sentence. This will make word order clearer.
- Check answers as a class.

a before   b after   c beginning

> **Reference and practice 2.1** Workbook page 115
>
> 1 2 We always train for two hours before breakfast.
>   3 Sarah never reads her text messages.
>   4 Ahmed and Natalie occasionally go cycling after work.
>   5 I'm often bored at the weekend.
>   6 My cousins are rarely at the sports centre on Sundays.
>
> 2 2 never goes to the cinema
>   3 sometimes play football in the park
>   4 'm usually late for school
>   5 occasionally drive to work
>   6 always sleeps on my bed

Exercise 5 page 27

- Remind students to think about the main verb when they put the adverb in the correct place.
- When they have finished, ask a few students to write the sentences on the board. The other students say if they think the sentences are correct.
- Check answers as a class.

1 I always play tennis at the weekend with my friends Grace, Jess and Sonia.
2 Grace and Sonia are sometimes late for the game, but Jess is never late. / Sometimes, Grace and Sonia are late for the game, but Jess is never late.
3 Jess usually wins the game. / Usually, Jess wins the game.
4 She often practises tennis after school.
5 I'm always very tired at the end of the game.
6 We don't often watch tennis matches on TV.

Exercise 6 page 27

- Focus attention on the table and the example sentence. Ask: *How often does Sue play football?* and elicit a full sentence reply. (*Sue usually plays football at the weekend.*)
- Remind students that we add *-s* or *-es* to the verb in the third person. Students then work individually to write the sentences before comparing answers in pairs.
- Check answers as a class.

David always plays football at the weekend.
David often goes cycling at the weekend.
Susan often does homework at the weekend.
Susan usually plays football at the weekend. / Usually, Susan plays football at the weekend.
Susan usually gets bored at the weekend. / Usually, Susan gets bored at the weekend.
David sometimes plays the guitar at the weekend. / Sometimes, David plays the guitar at the weekend.
Susan sometimes goes cycling at the weekend. / Sometimes, Susan goes cycling at the weekend.
David doesn't often get bored at the weekend.
David never does homework at the weekend.
Susan never plays the guitar at the weekend.

Exercise 7 page 27

- Ask two students to read out the example question and answer.
- Circulate and monitor, noting any common errors.

> **Extra activity: Fast finishers**
>
> Ask **fast finishers** to write four more questions with *How often …?* and the daily routine phrases from Unit 1, page 14. They then ask and answer questions in pairs.

Exercise 8 1·37 page 27

- Tell students to read Rose's notes first and try to predict her questions.
- Play the recording for students to check their answers. Then play it again.
- Check answers as a class.

Audio script
Rose Hey, Sarah, I've got this healthy lifestyle survey for my English homework. Can I ask you some questions?
Sarah Um, OK then.
Rose What time do you get up in the morning?
Sarah I usually get up at seven., but at the weekends, I sometimes get up at eight or nine.
Rose OK. And what do you usually have for breakfast?
Sarah I don't often have breakfast. I don't like eating in the morning.
Rose Oh, that's not very healthy. Well, how do you get to school? Do you take the school bus?
Sarah No, I never take the bus. I always cycle to school. Also when it rains!
Rose Very healthy! So, next question. How often do you do sport after school?
Sarah Well, you know I love playing basketball and I'm in the karate club. So I do sport three or four nights a week.
Rose OK, so that means you often do sport?
Sarah Yes, that's right. Any more questions?
Rose Yes, last one. What time do you go to bed?
Sarah I always go to bed at ten o'clock.
Rose Great. Thanks very much, Sarah. I think your lifestyle is quite healthy!

usually gets up at 7
sometimes gets up at 8 or 9 at the weekend
doesn't often have breakfast
never takes the bus to school – **always** cycles
always goes to bed at 10

Exercise 9 page 27

- Go through the questions with students. Check that they understand *team sport*, *individual sport* and *fast food*.
- Focus attention on Rose's notes again and remind students to write notes, not full sentences.
- Ask a few students to tell the rest of the class about their partner.

Vocabulary bank: Sports collocations page 127

1 **play** badminton, basketball, cricket, hockey, rugby, volleyball
  go canoeing, running, sailing, skiing
  do aerobics, archery, athletics, gymnastics, karate

2 a play   b go   c do

3 1 play   2 play   3 play   4 do   5 play   6 play
  7 play   8 do   9 do   10 do   11 go   12 do
  13 go   14 go   15 go

4 Students' own answers

Learning outcome

Ask students: *What have you learned today? What can you do now?* and elicit answers: *I can use adverbs of frequency. I can read an interview with a sportsperson. I can understand a healthy lifestyle survey. I can ask and answer questions about my lifestyle.*

2C Culture, vocabulary and grammar

Making music

Lesson summary
Topic: Music and abilities
Vocabulary: Musical instruments
Grammar: *can / can't* for ability
Reading: Music for everyone
Speaking: Planning a music camp
Communication worksheet 2B: Do you like … ?

Lead-in

- Write *MUSIC* in capital letters on the board.
- Ask students to work in pairs. Give them one minute to brainstorm words related to the theme of music, e.g. *piano, opera, CD*.
- When they have finished, ask the pair with the longest list to read out their words.

Exercise 1   page 28

- Focus attention on the photos and ask students to discuss the questions in pairs.
- When they have finished, ask students to share their ideas with the class. Do not expect full sentence answers to the question *What are they doing?* as students have not yet learned the present continuous.

Exercise 2 1·38   page 28

- Explain, if necessary, that the different instruments in an orchestra usually sit in 'sections' – the string section, the woodwind section, the brass section and the percussion section.
- Give students time to look at the photo and find the instruments. Then play the recording for them to listen and check their answers.
- Check answers as a class. Model and drill the words, pointing out the /tʃ/ in *cello* /ˈtʃeləʊ/, the /ɪ/ in *guitar* /ɡɪˈtɑː/ and the /ɔː/ in *keyboards* /ˈkiːbɔːdz/.

1 trumpet   2 guitar   3 flute   4 clarinet   5 drums
6 keyboards   7 violin   8 saxophone   9 piano
10 cello

Exercise 3   1·39   page 28

- Students who are musical or who are studying a musical instrument will find this activity much easier than others. Put students into small groups, making sure that each group includes a student who has some musical knowledge or who can play an instrument.
- Play the recording and then check answers as a class.

1 keyboards   2 flute   3 drums   4 violin
5 trumpet   6 cello

Alternative activity
Do the activity as a competition. Put students into three or four teams. Play the recording. As soon as a team thinks they can identify the instrument, they should stand up. If they answer correctly, they score a point.

Exercise 4   page 28

- Read out the sentences and the answer options and explain that Milton Keynes is the name of a large town in the UK.
- Give students two minutes to do the exercise.
- Check answers as a class.

1 the UK   2 has   3 tents

Culture note: National Youth Music Camps
The **National Youth Music Camps** were founded by Dr Avril Dankworth – sister of the famous jazz saxophonist Johnny Dankworth – in 1970. They are open to children aged eight to seventeen. The Camps practise an 'Allmusic' philosophy that encourages enthusiasm and creativity whatever the skill level of the child.

Exercise 5   page 28

- Tell students to read the sentences and to underline the key words. They should then look for these words in the text.
- Read out each sentence and ask students to put up their hands if they think it is true.
- Check answers as a class. Ask a few students to write correct versions of the false sentences on the board.

38   Unit 2 Time out

1 T
2 T
3 F: Some children are good musicians, but some can't play an instrument.
4 F: The children perform a special concert and their families come to it.
5 F: Tony thinks that it isn't important.
6 F: Yasmin plays classical music at home.

> **Extra activity: Game**
>
> Students work in pairs. One student reads out a sentence from the text but says *BUZZ* in place of a key word, e.g. *They have music lessons at the BUZZ*. The other student tries to remember the missing word (*campsite*) without looking at the text.

Exercise 6 page 28

- Remind students that they learned about antonyms on page 25.
- With a **weaker class**, go through the text with students. Elicit all the adjectives and write them on the board.
- Students work in pairs to find the antonyms.
- Check answers as a class.

big small   quiet noisy   unusual usual / ordinary
bad good   same different   difficult easy

> **Additional vocabulary**
>
> The following words are from the text *Music for everyone*:
> - *campsite* /ˈkæmpsaɪt/ (n) a place where you can stay in a tent
> - *musician* /mjuˈzɪʃn/ (n) a person who writes music or plays a musical instrument
> - *perform* /pəˈfɔːm/ (v) to be in something such as a play or a concert
> - *tent* /tent/ (n) a kind of small house made of cloth. You sleep in a tent when you go camping.

Exercise 7 page 28

- To prepare for this activity, ask students to read Tony and Yasmin's texts again and find four words for types of music (*rock*, *hip hop*, *classical*, *jazz*). Write them on the board and elicit or supply a few more words, e.g. *folk*, *punk*, *pop*.
- Students discuss the questions in pairs. Circulate and monitor, helping with vocabulary if necessary.

Exercise 8 page 29

- Read out the example sentences and tell students to find them in the text. Explain or demonstrate the meaning of *ability*; mime something that you *can* do, e.g. *sing*, *hop*, and something that you *can't* do, e.g. *fly*.
- Check answers as a class. Point out the /ɑː/ in *can't* /kɑːnt/.

a without   b can't   c the same

Reference and practice 2.2 Workbook page 116

1 2 a 3 b 4 a 5 b 6 c

2 2 can do   5 can make
   3 can play   6 can speak
   4 can't

3 2 Can she do karate? No, she can't.
   3 Can she play the drums? No, she can't.
   4 Can she sing? Yes, she can.
   5 Can she make a cake? No, she can't.
   6 Can she speak Spanish? Yes, she can.

Exercise 9 page 29

- Focus attention again on the example sentences in exercise 8 and ask students to identify the affirmative sentences, the negative sentence and the question.
- Students work individually to write the sentences. They then check answers in pairs.
- Check answers as a class.

1 Jane can play the piano.
2 Adam can't dance.
3 Can Tom take good photos?
4 Rose can't ride a bike.
5 Can Simon play the drums?
6 Maria can speak English.

Exercise 10 1·40 page 29

- Tell students to look at the table and think about the words they will hear in the recording.
- Play the recording for students to complete the table.
- They then work in pairs to write the sentences.
- Play the recording again for students to check their answers.
- Ask a few students to read out their sentences. Make sure that they are pronouncing *can* /kən/ and *can't* /kɑːnt/ correctly.

Audio script

Bella Wow! Omar, you're really good at the violin!
Omar Thanks, Bella. Can you play the violin?
Bella No, I can't. I can sing and I can play the flute, but I can't play the violin.
Omar Ah, I can't play the flute and … I can't sing.
Bella No, you can't. That's true. Do you want to be a professional musician?
Omar No. Actually, I want to be a dancer.
Bella Oh, so you can dance?
Omar Yes, I can. Can you dance?
Bella No way! I'm a terrible dancer. I can act, but I can't dance.
Omar And I can dance … but I can't act.
Bella Well, we've all got our own talents, I guess.

Omar can play the violin. Bella can't play the violin.
Omar can't play the flute. Bella can play the flute.
Omar can't sing. Bella can sing.
Omar can dance. Bella can't dance.
Omar can't act. Bella can act.

Exercise 11 (page 29)

- Ask: *Can you play a musical instrument?* and elicit *Yes, I can* or *No, I can't*.
- Students ask and answer in pairs.
- Circulate and monitor. **Fast finishers** can use the list of instruments on page 28 or the sports from the Vocabulary bank on page 127 to make more questions with *can*.

Exercise 12 (page 29)

- Explain to students that they are going to plan their own Music Camp. They must include answers to the questions and they can also add their own ideas.
- Give students five minutes to discuss their Music Camp and to make some notes. Then ask a few pairs to share their ideas with the class.
- Ask the class to vote for their favourite Music Camp.

> **Extra activity: Further discussion**
>
> Ask students to discuss these questions in groups:
> *Do you like listening to music when you study? Why? / Why not?*
> *Do you like the same kind of music as your parents?*
> *Do you sometimes go to music concerts? What kind of music?*
> *Do you prefer listening to recorded music (e.g. CDs, MP3s) or live music? Why?*

DVD extra | A famous music school

Learning outcome

Ask students: *What have you learned today? What can you do now?* and elicit answers: *I know the names of musical instruments. I can talk about ability with 'can' and 'can't'. I can describe what people can and can't do. I can plan a Music Camp.*

2D Listening, speaking and vocabulary

Superheroes

Lesson summary
Topic: People with amazing abilities
Vocabulary: Languages
Grammar: Adverbs of manner
Speaking: Making requests with *can* and *could*
Writing: A dialogue between two friends

Lead-in

- Ask students to work in groups to create their own superhero. Give them three minutes to think about their hero and to make notes. Tell them that their superhero has to have at least two 'superpowers', e.g. *He can fly*, and also one weakness, e.g. *He doesn't like water*.
- When they have finished, ask one student from each group to share their group's ideas with the class.
- Ask the class to vote for the best superhero.

Exercise 1 1•41 (page 30)

- Focus attention on the different languages and explain that the sentences all express the same thing.
- Give students two minutes to match the languages to the sentences. If necessary, explain that Chinese, Japanese and Russian all use different alphabets.
- Play the recording for students to check their answers.
- Check answers as a class.

1 Dutch   2 Japanese   3 French   4 Italian   5 Spanish
6 English   7 Portuguese   8 Hungarian   9 Polish
10 Russian   11 Chinese

> **Extra activity: Other languages**
>
> If you have any students from different countries in your class, ask them to write *Welcome to my country* in their language on the board and teach the class how to say it.

Exercise 2 (page 30)

- Go through the strategy together. Explain to students that English spelling is difficult even for English speakers, and therefore it is important for them to keep a record of different spelling patterns.
- Copy the headings on the board and ask different students to write the languages under the correct heading.

-ish   English, Polish, Spanish
-ian   Hungarian, Italian, Russian
-ese   Chinese, Japanese, Portuguese
-ch   Dutch, French

Exercise 3 (page 30)

- Model the questions and answers with a student.
- Students then work in groups, asking and answering the questions.

> **Alternative activity**
>
> Ask students to imagine a character from another country who speaks different languages. They then work in large groups. In the role of their character, they ask and answer the questions in exercise 3 and try to find other characters from the same country or who speak the same languages.

Exercise 4 1•42 (page 30)

- Ask students to read the questions. Remind them that they do not need to understand every word of the dialogue in order to answer the questions.
- Play the recording once.
- Check answers as a class.

Audio script

Girl Look at this article, *Vote for your Superhero!* It's really interesting.
Boy What's that about?
Girl It's an article about three people who are really into their particular hobby – learning languages, sport and music. So, for example, there's this guy called Richard Simcott.
Boy And why is he a superhero?
Girl Well, he loves learning languages. He travels around the world and he can speak more than sixteen languages.
Boy Really? Which ones can he speak?

40   Unit 2 Time out

Girl Oh, I can't remember all of them. But definitely English, French, Dutch, … erm, Portuguese, I think, Spanish, Italian …
Boy Wow, that's very impressive. Who else is in this 'superhero' article?
Girl Right, well, there's a woman called Amber Monforte. She works as a nurse, but she also loves sport. Every year, she does this event called Ultraman in Hawaii.
Boy And what do athletes do in an Ultraman event?
Girl They swim, cycle and run. First, they swim ten kilometres in the sea.
Boy Wow! OK.
Girl Then they cycle 421 kilometres.
Boy What! 421 kilometres?
Girl Yup, and finally, they run eighty-four kilometres.
Boy And how long does it take?
Girl Well, Amber usually completes the whole race in about twenty-four hours.
Boy And who's the third superhero in the article?
Girl It's Herbie Newson. He loves music and he can play twenty-two different instruments!

1 He can speak (more than) sixteen languages. English, French, Dutch, Portuguese, Spanish, Italian
2 Swimming, cycling and running.

Exercise 5 1·42 page 30

- With a **stronger class**, ask students to answer as many questions as they can before listening to the recording again.
- Play the recording again for students to check their answers.
- Check answers as a class.

1 b   2 a   3 c   4 a   5 a

See exercise 4 for audio script

> **Language note: Adverbs of manner**
> - Adverbs of manner usually come after the main verb if there is no object, or after the object. They do not come between the main verb and the object.
>   *She reads quickly.*
>   *She reads the book quickly.*
> - Other common irregular adverbs of manner include *fast* and *straight*.

Exercise 6 page 31

- Remind students that they have already studied adverbs of frequency. Say: *Adverbs of frequency answer the question 'How often … ?'. Adverbs of manner answer the question 'How … ?'.*
- Give students a minute to read the rules.
- With a **stronger class**, ask students to make adverbs from these adjectives: *noisy* (noisily), *sad* (sadly), *happy* (happily), *safe* (safely).

> **Reference and practice 2.3** Workbook page 117
> 1 2 well   3 fast   4 badly   5 easily   6 slowly
> 2 2 I play tennis badly.
>   3 They play the piano slowly.
>   4 We usually finish our homework quickly.
>   5 Dad sometimes shouts angrily at our dog.
>   6 Your little brother plays very noisily.
> 3 1 Kate plays the flute really beautifully.
>   2 Our teacher speaks very loudly.
>   3 I do quite well in tests.
>   4 The volleyball team trains very hard.
>   5 I eat breakfast really quickly.

Exercise 7 1·43 page 31

- Write the adverbs from exercise 6 on the board. Play the recording once and ask students to complete the sentences.
- Play the recording again. This time pause after each adverb.
- Check answers by asking individual students to read out the sentences.

Audio script
Boy I can learn to play new musical instruments easily, and I often learn songs from YouTube tutorials. I learn new songs quickly, but I practise hard every day, so that helps. My first instrument is the violin, and I can play it well. I can also play the guitar and the cello. But I'm a beginner at the cello. I play it badly! I can also play the recorder, the flute and the piano. But I usually play the piano very quietly because my girlfriend hates listening to piano music. I can play about twenty-two or twenty-three instruments in total.

1 easily   2 quickly   3 hard   4 well   5 badly
6 quietly

Exercise 8 page 31

- Read out the two problems and ask students to call out the correct letter.
- Ask:
  Where's the bag in picture A? (under the chair)
  Why is the girl cold in picture B? (because the window is open)

A She can't find her bag.   B She is very cold.

Exercise 9 1·44 page 31

- Play the recording and then check the answer as a class.
- Play the recording again and ask: *What is Sarah's other problem?* (She hasn't got a calculator.)

Audio script
Dad Sarah, you're late for school.
Sarah I know, but I can't find my bag. Can you help me, please?
Dad Sure. No problem. Look, here it is. Now, have you got everything?
Sarah Oh, no! I haven't got a calculator. Could you buy me one, please?
Dad Yes, of course.

A

Exercise 10 1·44 page 31
- Students work in pairs to complete the phrases.
- Play the recording again for students to check their answers.
- Check answers by asking individual students to read out the phrases. Make sure they use a rising intonation at the end of the sentence.

1 help   2 you (buy) me   3 Sure   4 problem
5 of course

See exercise 9 for audio script

Exercise 11 1·45 page 31
- Go through the phrases together. Ask students to identify two responses (*No, sorry, I can't. Yes, of course.*) and two requests (*Can you get my sweater? Could you close the window?*).
- Give students a minute to complete the dialogue. Then play the recording for them to check their answers.
- Check answers as a class.

1 Could you close the window
2 Yes, of course
3 Can you get my sweater
4 No, sorry, I can't

Exercise 12 page 31
- Elicit some ideas for problems and requests and write them on the board, e.g. *I'm hungry – make a sandwich; I'm hot – open the window; I can't do my homework – talk to the teacher.*
- Circulate and monitor as students write their dialogues, helping with vocabulary if necessary.
- When they have finished, ask a few students to act out their dialogue in front of the class.

Learning outcome
Ask students: *What have you learned today? What can you do now?* and elicit answers: *I know the names of different languages. I can understand a dialogue about people's abilities. I can use adverbs of manner. I can make requests with 'can' and 'could'.*

2E Writing

An informal letter

Lesson summary
Topic: Pen pals
Vocabulary: Linking words: *and, but, or*
Reading: An informal letter to a pen pal organization
Writing: An informal letter with personal information

Lead-in
- Write PEN PAL on the board. Elicit or explain the meaning (a person that you make friends with by writing letters).
- Ask:
  Has anyone in the class got a pen pal?
  Where is your pen pal from?
  How often do you write to your pen pal?
- If no one in the class has a pen pal, ask:
  Do you want a pen pal? Why / why not?
  How can a pen pal help your English?

Exercise 1 page 32
- Focus attention on the advertisement and explain, if necessary, that *global* means 'international'.
- Give students one minute to find the answers.
- Check answers as a class.

1 It finds pen pals for people.
2 It wants to know about school, daily life and hobbies.

Exercise 2 page 32
- Focus attention on Julia's letter. Ask:
  Who is the letter to? (Global PenPals)
  Who is it from? (Julia Mitchell)
- Ask students to read the letter and underline the phrases or sentences in the list.
- Check answers as a class by asking students to read out the relevant sentence for each thing.

Julia's letter mentions free-time activities, pets, friends, school, family and weekends.

Exercise 3 page 32
- Go through the strategy together. Explain that you use an *informal* style when talking or writing to friends and family.
- Students read the letter again and complete the strategy.
- With a **weaker class**, ask students to underline the following in the letter first: the address, *Best wishes*, the date, the name of the writer, *Dear …* .
- Check answers as a class.

1 Begin   2 Finish   3 address   4 date   5 bottom

Exercise 4 page 32
- Explain that the sentences are all from Julia's letter. Give students two minutes to complete them.
- Check answers as a class.

1 and   2 or   3 but / and   4 and   5 but   6 or

> **Language note: Linking words: *and, but, or***
> - We use *and* to add information.
> - We use *but* to contrast information.
> - We use *or* to combine two negative phrases (*I can't swim or ride a bike*) or to offer an alternative (*Do you want coffee or tea?*).

Exercise 5 page 32
- Students do the exercise on their own or in pairs.
- Check answers as a class.

1 but   2 or   3 and   4 but   5 or

Writing guide   page 33

- Read the **task** together, making sure students are clear that they have to write a letter similar to Julia's.
- Give students five to ten minutes to complete the **ideas** stage and **plan** their letter. Circulate and monitor, helping with language and ideas as necessary. Remind students to write notes, not full sentences.
- Circulate and monitor while students **write** their letters, encouraging them to use *and*, *but* and *or*. Remind them to activate the language they learned in the unit (*can* and *can't* for ability, adverbs of frequency, adverbs of manner).
- When students have finished, they **check** their work. Refer them to the checklist to make sure they have completed the task as well as they can.

Extension: Fast finishers
Ask **fast finishers** to swap letters with another student to read and check for mistakes.

Additional writing activity
Imagine you are one of these people:
- someone from another planet
- a ninety-year-old man/woman
- a five-year-old child
- a young person in the year 1850

Write a letter to Global PenPals with information about your family, your school and your free time.

Learning outcome
Ask students: *What have you learned today? What can you do now?* and elicit answers: *I can read and understand a letter from a pen pal. I can use linking words, 'and', 'but' and 'or'. I can write an informal letter about my home, school, family and free time.*

Review 2   page 33

1 1 drawing   2 painting   3 acting   4 dancing
    5 sailing   6 violin   7 flute   8 trumpet

2 1 My brother loves skateboarding.
    2 I'm into singing.
    3 Rob likes photography.
    4 We don't enjoy cooking.
    5 My sister isn't interested in dancing.
    6 Kate dislikes swimming.

3 1 Italian   2 French   3 Russian   4 Japanese
    5 Spanish   6 Polish   7 Dutch   8 English

4 1 Oliver never has fish for lunch.
    2 My sister often goes to bed late.
    3 We sometimes cycle to school. / Sometimes, we cycle to school.
    4 I'm always late for school.
    5 Mia usually plays tennis at the weekend. / Usually, Mia plays tennis at the weekend.
    6 My parents don't often use the internet.

5 1 can (you) do
    2 Can (you) act
    3 can't
    4 Can (you) sing
    5 can't
    6 can't dance
    7 can paint
    8 Can (you) take
    9 can
    10 Can (you) use
    11 can

6 1 quietly   2 hard   3 badly   4 well   5 quickly
    6 easily

Pronunciation insight 2   Workbook page 132
Answer key: Teacher's book page 154

Cumulative review Units 1–2

pages 34–35

1 🔊 1·46

1 T
2 F: They usually swim for 1,500 metres.
3 F: They cycle for forty kilometres.
4 F: They do all the sports on the same day.
5 T
6 F: His favourite sport is cycling.
7 F: He trains six days a week.
8 T
9 T
10 T

Audio script

Trisha Hello, and welcome to *The Sports Programme*. Triathlon is a very difficult sport. Andy Brown is a champion triathlon athlete and he's here with us today. Hello, Andy.
Andy Hi.
Trisha Now, Andy. There are three sports in the triathlon. What are they?
Andy Well, Trisha, the triathlon sports are swimming, cycling and running.
Trisha Right. So, how far do you swim?
Andy In the Olympics, we swim for 1,500 metres.
Trisha And how far do you cycle?
Andy We cycle for forty kilometres.
Trisha Do you stop and rest after the swimming and before the cycling?
Andy We don't rest. But we stop to change clothes. The triathlon is a continuous race and we do one sport after the other.
Trisha Right. So it's swimming for 1,500 metres, cycling for forty kilometres and then running. How far do you run?
Andy We run for ten kilometres.
Trisha Ten kilometres! That's a long way. Are you tired when you finish?
Andy Yes, I am. I'm very tired!
Trisha Which is your favourite sport, Andy? Swimming, cycling or running?
Andy I really enjoy cycling. I love going fast.
Trisha OK. Now, Andy, how often do you train?
Andy I train six days a week. Sunday is my day off, so I don't train then.
Trisha And do you train in the morning or in the evening?
Andy I train every evening from Monday to Saturday, and I go running three mornings a week. I get up early and I run for about five kilometres before I go to university.
Trisha So you're a student, Andy?
Andy Yes. I study sports science at the University of Manchester.
Trisha That's interesting. Andy, do you do any other activities in your free time, apart from sport?
Andy Yes, I love cooking. On Sundays, I often cook a special meal for my girlfriend and some friends. We usually have a curry, but sometimes I make some Japanese food. I'm really into sushi.
Trisha That sounds delicious! Andy Brown, thank you for talking to us. And good luck in your next triathlon.
Andy Thanks a lot, Trisha.

2 Students' own answers

3 C

4 1 d 2 c 3 c 4 a 5 c 6 a

5 1 b 2 b 3 a 4 c 5 b 6 c 7 a 8 a
9 c 10 a

6 Students' own answers

Additional materials			
Literature insight 1	Workbook page 92	Answer key:	Teacher's book page 151
Exam insight 1	Workbook page 102	Answer key:	See website

3 Home and away

Map of resources

Section A: Student's Book pages 36–37
Workbook page 28
Vocabulary bank, In the home page 128
Teacher's resource disk, Communication worksheet 3A

Section B: Student's Book pages 38–39
Workbook page 29
Grammar reference and practice 3.1, Workbook page 117
Vocabulary bank, Around town page 128
Teacher's resource disk, Communication worksheet 3A

Section C: Student's Book pages 40–41
Workbook page 30
Grammar reference and practice 3.2, Workbook page 118
Grammar reference and practice 3.3, Workbook page 118
Teacher's resource disk, DVD extra + worksheet, A room with a view? page 41

Section D: Student's Book pages 42–43
Workbook page 31
Teacher's resource disk, Communication worksheet 3B

Section E: Student's Book pages 44–45
Workbook page 34
Teacher's resource disk, Writing bank
Teacher's resource disk, Functional language bank

Review 3 page 45
Pronunciation insight 3, Workbook page 133
Progress check Unit 3, Workbook page 35
Language and skills tests 3A and 3B, Test Bank

3A Reading and vocabulary

House of the future

Lesson summary
Topic: Homes
Vocabulary: Inside and outside the home; prepositions of place; Vocabulary bank: In the home
Reading: Earthships
Speaking: Describing your home
Communication worksheet 3A: What's in the room?

Lead-in

- Write *House of the future* on the board. Elicit or explain the meaning of *future*. Students work in pairs and imagine a house of the future. Write some questions on the board:
Where is it? Is it big or small?
Is it on land, in the air or in the sea?
How many people live in it?
- Students can discuss their ideas in their own language.
- When they have finished, ask each pair to share their ideas with the class and write notes in English on the board, translating where necessary.

Exercise 1 page 36

- Use the photos on this page to explain the difference between a *house* and a *flat*. Talk briefly about your own home, e.g. *I live in a flat in the middle of town. My favourite thing in my flat is my piano because I love playing music.*
- Students work in pairs to tell each other about their homes.
- Discuss the final question – *What's the difference between a house* (a building where a person or a family lives) *and a home* (the place where you live)? – with the whole class.

Exercise 2 1·47 page 36

- Give students one minute to match the words to the pictures. Then play the recording for them to check and repeat.
- Point out that all the words are stressed on the first syllable, and that *-room* is pronounced /rʊm/.
- Check answers as a class.

1 bedroom 2 kitchen 3 hall 4 living room
5 bathroom 6 garden

Extra activity: Rooms
Write the following words on the board: *play football, sleep, watch TV, have breakfast, have a shower*. Ask **fast finishers**, in pairs, to match each activity to a room in exercise 2 and to say a sentence for each one, e.g. *I play football in the garden*. Tell them that one room (*hall*) is not needed. They can then think of one more sentence for each room.

Exercise 3 1·48 page 36

- Use things in the classroom to pre-teach *ceiling*, *cupboard*, *door*, *floor*, *table*, *wall* and *window*.
- Ask students to find the other things in the photos.
- Students exchange answers with a partner and then listen to the recording to check their partner's answers.
- Focus on the pronunciation of *ceiling* /ˈsiːlɪŋ/, *drawers* /drɔːz/, *cupboard* /ˈkʌbəd/ and *fridge* /frɪdʒ/.
- Check answers as a class.

A wall **B** bed **C** chest of drawers **D** ceiling
E cooker **F** cupboard **G** door **H** rug **I** window
J sofa **K** table **L** floor **M** toilet **N** bath **O** shower
P roof

Exercise 4 1·49 page 36

- Explain that the sentences are about homes in different countries. Ask students to skim-read the sentences and find out which country each sentence is about. They then work in pairs to circle the correct words, guessing if necessary.
- Play the recording for students to check their answers.
- Check answers as a class.

1 table; floor
2 bed; cupboard
3 fridges; cookers
4 windows
5 bathroom

Culture note: Earthships

Michael Reynolds, of Earthship Biotecture, pioneered the design of **Earthships** in the 1970s. There are now Earthships in Africa, Australia, North America and Europe. The design follows the principles of producing electricity from heat and wind, collecting water from rain and snow, heating and cooling the building from the sun and the earth, and using natural or recycled building materials.

Exercise 5 page 36

- Tell students that the photos on page 37 are all from an Earthship. Ask them to speculate what type of house this is, and if it is good or bad for the environment.
- Give students two minutes to read the text quickly to check their ideas.
- Check the answer as a class and ask students to give reasons for their answer.

It is good for the environment.

Exercise 6 page 36

- Tell students to read the questions carefully and then look for the key information in the texts.
- Check answers as a class.

1 F: You don't build an Earthship like an ordinary house.
2 T
3 F: You build the back wall from old car tyres.
4 F: There aren't (any) windows in the back wall.
5 F: Earthships are warm at night.
6 T
7 T
8 F: After a shower, you can use the water on plants and in the toilet.
9 F: She thinks her home is fantastic.
10 T

Additional vocabulary

The following words are from the text *Earthships*:

- *recycled* /ˌriːˈsaɪkld/ (adj) Something that is recycled has been used before.
- *rubbish* /ˈrʌbɪʃ/ (n) things that you do not want any more
- *filter* /ˈfɪltə(r)/ (v) to pass a liquid through a special device in order to hold back the solid parts in it
- *comfortable* /ˈkʌmftəbl/ (adj) nice to sit in, to be in, or to wear
- *modern* /ˈmɒdn/ (adj) of the present time; of the kind that is usual now

Exercise 7 page 37

- Brainstorm some ideas in favour of and against Earthships on the board first, e.g. *they are good for the environment, they are cheap to build, they look strange, you can't build them in the middle of a city*, etc.
- Suggest some different ways to help the environment, e.g. *use public transport, cycle or walk, recycle rubbish, don't use a lot of water, take a shower instead of a bath*.
- Circulate and monitor, helping with any vocabulary if necessary.

V insight Prepositions of place

The most commonly used prepositions of place are *at*, *on* and *in*. We often use:

- *at* with points, e.g. *at the bus stop, at the end of the road*.
- *in* with enclosed spaces, e.g. *in the house, in the garden*.
- *on* with surfaces, e.g. *on the floor, on a page*.

Encourage students to make a note of phrases with prepositions and to learn them in context.

Exercise 8 page 37

- Use objects in the classroom, e.g. a bag and a desk, to demonstrate the different prepositions.
- Students find the prepositions in the text and match them to the diagrams.
- Check answers as a class. Make sure students understand that *next to* is usually closer than *near*.

1 in **2** on **3** under **4** near **5** next to **6** in front of
7 behind **8** between **9** opposite

Extra activity: Where's the coin?

Ask one student to leave the classroom. Another student hides a coin somewhere in the classroom. Bring the first student back into the classroom. They ask questions to find out where the coin is, e.g. *Is it under the desk? Is it near the door?* The rest of the class answers the questions.

Exercise 9 page 37

- Students look at the photos of the Earthship again and use the prepositions to describe where things are.
- With a **weaker class**, write the prepositions (*in, opposite, in front of, next to*) on the board, and ask students to use them to complete the sentences.
- Check answers as a class.

1 in **2** next to **3** on **4** opposite **5** in front of

Unit 3 Home and away

Exercise 10 *page 37*

- Go through the strategy with students. Emphasize that they do not have to be good at drawing – stick figures and simple sketches will be fine – but the process of actively drawing something will help them to remember the word.
- Give students two minutes to draw their own diagrams for each preposition.

Exercise 11 *page 37*

- Focus attention on the picture on page 128. Students will need to use some of the new vocabulary on this page to describe where the different things are.
- Elicit answers from different students by asking questions, e.g. *Where's the wardrobe?*
- With a **stronger class**, you can play a memory game. Give students one minute to look at the picture and then ask them to close their books. Can they remember where the different things are?

Exercise 12 *page 37*

- Introduce the activity by telling students about your Earthship. Students then continue to work in pairs.
- Circulate and monitor, noting any common errors.

> **Extra activity: Further discussion**
>
> Ask students to discuss these questions in groups:
> *What do you like about your home? What don't you like?*
> *How important are these things in a home? Rank them in order of importance: size of rooms, big garden, close to shops / school, big kitchen, eco-friendly*
> *Some people live on boats, in buses or under the ground. Do you think you would like to live in an unusual house? What kind of house?*

> **Vocabulary bank: In the home** *page 128*
>
> **1** 1 shutters   2 wardrobe   3 shelf   4 rug
>   5 bedside table   6 lamp   7 washbasin   8 mirror
>   9 curtains   10 bidet   11 front door   12 stairs
>   13 armchair   14 fireplace   15 carpet   16 cushion
>   17 freezer   18 fridge   19 dishwasher   20 sink
>   21 washing machine
>
> **2** Suggested answers:
>   **bedroom** bedside table, carpet, curtains, cushion, lamp, mirror, rug, shelf, shutters, wardrobe
>   **bathroom** bidet, mirror, rug, shelf, shutters, washbasin
>   **dining room** carpet, curtains, fireplace, lamp, mirror, rug, shelf, shutters
>   **kitchen** dishwasher, freezer, fridge, rug, shelf, shutters, sink, washing machine
>   **living room** armchair, carpet, curtains, cushion, fireplace, lamp, mirror, rug, shelf, shutters, stairs
>   **hall** front door, mirror, rug, stairs
>
> **3** Students' own answers

Learning outcome

Ask students: *What have you learned today? What can you do now?* and elicit answers: *I can talk about rooms and furniture. I can understand a text about Earthships. I can use prepositions of place to describe where things are. I can describe my home.*

3B Grammar and listening

Enjoy the view

> **Lesson summary**
>
> **Topic:** Unusual hotels
> **Vocabulary:** Vocabulary bank: Around town
> **Grammar:** *there is / there are* with *some / any*
> **Listening:** Sam's holiday
> **Reading:** On the beach or in a tree?
> **Speaking:** Discussing places to stay on holiday
> **Communication worksheet 3A:** What's in the room?

Lead-in

Tell students that you are thinking of a word. They have to guess what the word is. Start by giving some clues, e.g. *It's a building. People sleep here, but it isn't a house.* Students can ask you questions but you can only answer *yes* or *no*.

When they guess the word (hotel), ask them to discuss these questions:
Do you sometimes stay in hotels on holiday?
What other places do people stay in on holiday? (e.g. *a tent, a villa, a friend's house, a hostel*)

Exercise 1 *page 38*

- Elicit the names of the hotels and write them on the board. Explain, if necessary, the meaning of *sand*. Ask: *Where do you usually see sand?* (on the beach)
- Brainstorm ideas for how the hotels are the same or different and write notes on the board. Accept suggestions in students' own language.

Exercise 2 *page 38*

- Give students two minutes to read the text quickly and check their ideas.
- With a **stronger class**, challenge students to find the answers to the following questions as quickly as possible:
How much is a night at the Sand Hotel? (£10)
Have the rooms at the Sand Hotel got ceilings? (no)
Why is the Vanya Tree House peaceful? (There aren't any other people.)
What can you hear in the morning? (birds and monkeys)

(Possible answers)
They have both got great views.
The Sand Hotel hasn't got a toilet but the Vanya Tree House has got a toilet.
The Sand Hotel is on the beach but the Vanya Tree House is in the jungle.
The Sand Hotel hasn't got electricity but the Vanya Tree House has got electricity.

> **Language note:** *there is / there are* **with** *some / any*
>
> We use *there is / there are* to introduce a topic or to say that something exists.
> *There is a pencil in my bag.   There are some books on the desk.*
> We use *There is a / an* with singular nouns.
> We use *There are some* with plural nouns.
> We also use *There is + some* with uncountable nouns, but students will not be studying this construction yet.

Unit 3 Home and away 47

Exercise 3   page 38

- Students find the examples and complete the sentences.
- They then compare sentences in pairs before matching the rules.
- Check answers as a class.

1 There is   2 There are   3 There isn't
4 There aren't   5 Is there; there is   6 Are there

a 2   b 1   c 5   d 3   e 4
a 3   b 2   c 1

Reference and practice 3.1   Workbook page 117

1   2 There is   5 There are
    3 There is   6 There are
    4 There are

2   2 an   3 Is; No   4 some   5 aren't   6 is

3   2 Is there an armchair in your room? No, there isn't.
    3 Is there a bin in your classroom? Yes, there is.
    4 Are there any curtains at the window? No, there aren't.
    5 Is there a university in your town? Yes, there is.

Exercise 4   page 38

- Tell students to use the rules in exercise 3 to help them complete the sentences.
- With a **weaker class**, tell students to look at the noun after each gap and decide if it is singular or plural. Remind them that we use *an* before singular nouns that begin with *a, e, i, o* or *u*.
- Check answers as a class.

1 some   2 a   3 any   4 some   5 any   6 a
7 some   8 a

1 the Sand Hotel   5 Vanya Tree House
2 Vanya Tree House   6 the Sand Hotel
3 the Sand Hotel   7 Vanya Tree House
4 Vanya Tree House   8 the Sand Hotel

Exercise 5   page 39

- Write *monkeys and birds* on the board and ask: *singular or plural?* (plural) Then tell students to look at the text about the Vanya Tree House and ask: *Are there any monkeys and birds there?* (yes) Elicit the full sentence: *There are some monkeys and birds outside the tree house hotel.*
- Students work in pairs to write sentences.
- Check answers as a class.

1 There are some monkeys and birds outside the tree house hotel.
2 There aren't any duvets for the beds at the sand hotel.
3 There isn't a roof at the sand hotel.
4 There is a toilet and washbasin at the tree house hotel.
5 There is a view of the stars from your bed at the sand hotel.
6 There is a wind turbine for electricity at the tree house hotel.
7 There isn't a road when you arrive at the tree house hotel.

Exercise 6   page 39

- Focus attention on the photos on page 39. Ask students to name the things they can see in the photos (*trees, lights, shelves, bed, cushions*).

- Students work individually to complete the questions.
- Choose two students to model the first question and answer for the rest of the class. Students then ask and answer in pairs.
- Check answers as a class.

1 Is there a; Yes, there is.
2 Are there any; Yes, there are.
3 Is there a; No, there isn't.
4 Is there a; Yes, there is.
5 Are there any; Yes, there are.
6 Are there any; No, there aren't.
7 Is there a; No, there isn't.
8 Is there an; No, there isn't.

Exercise 7   page 39

- Brainstorm reasons and write notes on the board, e.g. *good view, cold, uncomfortable, interesting*.
- Circulate and monitor as students discuss the hotel rooms.

Exercise 8   1•50   page 39

- Go through the words together and make sure students know what they mean.
- Play the recording for students.
- Check answers as a class.

Audio script
Mum   Hey, Sam, come and have a look at this website. There are lots of holiday homes on it. We can choose one for our next holiday.
Sam   Cool. That first place is nice – the one in Cornwall. It's got a nice garden, and the beaches in Cornwall are fantastic.
Mum   Yes, but we can't go there. There are only two beds, and there are four people in our family.
Sam   That's fine. Anna and I can sleep in the beds, and you and Dad can sleep on the sofa or the floor.
Mum   Hmm. Maybe not, Sam. But that second place is OK. It's got five beds and it's in the mountains in Wales. You can do lots of fun sports in the mountains. What do you think?
Sam   Well, there aren't any nice views of the mountains from the house. Look! It's in a horrible town.
Mum   That's true. And there aren't any beaches in the area.
Sam   Oh. I want a holiday near the sea.
Mum   OK. What about the third place, in Yorkshire? It's near some nice beaches. And look! It's got a swimming pool, too.
Sam   Cool. How many beds are there?
Mum   Four, so that's OK. There isn't a TV, but we can play games in the evenings.
Sam   No way! We can't stay in a place without a TV.
Mum   Oh, Sam. You're impossible.

beach, sports, good views, swimming pool, TV

Exercise 9   1•50   page 39

- Give students a minute to read the sentences. Then play the recording again.
- With a **stronger class**, ask students to try to choose the correct words before listening and then use the recording to check their answers.

1 garden   2 are some   3 two   4 five   5 aren't any
6 aren't any   7 are some   8 is   9 isn't

See exercise 8 for audio script

48   Unit 3   Home and away

Exercise 10 (page 39)

- Students look at the table and work individually to decide which are the most important features. They then discuss in pairs.
- Circulate and monitor, helping with vocabulary if necessary.
- Ask a few pairs of students to explain their choice.

Vocabulary bank: Around town (page 128)	
1 1 café	9 train station
2 restaurant	10 bank
3 park	11 hospital
4 leisure centre	12 library
5 stadium	13 museum
6 cinema	14 police station
7 theatre	15 shopping centre
8 bus stop	16 university

2 1 theatre 2 park 3 bus stop 4 leisure centre
5 stadium 6 university 7 museum 8 library
9 hospital 10 bank

3 Students' own answers

Learning outcome

Ask students: *What have you learned today? What can you do now?* and elicit answers: *I can use 'there is' / 'there are' with 'some' / 'any'. I can ask and answer questions about things in a room. I can understand a discussion about places to stay on holiday. I can talk about holiday homes.*

3C Culture, vocabulary and grammar

Underground city

Lesson summary
Topic: Unusual places
Grammar: Possessive 's; possessive pronouns and *whose*
Reading: Underground Montreal
Speaking: Talking about possessions

Lead-in

- Write the following questions on the board:
  What is your favourite place in your town? Why?
  What is special about your town?
  What do you want to change in your town? Why?
- Students discuss the questions in pairs or small groups.
- When they have finished, ask a few students to share their ideas with the class.

Exercise 1 (page 40)

- Ask students to call out the names of towns and cities that they have visited or would like to visit and write them on the board.
- Elicit reasons why students might like a town or city, e.g. it has good shopping facilities, parks, cultural life, friendly people, interesting architecture.

Exercise 2 (page 40)

- Ask students to see how many questions they can answer.

- They then read the text quickly to check their answers. Remind them that they do not need to understand every word in order to do this task.
- Check answers as a class.

1 c **2** b **3** a

Culture note: Underground Montreal
The first underground building in Montreal was the Place Ville-Marie shopping centre, which opened in 1962. After the Metro was built in 1966, more underground shops appeared and tunnels were built to link them together. The underground city is now known as RÉSO (a homonym for the French word *réseau*, meaning 'network'). It covers twelve square kilometres and there are more than 120 entrance points to the underground city.

Exercise 3 (page 40)

- Ask students to read the sentences and underline the key words. They then scan the text for these words or synonyms.
- Give students two minutes to complete the task.
- Check answers as a class.

1 snow **2** tunnels **3** 500,000 **4** music **5** concerts
6 winter

Additional vocabulary
The following words are from the text *Underground Montreal*:
- *complain* /kəmˈpleɪn/ (v) to say that you do not like something or that you are unhappy about something
- *entrance* /ˈentrəns/ (n) the door, gate or opening where you go into a place
- *ground* /ɡraʊnd/ (n) the surface of the road
- *natural* /ˈnætʃrəl/ (adj) normal or usual; made by nature, not by people
- *smile* /smaɪl/ (v) to move your mouth to show that you are happy or that you think something is funny
- *tunnel* /ˈtʌnl/ (n) a long hole under the ground or sea for a road or a railway

Exercise 4 (page 40)

- Give students two or three minutes to discuss the questions in pairs.
- Ask a few students to share their partner's ideas with the class.

Extra activity: Further discussion
Ask students to discuss these questions in groups:
What are the advantages and disadvantages of living in a city?
What are the advantages and disadvantages of living in the countryside?
Does it snow in winter in your country? For how long?
Do you like being outside or inside in the cold weather?

Extra activity: Internet research
Ask students to do some internet research into another underground city, for example, Kaymaklı in Turkey, or Beijing in China, and then write a small fact sheet about it.

Unit 3 Home and away 49

Language note: Possessive 's

With names ending in -s, e.g. *Chris*, we can use either 's or '.
Chris's bag   Chris' bag
With two or more names, e.g. *Mr and Mrs Smith*, the possessive 's comes after the final name.
This is Mr and Mrs Smith's house.

Exercise 5   page 40

- Copy the sentences on the board and underline the possessive 's in each sentence.
- Students work in pairs to complete the rules.
- Check answers as a class.

a 's: Everyone in Coralie's family … ; Winter is Olivier's favourite season.
b ': My parents' main interest is art.
c 's: In Montreal, people's first language is French.

Reference and practice 3.2   Workbook page 118

1   2 's   3 s'   4 's   5 's   6 's   7 s'   8 's
2   2 My children's room is very messy.
    3 This is my friends' new song. They are in a band.
    4 I've got one cat. The cat's bed is under the table.
    5 A: Are those bikes Tim's?
       B: Yes, they are. He's got five bikes!
    6 My sister's daughter's name is Alice.

Exercise 6   page 41

- Remind students that they should decide if the noun which indicates the possessor(s) is singular or plural.
- Ask **fast finishers** to write more prompts. They then swap with a partner and write the possessive 's version.
- Check answers as a class.

1 the students' bags
2 children's clothes
3 my grandmother's kitchen
4 her sisters' friend
5 my friend's brothers
6 a girls' school
7 Canadian people's favourite food
8 my aunt's office

Exercise 7   page 41

- Go through the first point together. Some students may point out that the sentence is false, but do not confirm this yet. Tell them that they will be looking at the sentences again in the next activity.
- Emphasize that there are eight missing apostrophes in total.
- Check answers as a class.

1 Boston's   5 London's
2 Queen's   6 people's
3 –   7 Tutankhamun's; Cairo's
4 president's   8 Egyptians'

Exercise 8   1·51   page 41

- Students do the exercise in pairs.
- With a **strong class**, encourage students to correct the false sentences.
- Play the recording for students to check their answers.
- Check answers as a class.

Audio script
1 In the USA, the name of Boston's famous university is Cambridge.
   False. There are two famous universities in Boston: Harvard and MIT. Cambridge University is in the UK.
2 Big Ben is the British Queen's home in London.
   False. Her home is Buckingham Palace.
3 You can see ancient Roman theatres in many countries, including Spain, Turkey, Syria, Libya and France. True.
4 The Chinese president's home and office is in the Kremlin.
   False. The Kremlin is in Moscow, Russia, and it's the home and office of the Russian president.
5 London's famous football stadium is at Wembley. True.
6 In the Canadian Arctic, the Inuit people's homes are igloos.
   False. Inuit people don't live in igloos now.
7 Tutankhamun's gold mask is in Cairo's Egyptian Museum.
   True.
8 Some of the ancient Egyptians' pyramids are now hotels.
   False. There aren't any hotels in Egyptian pyramids.

See audio script for answers

Language note: *whose* and possessive pronouns

It is a good idea to clarify the difference between subject pronouns, possessive adjectives and possessive pronouns before students attempt exercise 9.

Write the subject pronouns on the board: *I, you, he, she, we, they*. Point to *I* and give an example sentence: *I've got a blue bag*. Then write *my* next to *I* and say: *It's my blue bag*. Finally, write *mine* next to *my* and say: *The blue bag is mine*.

Exercise 9   1·52   page 41

- Elicit the highlighted words in the text and write them on the board. Ask students to identify the question word (*whose*). Then give students two minutes to complete the sentences.
- With a **weaker class**, ask students to match the possessive pronouns to the subject pronouns and possessive adjectives on the board before they complete the sentences.
- Play the recording for students to check their answers and repeat.
- Check answers as a class.

1 Whose   2 mine   3 his   4 hers   5 theirs

Exercise 10   page 41

- Ask students to look again at the sentences in exercise 9 and then do the matching activity in pairs.
- Check answers as a class.

a 3   b 1   c 2

Reference and practice 3.3   Workbook page 118

1   2 b   3 a   4 a   5 a   6 c
2   1 B: her; ours
    2 A: your; my   B: your; mine
    3 yours; ours
    4 A: your   B: theirs; my
    5 A: my; yours   B: mine
    6 Your; hers
3   2 theirs   3 ours   4 yours   5 his   6 mine

50   Unit 3   Home and away

Exercise 11 (page 41)

- Tell students to look at the rules about possessive 's in exercise 5 again and remind them that possessive adjectives come before nouns, whereas there is no noun after a possessive pronoun.
- Students work individually or in pairs to do the exercise.
- When they have finished, ask two students to read out the dialogue. The rest of the class listen and call out if they think there is a mistake.
- Check answers as a class.

1 ours   2 Our   3 Whose   4 yours   5 mine   6 Her
7 David's   8 grandparents   9 Lucy's   10 Theirs

Exercise 12 (page 41)

- Ask two students to read out the example questions and answers. Remind them to use falling intonation for *Wh*- questions, with the voice starting at a higher pitch and falling to a lower pitch at the end of the question.
- Circulate and monitor, helping with vocabulary if necessary.

DVD extra A room with a view?

Learning outcome

Ask students: *What have you learned today? What can you do now?* and elicit answers: *I know about an underground city in Montreal. I can use possessive 's, 'whose' and possessive pronouns. I can ask and answer about possessions.*

3D Listening, speaking and vocabulary

Around town

Lesson summary
Topic: Town and country
Vocabulary: City to country
Speaking: Describing your perfect home; asking for and giving directions
Listening: Where we live
Communication worksheet 3B: Where's the bank?

Lead-in

- Write TOWN and COUNTRY in capital letters on the board. Ask students to work in groups and brainstorm as many words as possible for each heading. Give them three minutes for this.
- When they have finished, ask students to share their ideas with the class and write their ideas on the board, helping with translations if necessary.

Exercise 1 1·53 (page 42)

- Give students one minute to write the words.
- Play the recording for students to check their answers. Point out the weak pronunciation of *a* in *village* /ˈvɪlɪdʒ/ and the third syllable of *capital* /ˈkæpɪtl/.
- Check answers as a class.

1 town   2 city   3 village   4 city centre   5 suburb
6 countryside

Exercise 2 (page 42)

- Ask students to brainstorm some advantages and disadvantages of cities and villages and write their ideas on the board, e.g. *quiet, busy, crowded, interesting.*
- They then answer the questions in pairs. Circulate and monitor, helping with vocabulary if necessary.

Culture notes: Town and country

Alsace is a small region in the north-east of France, bordering Germany and Switzerland. It is a popular destination for tourists because of its picturesque villages, old churches and castles. It is also a major wine-growing area.

Darjeeling is a town in the north of India, close to Bhutan. It is situated in the mountains, 2,045 metres above sea level. Darjeeling is famous for its production of black tea. The Darjeeling Himalayan Railway is over 120 years old, 78 kilometres long and is a UNESCO World Heritage site.

Houston is a large city in Texas, USA. It is also known as the 'space city' because NASA (the National Aeronautics and Space Administration) built a large space centre in the city in 1961. It suffers from some extreme weather conditions including flooding and hurricanes. Its main industries are oil, natural gas, aeronautics and biomedical research.

Times Square is a large pedestrianized square in Manhattan, New York. It is famous for being the heart of Broadway – the theatre district of the city – and its brightly illuminated billboards are an iconic image of New York. On New Year's Eve, many people gather in Times Square to welcome the New Year and watch the Time Ball drop from the top of the One Times Square building.

Scarborough is a large holiday resort on the North Yorkshire coast of the UK. It has the ruins of a fine 12th century stone castle, which was destroyed during the English Civil War of 1645.

Snowshill is a small village in the Cotswolds, an area of outstanding natural beauty in the UK. It is a typically English village, with ancient pretty cottages and a church, all set around a village green.

Exercise 3 1·54 (page 42)

- Go through the place names with students and ask if they know in which countries the places are. They most probably will not know Snowshill (a small village in the UK) or Scarborough (a town in the UK), but they may be able to name the other countries (Alsace – France; Darjeeling – India; Houston – USA; Times Square – USA).
- Students work in pairs to match the places to the photos. Play the recording for them to check their answers.
- Check answers as a class.

1 Darjeeling   2 Houston   3 Snowshill   4 Times Square
5 Scarborough   6 Alsace

Extra activity: Places

Students work in groups to prepare a geography quiz. On a piece of paper, they write the names of four places in different countries: a capital city, a city (not a capital), a town and a village. Tell them to write the names in random order. When they have finished, they swap quizzes with another group. Can they match the words *capital city*, *city*, *town* and *village* with the place names?

Exercise 4 1·55 page 42

- Go through the strategy together and then tell students to underline the key words in sentences 1–9.
- Check that students have correctly identified the key words before you play the recording (1: *home*, *important place*, *tea*; 2: *lives*, *suburb*; 3: *hasn't got*, *cafés*, *leisure centres*; 4: *hear*, *musical instruments*, *favourite place*; 5: *likes*, *countryside*; 6: *dances*, *favourite place*; 7: *likes*, *cinema*; 8: *chats*, *friends*, *shop*; 9: *favourite place*, *centre of town*).
- Check answers as a class.

Audio script

Su-Lin My home is the city of Beijing. It's the capital of China, and it's very big – about 20 million people live here. The flats in my suburb haven't got gardens, so everyone goes to the park. The park near my flat is my favourite place. It's very relaxing, and there are always lots of interesting things to see there. In the early morning, people do tai chi together – that's a type of Chinese exercise. At other times of the day, they play musical instruments and people dance together. I sometimes dance with them.

Yasmin I'm from a small village in England. Only 800 people live here, and there aren't any cafés or leisure centres. There isn't even a bus stop! But the people here are great. When I'm with my friends from the village, I always have a good time. We often cycle to town – the journey takes about half an hour. We also enjoy cycling in the fantastic countryside nearby. After that, we sit on the wall next to the village shop. It's our favourite place. We chat there for hours.

Hari I live in Darjeeling. It's a town in India, in the Himalayan mountains. Darjeeling is famous for its tea – we grow lots of tea in the mountains here. But my favourite place is the cinema in the centre of town. My dad works there, so I can watch the films for free. Indian films – people call them Bollywood films – are fantastic. They've got lots of singing and dancing, and they're very exciting.

1 H 2 S 3 Y 4 S 5 Y 6 S 7 H 8 Y 9 H

Exercise 5 page 42

- Give students two minutes to work individually and make notes about their perfect home.
- They then work in pairs and discuss their perfect home.
- When they have finished, ask a few students to share their partner's ideas with the class.

Exercise 6 page 43

- Check that students remember the prepositions of place they learned on page 37: *opposite*, *next to*, *on* and *between*.
- Students find the places on the map.
- Ask **fast finishers** to write more questions about places on the map using prepositions. They then work with a partner, taking it in turns to ask and answer questions.
- Check answers as a class.

1 shopping centre   2 theatre   3 museum   4 library

Exercise 7 1·56 page 43

- Tell students that they are going to listen to someone asking for directions. Make sure that they have found the leisure centre on the map and are ready to draw the route before you play the recording.
- Play the recording.
- Check answers as a class.

Audio script

Jane Excuse me. Where's the park?
Man The park? There are two parks. Do you want Green Park or South Park?
Jane South Park. How do you get to South Park, please?
Man Oh, OK. First cross the road outside the leisure centre. Take the second road on the left. That's Fox Street.
Jane Fox Street. OK …
Man: Go straight up Fox Street. Then, at the cinema, turn right into Friday Street. The park is on the left, opposite the theatre.
Jane Thank you very much for your help.

Jane wants to go to South Park.

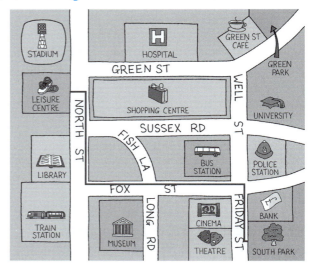

Exercise 8 1·56 page 43

- Students work in pairs to complete the phrases.
- When they have finished, play the recording again so they can check their answers.
- To check answers, ask individual students to read out the complete phrases.

1 Where's   2 How   3 Cross   4 second   5 Go
6 at   7 right   8 on

See exercise 7 for audio script

Exercise 9 1·57 page 43

- Ask students to read the dialogue quickly. Then elicit the first sentence in the dialogue.
- They then continue to work individually to do the exercise.
- With a **weaker class**, you can also identify the final sentence in the dialogue.
- Play the recording for students to check their answers.
- Play the recording again for them to draw the route.
- Check answers as a class.

52   Unit 3 Home and away

Audio script

Amy Excuse me. How do you get to the station, please?
Ben The train station or the bus station?
Amy The train station.
Ben Outside the café, turn right. Then take the first road on the left.
Amy Do you know the name of the road?
Ben Well Street, I think. Go past the shopping centre and the bus station. Then turn right into Fox Street. Go straight on. When you get to North Street, the train station is opposite you.
Amy Thank you very much for your help.

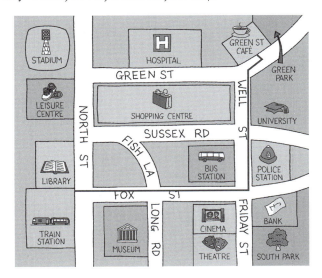

Exercise 10 page 43

- Ask students to identify the questions first.
- Write the question on the board and tell students to copy them into their notebooks.

Asking for directions How do you get to … ?   Do you know the name of the road? **Giving directions** outside (the café), turn (right)   take the (first) road on the (left)   Go past … turn (right) into …

Exercise 11 page 43

- Make sure students can find all the places on the map before they begin their pairwork.
- Circulate and monitor, noting any common errors.

Students' own answers

Exercise 12 page 43

- Read out the example directions.
- Students work in pairs to give directions and guess the place. Alternatively, invite different students to give directions for the rest of the class to guess the place.

Alternative activity
Ask students to give directions from their classroom to another place in the school building. Can their partner guess the place?

Learning outcome

Ask students: *What have you learned today? What can you do now?* and elicit answers: *I know town and country words. I can understand a description of a place. I know how to listen for key words. I can describe my perfect home. I can ask for and give directions.*

3E Writing

A tourist guide

Lesson summary
Topic: Edinburgh
Vocabulary: Sequencers: *first, then, after that, next, finally*
Reading: A tourist guide about Edinburgh
Writing: A tourist guide about a city you like

Lead-in

- Put students into groups and tell them that they are going to do a quiz about famous European cities.
- Write the following landmarks on the board: *Eiffel Tower*; *Sagrada Familia*; *Big Ben*; *Brandenburg Gate*; *St Basil's Cathedral*; *Acropolis*.
- Students work in groups to decide the city in which each landmark is located (Eiffel Tower – Paris; Sagrada Familia – Barcelona; Big Ben – London; Brandenburg Gate – Berlin; St Basil's Cathedral – Moscow; Acropolis – Athens). The first group to find the correct answers is the winner.

Exercise 1 page 44

- Introduce the activity by telling students what you do when you visit a city for the first time, e.g. *When I visit a new city, I usually take a bus around the city and then I visit a museum or an art gallery.*
- Students discuss their ideas in pairs. To get the discussion going, you can write the following questions on the board:
What do you do?
Where do you go?
How do you travel around the city?

Exercise 2 page 44

- Students read the guide quickly to see if their ideas are included.
- Focus attention on the heading and ask why they think Edinburgh is called *the Athens of the north*. (because many of its public buildings were built in the neo-classical style)

Language note: Sequencers
We often use sequencers to give instructions, e.g. in a recipe or in a science experiment.
Explain to students that sequencers help them to write a fluent informative text, which clearly shows the order of events or steps in a process.

Exercise 3 page 44

- Give students a minute to find and underline the sequencers in the text.
- Explain that *next*, *then* and *after that* can go in any order; they do not follow a specific sequence. However, *first* is used for the first event or step in a sequence, and *finally* is used for the last.
- Check answers as a class.

1 first
2 then, after that, next
3 finally

Unit 3 Home and away 53

Exercise 4 (page 44)

- Read through the sentences with the class. Explain that *loch* is the Scottish word for lake and that some people believe that a monster lives in Loch Ness. You could also tell students that the photo shows the town of Tobermory, and Ben Nevis is the highest mountain in Scotland.
- Students work individually to do the exercise.
- Check answers as a class.

1 First
2 Then / After that / Next
3 Then / After that / Next
4 Then / After that / Next
5 Finally

Exercise 5 (page 44)

- Go through the strategy together and explain to students that in this book they will always have a model text to study before they do their writing task. Encourage them to analyze texts and to think about their structure; this is a good way to improve their writing in their own language, as well as in English.
- Explain, if necessary, the meaning of *bullet point*, *summary*, *conclusion* and *details*.
- Students work in pairs to do the exercise.
- Check answers as a class.

1 bullet points
2 introduction
3 conclusion
4 imperatives
5 Students' own answers

Writing guide (page 45)

- Read the **task** together, making sure students understand that they have to write a tourist guide similar to the guide about Edinburgh.
- Give students five to ten minutes to complete the **ideas** stage and **plan** their letter. Circulate and monitor, helping with language and ideas as necessary. Remind students to write notes, not full sentences.
- Circulate and monitor while students **write** their tourist guides, encouraging them to use the sequencers *first*, *next*, *after that*, *then* and *finally*. Remind them to activate the language they learned earlier in the unit (prepositions of place, *there is / there are* with *some / any*, vocabulary for places in a town, possessive pronouns).
- When students have finished, they **check** their work. Refer them to the checklist to make sure they have completed the task as well as they can.

> **Extension: Fast finishers**
> Ask **fast finishers** to swap tourist guides with another student to read and check for mistakes.

> **Additional writing activity**
> Write a tourist guide for a day at your favourite holiday destination. Include information about places to stay, good restaurants or cafés, things to do and see and how to travel around.

Learning outcome

Ask students: *What have you learned today? What can you do now?* and elicit answers: *I can read and understand a tourist guide to a city. I can use the sequencers 'first', 'next', 'after that', 'then' and 'finally'. I can write a tourist guide to a city.*

Review 3 (page 45)

1 1 armchair/chair   5 cupboard
   2 bathroom   6 fridge
   3 bed   7 kitchen
   4 rug/carpet   8 cooker

2 1 in 2 in front of 3 near 4 behind 5 on
   6 opposite 7 under 8 next to

3 1 village 2 town 3 city 4 suburb 5 city centre
   6 countryside

4 1 are 2 there 3 is 4 Is 5 There's 6 isn't 7 a
   8 any 9 aren't 10 some

5 1 John's book
   2 women's shoes
   3 my grandparents' house
   4 men's shirts
   5 my friends' class
   6 my sister's computer
   7 children's game

6 1 mine 2 ours 3 yours / hers / his 4 hers
   5 theirs 6 his

> **Pronunciation insight 3** Workbook page 133
> **Answer key:** Teacher's book page 154

4 The natural world

Map of resources

Section A: Student's Book pages 46–47
Workbook page 36
Vocabulary bank, Animals page 129

Section B: Student's Book pages 48–49
Workbook page 37
Grammar reference and practice 4.1, Workbook page 119
Vocabulary bank, Pets page 129
Teacher's resource disk, Communication worksheet 4A

Section C: Student's Book pages 50–51
Workbook page 38
Grammar reference and practice 4.2, Workbook page 120
Teacher's resource disk, DVD extra + worksheet, Measuring the weather page 51
Teacher's resource disk, Communication worksheet 4A

Section D: Student's Book pages 52–53
Workbook page 39
Teacher's resource disk, Communication worksheet 4B

Section E: Student's Book pages 54–55
Workbook page 42
Teacher's resource disk, Writing bank
Teacher's resource disk, Functional language bank

Review 4 page 55
Pronunciation insight 4, Workbook page 133
Progress check Unit 4, Workbook page 43
Language and skills tests 4A and 4B, Test Bank

Cumulative review Units 1–4 pages 56–57
Literature insight 2, Workbook page 94
Exam insight 2, Workbook page 104

4A Reading and vocabulary

It's wild!

> **Lesson summary**
> **Topic:** Symbiotic relationships in the natural world
> **Vocabulary:** The natural world; animal verbs; Vocabulary bank: Animals
> **Reading:** Working together
> **Speaking:** Describing a symbiotic relationship

Lead-in

- Explain to students that they are going to find out about different wild animals. Give them one minute to brainstorm, in pairs, as many English words for wild animals as possible.
- When they have finished, ask the pair with the longest list to read it out. Write the animal names on the board and leave them there for exercise 3.

Exercise 1 page 46

- Explain that the definitions are from a dictionary and that the words describe different types of landscape.
- Ask a few students to read out the definitions. Model and drill the words, focusing on the /z/ in *desert* /ˈdezət/ and /ɪ/ in *forest* /ˈfɒrɪst/.
- Check answers as a class.

A forest   **B** desert   **C** grassland

Exercise 2 page 46

- Focus attention on the words and say: *What things can you find in photo A?* Students call out the answers.
- They then find the things in photos B and C. Explain that one thing (*cloud*) is in more than one photo.
- Check answers as a class.

Photo A tree, mountain, snow, cloud, ice
Photo B cactus, sand
Photo C flower, grass, plant, cloud

Exercise 3 page 46

- Students work in groups. They can refer to the list of animals on the board from the lead-in activity or use dictionaries to find names of other animals.
- Circulate and monitor, helping with vocabulary if necessary.
- When they have finished, ask a few students to share their ideas with the class.

> **Culture notes: Symbiotic relationbships**
> There are three types of symbiotic relationship.
> **Mutualism:** This is when both partners benefit from the relationship. The examples in the text are all of mutualism.

Commensalism: This is when one partner benefits and the other partner is neither helped nor harmed. For example, small remora fish attach themselves to sharks and eat the scraps that the sharks do not want. The fish get the food but there is no benefit to the shark.

Parasitism: This is when one partner benefits and the other partner suffers. For example, ticks feed on other animals' blood. The ticks benefit, but the host animals suffer from blood loss and may be infected by diseases.

Exercise 4 page 46

- Remind students that they do not need to understand every word to do this task. Give them two minutes to complete it.
- Students compare answers in pairs.
- Check answers as a class.

Eritrea baboon, elephant, lion
Kenya oxpecker bird, rhinoceros
Canada raven, wolverine

Extra activity: Game

Play a game to revise the animal vocabulary in this unit, in the Vocabulary bank and in the lead-in activity. Remove all the animal names from the board and tell students to close their books. Say: *A is for alligator*. Then go round the class asking individual students to name an animal for each of the letters of the alphabet. If students cannot think of an animal, move on to the next letter.

Exercise 5 page 46

- Go through the sentences together. Ask students to underline the verb in each sentence and then find the verbs in the text.
- With a **weaker class**, tell students that sentences 1 and 2 are about Eritrea, 3 and 4 are about Kenya, and 5 and 6 are about Canada.
- Check answers as a class.

1 elephant 2 baboon 3 rhinoceros 4 oxpecker bird
5 raven 6 wolverine

Additional vocabulary

The following words are from the article *Working together*:

- *towards* /təˈwɔːdz/ (prep) in the direction of somebody or something
- *tick* /tɪk/ (n) a small insect that bites humans and animals and sucks their blood.
- *relationship* /rɪˈleɪʃnʃɪp/ (n) the way people, groups, animals etc. behave towards each other
- *dead* /ded/ (adj) not alive now
- *together* /təˈgeðə(r)/ (adv) with each other or close to each other

Exercise 6 page 47

- Tell students to read the sentences carefully, underline the key words and then find the information in the text. You could put students into pairs with one **stronger student** and one **weaker student**.
- Check answers as a class.

1 F: The elephant digs the hole.
2 F: When it sees a lion, it makes a loud noise. / When the elephant sees a lion, it runs away.
3 T
4 F: The oxpecker eats small insects.
5 T
6 F: The raven makes a loud noise when it finds food.

Extra activity: Further discussion

Ask students:

- *Do you like watching wildlife documentaries on TV? Why? / Why not?*
- *What interesting facts do you know about animals in Africa?*
- *Do you know any examples of humans helping animals or animals helping humans?*

Language note: Phrasal verbs

Look for and *run away* are phrasal verbs – verbs that are followed by another word e.g. a preposition or an adverb. The second word often changes the meaning of the verb.

English has many phrasal verbs, and it is a good idea for students to keep a section in their notebooks for them.

Exercise 7 page 47

- Students read the highlighted words in the article in context before they do the exercise. The context will help them to understand the meaning of the word.
- Check answers as a class.

1 bite 2 follow 3 carry 4 look for
5 hunt, run away 6 dig

Exercise 8 page 47

- Go through the strategy together.
- Give an example of a word with a different meaning in a different context, e.g. *Your answer is right* (i.e. 'correct'). *Turn right* (i.e. the opposite of *left*) *at the post office*.
- Read out the example sentence and ask students to write sentences for each of the verbs in exercise 7. **Weaker students** can copy the sentences from the article, but **stronger students** write new sentences.

Exercise 9 page 47

- Show students how to make useful notes. Write *elephant* and *baboon* on the board and elicit words or phrases that will help students to describe their relationship, e.g. *Eritrea: hot and dry; elephant dig hole, look for water; baboon sit in tree, watch elephant, make noise; drink water together.*
- Ask a student to use the notes to talk about the baboon and the elephant.
- Students make similar notes about the other animal pairs and use them to describe their relationships.
- Circulate and monitor, helping with vocabulary and ideas as necessary.

Extra activity: Internet research

Ask students to find out about other symbiotic relationships. They can choose one of the following: *crocodile* and *Egyptian plover*; *clownfish* and *sea anemone*; *bee* and *flower*; *human* and *dog*. Tell them to write notes and then make a presentation to the class.

Vocabulary bank: Animals page 129

1   1 spider   2 whale   3 eagle   4 butterfly   5 horse
    6 cow   7 chicken   8 pig   9 sheep   10 fox
    11 tiger   12 wolf   13 elephant   14 monkey
    15 giraffe   16 bear

2   1 chicken   2 tiger   3 monkey   4 horse
    5 elephant   6 pig   7 wolf   8 sheep   9 giraffe
    10 butterfly   11 bear   12 spider   13 whale
    14 fox   15 eagle   16 cow

Learning outcome

Ask students: *What have you learned today? What can you do now?* and elicit answers: *I know the names of different things in the natural world. I can understand a text about symbiotic relationships. I can use verbs to describe animal actions. I can discuss and describe symbiotic relationships.*

4B Grammar and listening

What are you watching?

Lesson summary	
Topic:	Animal activities
Vocabulary:	Vocabulary bank: Pets
Grammar:	Present continuous
Listening:	Where is Raj?
Reading:	Watching animals
Speaking:	Asking and answering about things happening now
Communication worksheet 4A:	Find someone who …

Lead-in

- Students discuss the following questions in groups:
  Do you like animals?
  Have you got any pets?
  What are the advantages and disadvantages of having a pet? (e.g. they are friendly, they are interesting; they are sometimes expensive, some visitors don't like them)
- When they have finished, ask one student from each group to share their group's ideas with the class.

Exercise 1 page 48

- Explain, if necessary, what a social networking site is, and give some examples (Facebook, Google Plus+, MySpace).
- Focus attention on the tweets in exercise 2 and ask if anyone reads or writes tweets.
- Ask students to look at the title (*Green Magazine*) and the introductory text in exercise 2. Ask: *What are these tweets about?* (animals)

Exercise 2 page 48

- Explain that *Green Magazine* is asking the question on Twitter, and that SafariGirl, PetCrazy, TeenVet and LazyBoy are the names of people writing replies on Twitter. Students read the replies to answer the questions.
- With a **weaker class**, tell students to write the Twitter users' names for six of the activities, but for *eating plants in a garden* and *sleeping* they write the name of the animal.

- Give students two minutes to read the tweets and match the names with the activities.
- Check answers as a class.

1 PetCrazy
2 SafariGirl
3 TeenVet
4 TeenVet
5 LazyBoy
6 two elephants
7 TeenVet and his sister
8 LazyBoy's cat

Extra activity: Quiz

Ask students to work in pairs and make questions from the following prompts:

1 *How much food / elephants / eat?*
2 *How fast / pigeons / fly?*
3 *How fast / dogs / run?*
4 *How much / adult rhinos / weigh?*
5 *How many / black rhinos / be / in the wild?*
6 *How many hours / cats / sleep?*

Check that they have formed the questions correctly. They then look at the article to find the answers. One student then closes the book. The other student asks one of the questions. Can the first student remember the answer?

How much food do elephants eat? (125–250 kg a day)
How fast do pigeons fly? (ninety km per hour)
How fast do dogs run? (thirty km per hour)
How much do adult rhinos weigh? (1,300 kg)
How many black rhinos are (there) in the wild? (3,600)
How many hours do cats sleep? (13–16 hours a day)

Language note: Present continuous

- We use the present continuous:
  – to talk about what is happening at the moment.
    I'm watching a film about a whale.
  – to talk about what is happening around now.
    I'm studying French at university.
  – a temporary situation.
    We're staying with my aunt this summer.
  – with *always* to talk about a repeated annoying action.
    My sisters are always arguing.
- Some verbs do not take the present continuous. They are called stative verbs and include *feel, hear, see, love, like, want, think, understand, believe, know.*

Exercise 3 page 48

- Point out that the forms in brackets are the contracted forms, and remind students that we usually use these in speech and in informal texts, for example, in tweets.
- Give students two minutes to complete the table.
- Check answers as a class.

1 'm   2 is   3 're   4 'm not   5 isn't   6 Are

Unit 4 The natural world   57

Exercise 4 page 48

- Students look at the example sentences and complete the rules.
- Point out that for rule a, students need to understand *why* we use the present continuous, and for rules b and c, they need to understand *how* we form it.
- Check that students understand the meaning of *auxiliary verb* and *main verb*. Write *I am sleeping* on the board and ask students to identify the auxiliary verb (*am*) and the main verb (*sleeping*).

a things happening at the moment
b *be*
c after, before

Reference and practice 4.1 Workbook page 119

1 2 are preparing
   3 A: Are you looking
      B: 'm looking
   4 isn't talking; 's sleeping
   5 're learning
   6 A: Is your brother listening
      B: isn't

2 2 My dog is chasing a cat in the garden.
   3 We're taking photographs of tigers at London Zoo.
   4 The foxes are digging a hole in the ground.
   5 The hungry wolves are looking for food.
   6 I'm not doing my homework. I'm drinking a cup of tea.
   7 She's listening to some music at the moment.
   8 Why are you laughing?

3 1 Is (he) chatting; b
   2 Are (you) downloading; c
   3 Is (she) doing; a
   4 Are (they) enjoying; d

Exercise 5 page 49

- Focus attention on the picture and use it to teach *flamingos* and *tourists*.
- Ask two students to read out the example exchange.
- Students write the questions individually. They then work in pairs, asking and answering them.
- Check answers as a class.

1 Is the elephant eating? Not, it isn't. It's drinking (water).
2 Are the tourists sleeping? No, they aren't. They're watching the animals.
3 Is the giraffe drinking water? No, it isn't. It's eating.
4 Are the flamingos walking? No, they aren't. They're flying.
5 Is the rhinoceros digging a hole? No, it isn't. It's sleeping.
6 Are the monkeys running away? No, they aren't. They're sitting (in a tree).

Exercise 6 1·58 page 49

- Students work individually to complete the dialogue.
- When they have finished, they exchange dialogues with a partner. They then listen to check their partner's answers.
- Check answers as a class.

1 'm watching
2 Is (your brother) watching
3 isn't
4 's playing
5 's singing
6 Are (your parents) listening
7 aren't
8 're playing
9 are (you) doing
10 Are (you) listening
11 'm not listening
12 'm doing
13 's shouting
14 is (he) shouting
15 is digging

Exercise 7 page 49

- Ask a student to complete the first question and then ask another student. Make sure that students understand that they have to guess what their mother / father is doing now. Ask students to complete the questions first. They then ask and answer in pairs.
- Check answers as a class.

1 is (your mum / dad) doing
2 is (your teacher) doing
3 are (you) reading
4 Are (you) watching
5 Are (you) listening
6 are (you) doing

Students' own answers

> **Extra activity: Present continuous pictionary**
>
> Prepare some cards, each with a different present continuous sentence, e.g. *The boy is eating a banana. The baby is sleeping on the sofa. The cat is running away from the dog. The girl is reading a book. The man is playing the violin.* Ask one student to come up to the board and try to draw the sentence. The first person to guess the sentence correctly can be the next person to draw on the board.

Exercise 8 1·59 page 49

- Play the recording once.
- Check answers as a class.

Audio script

Sarah Hello?
Raj Hi, Sarah. It's Raj.
Sarah Hi, Raj. This isn't your number. Have you got a new phone?
Raj No, I'm using Mum's phone. I'm having a lot of problems with mine.
Sarah I see. So, what are you doing?
Raj I'm in Scotland with my family. We're driving to my cousin's house.
Sarah Are you using the phone and driving at the same time?
Raj No! Don't worry! My dad's driving. I'm learning to drive, remember? Anyway, we're not driving at the moment. We're in a café. It's a long journey and we're all hungry, so we're having lunch now.
Sarah Oh. So what's wrong with your phone?
Raj I don't know. I'm trying to take a photo of my sister. She's eating a big chocolate ice cream and she's got chocolate all over her face.

Sarah Urgh! And … ?
Raj Well, the camera isn't working. You've got the same phone, right? What am I doing wrong?
Sarah Ah … is there a small red button at the bottom of the screen?
Raj Yes, there is.
Sarah The camera is locked. It's red because the camera's locked! Press the button. Then try taking the photo.
Raj OK. I'm pressing the button and … Yes! It's working now. Thanks, Sarah! So, what are you doing at the moment?
Sarah: I'm writing my geography essay and I'm helping you, Raj!

Raj can't take a picture with his phone.
a

Exercise 9 1·59 page 49

- Go through the questions together and remind students to listen for key words.
- With a **stronger class**, ask students to try to answer some of the questions before listening to the recording again.
- Play the recording several times if necessary.
- Check answers as a class.

1 He's in Scotland.
2 He's going to his cousin's house.
3 His dad is driving.
4 They're having lunch in a café.
5 He's trying to take a photo of his sister.
6 She's eating a big chocolate ice cream.
7 The camera isn't working.
8 She's writing her geography essay and she's helping Raj.

See exercise 8 for audio script

Exercise 10 page 49

- Students work on their own to form questions.
- Check answers as a class.
- Encourage students to use their imagination. Give some examples: *I'm staying at the Taj Mahal. I'm playing tennis with Rafa Nadal.*
- Circulate and monitor, noting any common errors.

Where are you staying?
What are you doing?
Who are you spending time with?
What are you looking at now?

Students' own answers

> **Vocabulary bank: Pets** page 129
>
> 1 1 dog 2 rabbit 3 tortoise 4 hamster
>   5 budgie 6 mouse 7 cat 8 snake 9 fish
>   10 parrot 11 guinea pig 12 lizard
> 2 1 tortoise 2 budgie 3 lizard 4 dog 5 hamster
>   6 fish 7 cat 8 rabbit
> 3 Students' own answers

Learning outcome

Ask students: *What have you learned today? What can you do now?* and elicit answers: *I can use the present continuous. I can read and understand tweets about animals. I can describe what I am doing. I can understand a conversation about a problem with a phone.*

4C Culture, vocabulary and grammar

What's the weather like?

> **Lesson summary**
> **Topic:** Weather and climates around the world
> **Vocabulary:** Weather; adjective suffix -y
> **Grammar:** Present simple or present continuous
> **Reading:** What's the weather like with you?
> **Speaking:** Asking and answering about weather and activities
> **Communication worksheet 4A:** Find someone who …
> **Communication worksheet 4B:** What's the weather like?

Lead-in

- Write the following temperatures in a large word cloud on the left hand side of the board: *20°C, 12°C, 8°C, 27°C, –1°C*. Write the following places in a large word cloud on the right hand side of the board: *London, Moscow, Sydney, Tokyo, Singapore*.
- Explain that the numbers on the left represent average temperatures in the month of November for the places on the right. Give students, in pairs, two minutes to try to match the average temperatures to the cities.

London 8°C   Moscow –1°C   Sydney 20°C   Tokyo 12°C
Singapore 26°C

Exercise 1 page 50

- Explain that the photos show people in different parts of the world. It is the same date, but the seasons are different. Give students one minute to look at the photos and guess where the people are and what they are doing.
- Elicit suggestions but do not say whether they are correct.

> **Culture notes: Cities around the world**
>
> **Brighton** is a city in the south east of England. It has a popular pier with a funfair, arcade halls and cafés. The Royal Pavilion is a well-known landmark in Brighton. This palace was built for the Prince Regent in the early nineteenth century and is famous for its Indian architectural style. In May, Brighton hosts the biggest arts festival in England – the Brighton Festival.
>
> **Iqaluit** is the capital city of the Canadian territory of Nunavut. It was originally called Frobisher Bay and was founded in 1942 as an American airbase. It has the smallest population (6,699) of any capital city in Canada. Its climate is Arctic and there are very few trees in the area because the ground is always frozen.
>
> **Cairns** is a city in the north east of Australia, in the state of Queensland. It was founded in 1886. It is popular with tourists because of its tropical climate and its proximity to the Great Barrier Reef. There are often thunderstorms and tropical cyclones in Cairns between December and March.
>
> **Cape Town** is the provincial capital city of the Western Cape and the second largest city in South Africa. It is one of the most multicultural cities in the world, with a population of 3.74 million. Cape Town is famous for its picturesque harbour and for the imposing-looking Table Mountain.

Unit 4 The natural world

Exercise 2 page 50

- Ask students to look at the photos again and predict what words they might find in the texts to describe them, e.g. *water*, *raft*, *dog*, *snow*, *walk*.
- Students read the text quickly and match the photos to the paragraphs. They then find out what season it is.
- Check answers as a class.

A Paragraph 3. It's summer in Cairns.
B Paragraph 4. It's spring in Cape Town.
C Paragraph 2. It's the cold season / winter in Iqaluit.
D Paragraph 1. It's autumn in Brighton.

Exercise 3 page 50

- Students read the text in detail to answer the questions.
- Check answers as a class.

1 She's walking on the beach with her dog, Jet, and throwing a stick.
2 She walks on the beach with Jet every day.
3 He lives in Iqaluit in Northern Canada.
4 He's playing ice hockey with his friends.
5 She's white water rafting with her cousins.
6 There are two seasons.
7 They are walking in Table Mountain National Park.
8 It begins in December.

Exercise 4 page 50

- Focus attention on the weather icons and elicit the words for each icon in the students' own language first.
- Students then work in pairs to match the highlighted adjectives to the icons.
- Check answers as a class.

1 rainy 2 sunny 3 snowy 4 windy 5 cloudy
6 stormy 7 hot 8 warm 9 cool 10 cold

Exercise 5 page 50

- Point out to students that they have to make both adjectives and nouns; they add *-y* to the nouns to form adjectives and they remove the *-y* from the adjectives to form nouns.
- Ask **fast finishers** if they can think of any other adjectives that are formed by adding *-y* to the noun, e.g. *mess – messy*; *fun – funny*; *dirt – dirty*; *noise – noisy*.
- Check answers as a class.

1 sun 2 snow 3 wind 4 stormy 5 cloudy

Exercise 6 page 50

- Ask students to predict in which paragraph they will find these two expressions. They should guess that the synonym for *snowy* is in the text about Iqaluit, and the synonym for *rainy* is in the text about Brighton.
- Check answers as a class. Point out the difference in structure between *It is snowy* (*it + be* + adjective) and *It is snowing* (*it* + present continuous of *snow*).

1 It's snowing.
2 It's raining.

Additional vocabulary

The following words are from the article *What's the weather like with you?*:

- *umbrella* /ʌmˈbrelə/ (n) a thing that you hold above your head to keep you dry when it rains
- *stick* /stɪk/ (n) a long thin piece of wood
- *popular* /ˈpɒpjələ(r)/ (adj) liked by a lot of people
- *tropical* /ˈtrɒpɪkl/ (adj) typical of the parts of the world where it is very hot and wet
- *view* /vjuː/ (n) what you can see from a place

Exercise 7 1·60 page 50

- Give students two minutes to discuss the sentences in pairs. Then ask them to vote on whether the sentences are true or false. Write the results of the vote on the board.
- Play the recording for students to check their answers.
- Check answers as a class.

Audio script

1 A tornado can pick up a truck. This is true. A tornado is a very strong wind. Tornadoes can pick up cars, trucks, even houses and carry them to a different place.
2 It rains every day in the Amazon Rainforest. This is false. It's called the Amazon Rainforest, but it isn't always rainy! It rains about 250 days a year in the Amazon Rainforest. In total, the Amazon gets about 250 cm of rain per year.
3 All deserts are hot and dry. This is false. All deserts are dry, but not all deserts are hot. In fact, many deserts are very cold at night time. Some deserts are also cold during the day. Antarctica is a desert because it doesn't rain there.
4 Mount Baker in the USA has more snow per year than Antarctica. This is true. Mount Baker is very snowy! It gets about sixteen metres of snow every year. Antarctica gets five centimetres of snow per year.
5 There are 400 thunderstorms every day around the world. This is false. There are, in fact, 40,000 thunderstorms every day around the world.

1 T 2 F 3 F 4 T 5 F

Exercise 8 page 51

- Write a present simple and a present continuous sentence on the board: *I usually walk to school. Today I'm taking the bus.* Ask students to identify the present simple verb (*walk*) and the present continuous verb (*'m taking*). Remind them how we form the present continuous.
- To check answers, ask students to read out a sentence and say if it is present simple or present continuous.

1 PC 2 PS 3 PS 4 PC 5 PS 6 PC

Exercise 9 page 51

- Ask students to work in pairs to complete the rules.
- Write four headings on the board: *General truths*, *Habits and routines*, *Actions happening now*, *Things happening around now*. Then ask individual students to write the correct sentence from exercise 8 under each heading. Remind students that there are two sentences for some headings.

a present simple; sentence 3
b present continuous; sentences 1 and 4
c present simple; sentences 2 and 5
d present continuous; sentence 6

60 Unit 4 The natural world

> **Reference and practice 4.2** Workbook page 120
>
> **1** 2 PC 3 PC 4 PS 5 PC 6 PS 7 PS 8 PC
>
> **2** 1 I do
> 2 are cooking
> 3 isn't reading; 's listening
> 4 visit
> 5 watch
> 6 are you doing; 'm writing
>
> **3** 2 don't ride; take
> 3 A: Is (she) swimming
>   B: isn't; goes
> 4 aren't studying; 're visiting
> 5 A: Do (you usually) meet
>   B: do; 'm staying
> 6 are working
> 7 A: do you do
>   B: go
> 8 're watching

Exercise 10 page 51

- Give students two minutes to complete the text.
- With a **weaker class**, write both options for each gap on the board, e.g. 1 *play / am playing*. Students choose and copy the correct option.
- Check answers as a class.

1 play
2 're staying
3 's raining
4 're listening
5 is hiding
6 have
7 's
8 Is (it) raining

DVD extra Measuring the weather

Exercise 11 page 51

- Go through the first sentence together and elicit an answer.
- With a **weaker class**, remind students that words and phrases like *now* and *at the moment* indicate that the present continuous is needed. Adverbs of frequency like *always* and *usually* indicate that the present simple is needed.
- Check questions as a class. Students then work in pairs, asking and answering the questions.

1 What's the weather like today?
2 Is it raining at the moment?
3 What do you usually do at the weekend?
4 What are you doing now?
5 How many books do you read every month?
6 What book are you reading now?
7 What music do you usually listen to?
8 Are you listening to music now?

Learning outcome

Ask students: *What have you learned today? What can you do now?* and elicit answers: *I can describe different types of weather. I know about the seasons and weather in different parts of the world. I can use the present simple and the present continuous.*

4D Listening, speaking and vocabulary

Get active

> **Lesson summary**
> **Topic:** Outdoor life
> **Vocabulary:** Outdoor activities
> **Reading:** A flyer for an activity centre
> **Speaking:** Making and responding to suggestions
> **Writing:** A dialogue with two people trying to decide what to do

Lead-in

- Write *Outdoor activities* on the board and explain, if necessary, that *outdoor* means 'outside'.
- Ask students to work together in groups and brainstorm some outdoor activities. They can be very simple, e.g. *play football in the garden*, *take the dog for a walk*, or they can be more unusual, e.g. *bungee jumping*. Help with translations if necessary.
- Ask one student from each group to write their ideas on the board.
- Then ask students to open their books and look at the photos on page 52. Are any of their ideas included?

Exercise 1 page 52

- Students match the words to the pictures. Point out that four of the words do not have pictures.
- Check answers as a class. Then go through the remaining words (*canoeing*, *horse riding*, *mountain biking* and *surfing*) and elicit their meaning.

A zorbing B bouldering C snowboarding D caving
E diving F rock climbing G bungee jumping

Exercise 2 page 52

- Students discuss the questions in pairs. Remind them that with all these activities we use *go*, not *do* or *play*, e.g. *go bouldering*, *go canoeing*.
- Circulate and monitor, helping with vocabulary and ideas if necessary.
- Ask a few students to tell the class about the activities that people in their group do.

> **Extra activity: Game**
> Play a game to revise the sporting and outdoor activities that students have learned so far. Start by saying: *I love my weekends. I always play football.* Then ask a student to repeat your sentence, but to add another activity: *I love my weekends. I always play football and go zorbing.* Continue round the class, with each student adding another activity. For how long can they continue without forgetting an activity or making a mistake?

Unit 4 The natural world 61

Exercise 3 1·62 page 52

- Focus attention on the strategy and go through the examples of visual clues.
- Give students a minute to look at the flyer, identify the visual clues and think about what type of information is need to complete each gap.
- Play the recording.
- Students compare answers in pairs before listening to the recording again to check.
- Check answers as a class.

Audio script

It's holiday time at Redingly Activity Centre, and we've got some amazing activities this week. Try bouldering or horse riding! Maybe mountain biking is more your thing. Or you can go zorbing in our amazing new zorbing area. And don't forget, we have a wonderful lake, so you can also go canoeing.

Our holiday offer is now on: just £25 for a morning or afternoon session with two activities, or £42 for the day with four activities. We start early – we're open from eight in the morning until half past five in the afternoon, Monday to Saturday. So come to Redingly Activity Centre and have some fun!

1 horse riding / canoeing
2 canoeing / horse riding
3 42
4 8.00
5 Saturday

Exercise 4 1·61 page 52

- Focus attention on the flyer and explain that people can do lots of different outdoor sports at Redingly Activity Centre. Ask: *Are there places like this in your area?*
- Explain to students that they are going to listen to two instructors from the activity centre, Jeff and Maria. Read out the questions and remind students that they should focus on listening for the answers to those questions.
- Check answers as a class.

Audio script

Interviewer So, Jeff, you're an instructor here at Redingly Activity Centre. Can you explain for our listeners, what are you doing at the moment?
Jeff At the moment, I'm teaching a bouldering session.
Interviewer Bouldering. What's that?
Jeff Well, a boulder is a small rock, about three or four metres high. At the moment, we're outside, and as you can see, there are lots of boulders here. The students are climbing the boulders.
Interviewer Right, yes. So … what's the difference between rock climbing and bouldering?
Jeff Well, with rock climbing, you climb mountains or very big rocks and you also have lots of equipment. You use ropes, you wear a helmet and you usually climb with a partner. Bouldering uses no equipment.
Interviewer No equipment?
Jeff That's right. No ropes, no helmet. But, of course, the rocks are small – just three or four metres high. And there's a crash pad on the ground.
Interviewer A crash pad?
Jeff Yes, that's a thick cushion.
Interviewer OK, thanks very much, Jeff. Now I'm talking to another instructor here … This is Maria. Maria, what are you doing today?
Maria Hi! Today I've got three people with me and they're doing a zorbing session.
Interviewer Zorbing?
Maria Yes. Each person stands inside a big plastic ball, called a zorb. And then the zorb rolls down the hill.
Interviewer Is it difficult to do?
Maria No, it's not difficult, but it's fun. Guys, is it fun?
Voices Yeah! / Yes! / Woohoo!

Jeff talks about rock climbing and bouldering. He's teaching bouldering.
Maria talks about zorbing. She's teaching zorbing.

Exercise 5 1·61 page 52

- Focus attention on photos A, B and F and tell students that they can find the things in these photos.
- Play the recording again. Then ask different students to point to the things in the photos.

Photo A   zorb, hill
Photo B   crash pad, boulder
Photo D   helmet
Photo F   partner, helmet, rope
Photo G   rope

See exercise 4 for audio script

> **Extra activity: Further discussion**
>
> In small groups, students discuss the following questions:
> *Do you do any sports or outdoor activities with your friends or family?*
> *Do you like watching these kinds of activities on TV?*
> *Which activities are winter activities?*
> *Which activities are summer activities?*
> *Which activities are all-year activities?*

Exercise 6 page 53

- Demonstrate the activity. Say: *I'm not in a building, but it's very dark. I can't see anything. It's cold. I'm moving very slowly. I'm using a rope and I'm wearing a helmet.* Ask students to put their hands up when they guess the activity. (caving)
- Students play the game in pairs.
- When they have finished, ask a few students to talk about their activities for the rest of the class to guess.

Exercise 7 page 53

- Focus attention on the advertisement. Ask: *Do you stay in holiday parks on holiday? What things can you do there?*
- Give students one minute to read the advertisement quickly and answer the questions.

1 outdoor swimming, skateboarding
2 indoor swimming, climbing, tennis
3 outdoor swimming, horse riding, skateboarding, mini golf

Unit 4 The natural world

Language note
Focus on the verb forms used with these expressions:
What about + *-ing* form
How about + *-ing* form
Let's + verb
Why don't we + verb
I'd rather + verb
I'd prefer + *to* infinitive

Exercise 8 1·63 page 53
- Explain to students that Tarek and Steph are at Southview Holiday Park. They are trying to decide what to do.
- Play the recording.
- Check answers as a class.

Audio script
Tarek OK, so what do you want to do this morning, Steph?
Steph Um, how about mini golf?
Tarek Sorry, I'd rather not. I really don't like golf.
Steph Oh, all right then. Why don't we go horse riding?
Tarek I like horses, but it costs £25 and I haven't got any money.
Steph How about swimming, then? That's free.
Tarek Good idea!

They choose outdoor swimming.

Exercise 9 1·63 page 53
- Students work in pairs to complete as many phrases as they can.
- Play the recording for them to check their answers.
- To check answers as a class, ask individual students to read out the phrases. Then ask them which phrase is a negative response (*Sorry, I'd rather not.*) and which is a positive response (*Good idea!*).

1 want   2 about   3 don't we   4 rather not   5 Good

See exercise 8 for audio script

Exercise 10 1·64 page 53
- Go through the phrases with students. Ask them to identify two phrases for suggestions (*What about*, *Let's*) and two responses (*That sounds great*, *I'd prefer to*).
- Give students one minute to complete the dialogue. Then play the recording for them to check their answers.
- Check answers as a class.

Audio script
Steph Oh no! The swimming pool's closed.
Tarek What about going to the skateboarding park?
Steph That sounds great, but we haven't got a skateboard.
Tarek Yes, that's true. Let's go to the sports hall and play tennis. It's only £3.50 for a game.
Steph I'd prefer to go on the climbing wall.
Tarek Fine, I love climbing. Let's go!

1 What about
2 That sounds great
3 Let's
4 I'd prefer to

Exercise 11 page 53
- Tell students to look at the Redingly Activity Centre flyer again. Brainstorm some reasons for **not** wanting to do something, e.g. *I don't like it. It's boring. I can't ride a bike. I don't like water sports.*
- Students work in pairs. Circulate and monitor, helping with vocabulary and ideas if necessary.
- Ask pairs of students to perform their dialogues for the rest of the class.

Learning outcome
Ask students: *What have you learned today? What can you do now?* and elicit answers: *I know the names of different outdoor activities. I can understand a description of an unusual sport. I know how to make and respond to suggestions.*

4E Writing
Describing a photo

Lesson summary
Topic: Safari holiday
Vocabulary: Describing a photo
Reading: A description of a photo
Writing: A description of a photo

Lead-in
- To introduce the subject of photos, ask students: *Who likes taking photographs?* Then students discuss the following questions in pairs:
Do you take photos when you go on holiday?
Describe a good photo from your last holiday.
What do you prefer to photograph: people, animals or scenery?
Do you like it when people take photos of you?
- Ask a few students to share their partner's answers with the class.

Exercise 1 page 54
- Students discuss the questions in pairs.

Exercise 2 page 54
- Read out each question in exercise 1 and ask students to find the sentence or sentences that answer it. There is more than one possible answer for some of the questions, so be prepared for discussion.

(Possible answers)
It was taken at a safari park / on safari / in Africa.
The sun is shining and it looks hot. / It's hot and sunny.
An elephant.
It's standing and looking away from the people.
There are four people in the photo.
They are sitting in the jeep and looking at the elephant.

Unit 4 The natural world 63

Exercise 3 (page 54)

- Read out the examples and explain that *uncertainty* means 'not being sure about something'. Point out that after we express an opinion with *probably* or *I think*, we often explain, using the word *because*.
- Do the first sentence together and then ask individual students to write their answers to 2–4 on the board.

1 The people are probably in a desert because there is a lot of sand.
2 The elephants are in the jungle. Perhaps they are looking for food.
3 The weather is probably very cold because there is snow on the ground.
4 I think the old man is the children's grandfather.

Exercise 4 (page 54)

- Ask students to read the description in exercise 2 again and find *foreground* and *background*. Explain, if necessary, that they are similar in meaning to 'the front' and 'the back', but they are special terms used to describe pictures.
- Remind students that they already used the expressions *on the left* and *on the right* when they were giving directions.

1 in the background 2 in the middle 3 on the left
4 on the right 5 in the foreground

Exercise 5 (page 54)

- Give students a minute to look back through Unit 4 and identify another photo to describe.
- Circulate and monitor, helping with vocabulary and ideas if necessary.

> **Alternative activity**
>
> If you have any wildlife magazines or other pictures of animals, bring them to class. Choose one and invite students to look at it for one minute. Then cover the photo. Challenge a student to describe the photo from memory. The rest of the class listen and call out if they think there are any mistakes. Repeat the activity with other photos, each time challenging a different student to describe the photo from memory. Who has the best memory in the class?

Exercise 6 (page 54)

- Go through the strategy together. Explain that using questions to plan your writing is a useful way of checking that all the important information is included.
- Students describe the photo they chose in exercise 5 again, this time trying to include answers to all the questions in the strategy box.

Writing guide (page 55)

- Read the **task** together, making sure students are clear that they have to write a description of a photo.
- Give students five to ten minutes to complete the **ideas** stage and **plan** their description. Circulate and monitor, helping with language and ideas as necessary. Remind students to use expressions of uncertainty.
- Circulate and monitor while students **write** their descriptions, encouraging them to use words like *background* and *foreground* to describe where things are in photos. Remind them to activate the language they learned earlier in the unit (vocabulary for animals and the natural world, the present continuous and present simple).
- When students have finished, they **check** their work. Refer them to the checklist to make sure they have completed the task as well as they can.

> **Extension: Fast finishers**
>
> Ask **fast finishers** to swap descriptions with another student to read and check for mistakes.

> **Additional writing activity**
>
> Choose your favourite family photo. Describe what is happening in the photo. Include details about where things are, what the people are doing and what they are wearing.

Learning outcome

Ask students: *What have you learned today? What can you do now?* and elicit answers: *I can read and understand a description of a photo. I can use expressions of uncertainty. I can describe where things are in a photo. I can write a description of a photo.*

Review 4 (page 55)

1 1 follow 2 bite 3 carries 4 hunt 5 dig
   6 run away 7 look for

2 1 sunny 2 snowy 3 windy 4 rainy 5 stormy
   6 cloudy

3 1 bungee jumping   5 surfing
   2 mountain biking   6 zorbing
   3 snowboarding   7 white water rafting
   4 bouldering   8 diving

4 1 is it doing   7 are they doing
   2 it's hiding   8 They're looking
   3 it isn't hiding   9 I'm not pushing
   4 It's waiting   10 They're running away
   5 are you going   11 you're making
   6 I'm getting

5 1 do (people) go
   2 live
   3 organizes
   4 doesn't go
   5 starts
   6 isn't moving
   7 is showing
   8 aren't swimming
   9 are wearing
   10 are (they) listening to
   11 use
   12 are listening to
   13 does (a whale watching tour) cost

> **Pronunciation insight 4** Workbook page 133
> **Answer key:** Teacher's book page 154

64 Unit 4 The natural world

Cumulative review Units 1–4

pages 56–57

1 1·65

1 b   2 c   3 c   4 b   5 a

Audio script

1
This is a request for helpers to go to Westbrook Beach to help save some dolphins. We need volunteers to get the animals back into the sea. The dolphins have been out of the water for two hours, so they want to begin the rescue as soon as possible. The official start time is half past two, so you have forty-five minutes to get down to Margate and help.

2
Girl Is it real?
Boy What? The tiger?
Girl Yes. It looks real to me. It's really scary!
Boy It's in a boat with the boy – that's really dangerous.
Girl Maybe it's a trained tiger. It's a beautiful animal, anyway.
Boy Yes, it is, but I don't think it's real. It's probably a computer image. They don't use wild animals to make films.

3
Commentator … and City win the ball from United. City's Matt Enrico passes to Lucas Talin, and they're in front of the United goal. Talin shoots! Oh, and what a save from the United goalkeeper! That was a great try. The United goalkeeper kicks the ball out to Jones, and he passes it to Dankot. Dankot is going to take a shot. Ooh, that's unlucky he missed. With only minutes to go before half-time, it's a draw with no goals – nil, nil. This is a very exciting game at the stadium of …

4
Mum Do you know what you want for your birthday, Amy?
Amy Yes, I do. I'd really like to have a puppy.
Mum A puppy? What about a cat? Puppies don't stay small forever, Amy. They grow into dogs. Some of them grow into big dogs. A cat stays small.
Amy Yes, I know, but I don't mind.
Mum What about a rabbit? Dogs need exercise, too. What about taking it for walks? Rabbits can run around in the garden.
Amy No problem. I can take it for a walk before I go to school and in the evening after I get home.
Mum Well, let's wait and see what your father says, OK?

5
Wow! Look at that! Look at those dolphins! Can you see them? Is that a mother with her babies? They're playing in the waves. They're so playful! They're playing around that boat. Get the camera out of the bag. Don't get sand on it. They're swimming out to sea now.

2 Students' own answers

3 1 E   2 B   3 F   4 A   5 D

4 1 c   2 a   3 c   4 b   5 a   6 a   7 b   8 b   9 a
   10 c

5 Students' own answers

Additional materials

Literature insight 2 Workbook page 94   **Answer key:** Teacher's book page 152

Exam insight 2 Workbook page 104   **Answer key:** See website

5 Food, glorious food

Map of resources

Section A: Student's Book pages 58–59
Workbook page 44
Vocabulary bank, Food page 130

Section B: Student's Book pages 60–61
Workbook page 45
Grammar reference and practice 5.1, Workbook page 120
Grammar reference and practice 5.2, Workbook page 121
Teacher's resource disk, Communication worksheet 5A

Section C: Student's Book pages 62–63
Workbook page 46
Grammar reference and practice 5.3, Workbook page 121
Vocabulary bank, Food quantities page 130
Teacher's resource disk, DVD extra + worksheet, Borough Market page 63
Teacher's resource disk, Communication worksheet 5A

Section D: Student's Book pages 64–65
Workbook page 47
Teacher's resource disk, Communication worksheet 5B

Section E: Student's Book pages 66–67
Workbook page 50
Teacher's resource disk, Writing bank
Teacher's resource disk, Functional language bank

Review 5 page 67
Pronunciation insight 5, Workbook page 134
Progress check Unit 5, Workbook page 51
Language and skills tests 5A and 5B, Test Bank
Cumulative language and skills tests 1–5A and 1–5B, Test Bank

5A Reading and vocabulary

Food matters

Lesson summary
Topic: Eating habits
Vocabulary: Food, compound nouns, Vocabulary bank: Food
Reading: Unusual diets
Speaking: Talking about diets and food waste

Lead-in

- Write *FOOD* in capital letters on the board. Ask students to work in pairs and give them two minutes to brainstorm as many food words as possible. The pair with the longest list writes their words on the board.
- With a **stronger class**, ask students to categorize the food into *healthy food* and *unhealthy food*. This is subjective to some degree, so allow the class to vote if there are disagreements.

Exercise 1 page 58

- Make sure students understand the difference between *a million* and *a billion*. Write the two words on the board and ask a student to write the numbers in digits (1,000,000 = a million; 1,000,000,000 = a billion).
- Write the symbol *%* on the board and elicit or say *per cent*. Then write a few percentages on the board, e.g. *52%*, *17%*, and ask different students to say them.
- Students work individually to complete the sentences. They then check their ideas in pairs before looking at the answers at the bottom of the page.

Extra activity: Present continuous
Students work in pairs and try to remember the information in exercise 1. One student reads out a sentence from exercise 1 but says BUZZ in place of the bold words or numbers. The other student tries to remember the correct word or number to complete the sentence.

Exercise 2 2·01 page 58

- Focus attention on the letters of the title, *Unusual diets*, and explain that each letter contains the picture of a different type of food.
- Give students a minute to match the words to the letters in the title before playing the recording.
- Check answers as a class. Point out that *chocolate* /ˈtʃɒklət/ has only two syllables, and make sure that students are pronouncing the /juː/ in *cucumber* /ˈkjuːkʌmbə(r)/ correctly and the /ɪ/ in *orange* /ˈɒrɪndʒ/.

66 Unit 5 Food, glorious food

U tomato	D cheese
N cucumber	I nuts
U carrot	E mushroom
S bread	T lettuce
U apple	S coffee
A chocolate	
L orange	

Exercise 3 page 58

- Go through the strategy together. Give an example of a mind map by revising the animal words from Unit 4. Write ANIMALS on the board in capital letters as the main topic word. Around this write the sub-topics SEA, LAND and AIR, and elicit two animals for each sub-topic, e.g. SEA: fish, whale; LAND: elephant, giraffe; AIR: eagle, butterfly.
- Students copy the mind map and complete it with the words in exercise 2. Tell them to leave space so that they can add more food words later.
- Check answers as a class. Students may point out that a tomato is actually a fruit, lettuce is a plant and a mushroom is a fungus, but most people would class them as vegetables.

carbohydrates: bread
vegetables: carrot, cucumber, lettuce, mushroom, (tomato)
fruit: apple, nut, orange, (tomato)
sugar and fats: chocolate, (cheese)
dairy products: cheese
drinks: coffee

Exercise 4 page 59

- Write the following words on the board: *freegan, fruitarian* and *locavore*. Explain to students that these are names for people who eat only a particular kind of food. Students work in pairs and guess what kinds of food each of these people eats.
- Remind students that they do not need to understand every word in order to answer the questions; they should look for the main gist.
- Check answers as a class.

a Simon Pilcher   b Lucy Friend   c Tim Jenson

Exercise 5 page 59

- Tell students to read the questions and underline the key words. Then give them three minutes to read the text and answer the questions.
- Check answers as a class.
- With a **weaker class**, give students the line numbers where they can find the answers (1: lines 17–18; 2: lines 23–26; 3: line 30; 4: lines 31–32; 5: lines 37–39; 6: lines 39–40; 7: lines 43–44; 8: lines 46–48; 9: lines 49–52)

1 Because when you eat a carrot the carrot plant dies.
2 It doesn't provide enough calcium, iron or vitamin B.
3 It is very popular in India.
4 Because it uses a lot of petrol, which causes global warming.
5 No, because the ingredients come from abroad.
6 It's sometimes difficult for him.
7 Because of the way it treats animals and the environment.
8 From his garden, the countryside and from bins outside big shops.
9 Freegans eat food that shops throw away.

Additional vocabulary

The following words are from the text *Unusual diets*:
- *vegetarian* /ˌvedʒəˈteəriən/ (n) a person who does not eat meat or fish
- *treatment* /ˈtriːtmənt/ (n) the way that you behave towards somebody or something
- *fair* /feə(r)/ (adj) treating people equally or in the right way
- *throw away* /ˌθrəʊ əˈweɪ/ (v) get rid of something you do not want
- *waste* /weɪst/ (n) something that has not been used in a useful way
- *ingredient* /ɪnˈɡriːdiənt/ (n) one of the things that you put in when you make something to eat

Extra activity: Further discussion

Ask students to discuss these questions in groups:
Do you read the labels on food?
Do you know where your food comes from?
Does your family usually buy food from the supermarket or from smaller shops?

Exercise 6 page 59

- Introduce the discussion by eliciting reasons why people might have an unusual diet, e.g. because of their religious, political or ethical beliefs; health reasons.
- Find out if anyone in the class has an unusual diet, but treat this subject with caution as some students may be sensitive about the food they eat or may feel uncomfortable talking about their religious or political convictions.
- Students discuss the questions in pairs.
- When they have finished, ask a few students to report back on the types of food they would find it most difficult to live without.

V insight Compound nouns

- Most compound nouns in English are formed by combining two nouns or an adjective and a noun to make a new word. The first word in a compound noun usually modifies the second word, e.g. *goldfish – gold* gives more information about *fish*.
- We can also form compound nouns by combining a preposition and a noun, e.g. *underground*.
- Most compound nouns are one word, e.g. *bedroom*.
- Some compound nouns have a hyphen, e.g. *check-in*.
- Some compound nouns are written as two separate words, e.g. *swimming pool*.

Exercise 7 page 59

- Do the first sentence together, demonstrating that students need to choose one word from the first group and one word from the second group to make a compound noun.
- Check answers as a class. Remind students to record the words in their vocabulary notebooks.
- With a **weaker class**, give students the second word in each compound noun and ask them to find the first word.

1 orange juice
2 ham sandwich
3 ice cream
4 mushroom pizza
5 chocolate cake
6 tomato sauce
7 fruit salad
8 olive oil

Exercise 8 page 59

- Explain, if necessary, the meaning of *waste*. Say: *I buy a big cheese sandwich. I eat half and I put the other half in the bin. That's a waste of food! Do you ever waste food?*
- Circulate and monitor, helping with vocabulary and ideas if necessary.
- Ask a few pairs of students to share their ideas with the class.

> **Vocabulary bank: Food** page 130
> 1 1 ketchup, potatoes, steak, onions
>   2 peas, salmon, pepper
>   3 cream, strawberries, sugar
>   4 pasta, rice
>   5 grapes, peaches
>   6 sweets, crisps
> 2 **Carbohydrates** pasta, potatoes, rice
>   **Meat and fish** salmon, steak
>   **Fruit** grapes, peach, strawberries
>   **Vegetables** onions, peas, potatoes, spinach
>   **High in sugar or fat** cream, crisps, sugar, sweets
>   **Condiments** ketchup, pepper, salt
> 3 Students' own answers

Learning outcome

Ask students: *What have you learned today? What can you do now?* and elicit answers: *I can name different types of food. I can read and understand a text about unusual diets. I know some compound nouns. I can talk about diets and wasting food.*

5B Grammar and listening

School food with a difference

Lesson summary
Topic: Farms
Grammar: Countable and uncountable nouns; *much, many, a lot of*
Listening: A radio programme about a farm school
Reading: Farm school
Speaking: Planning a farm for your school
Communication worksheet 5A: Party time!

Lead-in

- Write the following words on the board and ask students what place links them all: *pig, cow, vegetables, fruit, field, tractor*. Translate *field* and *tractor* if necessary.

- When students have guessed the place (farm), ask them to discuss the following questions:
  Do you live on or near a farm?
  Do you visit farms?
  Do you think farms are interesting places?

Exercise 1 page 60

- Elicit and write two or three food words on the board, e.g. *milk, potatoes, cabbages*.
- Students work in pairs. For the second question, tell them not to read the text but just look at the photos.
- Give students two minutes to discuss their ideas and then get feedback from a few pairs. Explain that we use *beef* for meat from cows, *lamb / mutton* for meat from sheep, *chicken* for meat from hens, and *pork* for meat from pigs.
- Check answers as a class.

1 Students' own answers
2 Hens, cows and milking machines. The farm produces eggs, chickens and milk. It's unusual because school students are working there.

Exercise 2 page 60

- Give students two minutes to read the text quickly and check their ideas.
- Ask the class to vote on whether they like the idea of a school farm.
- With a **stronger class**, ask students for ideas on how the school uses the farm to teach maths, art and science.
- Check the answer as a class.

The farm produces honey, apples, potatoes, cabbages, other vegetables, eggs, milk, lamb and pork.

> **Language note: Countable and uncountable nouns**
>
> Countable nouns are things we can count, e.g. *pencils, computers, chairs*. They can be singular or plural. When a countable noun is singular, we must use a determiner or a possessive adjective before it.
> *This is a book. It's my book.*
>
> Uncountable nouns are things we cannot count, e.g. *rice, money, love*. We do not use *a / an* with uncountable nouns. We usually use a singular verb.
> *This bread is delicious.*
>
> Some words can be countable or uncountable, depending on the meaning in context.
> *I've got a new light for our sitting room.* (light = countable)
> *I can't see because the light is poor.* (light = uncountable)

Exercise 3 page 60

- You could use a bottle of water to demonstrate the difference between something countable (*bottle*) and something uncountable (*water*).
- Students look at the example words and decide which are countable and which are uncountable.
- Check answers as a class.

Countable apple, sausage
Uncountable honey, milk

Exercise 4 page 60

- Go through the explanation together. Then give students two minutes to complete the table.
- Students compare answers in pairs.
- With a **stronger class**, explain to students that uncountable nouns are often abstract concepts, e.g. *time*, *happiness*. Then ask them to think of two more examples for each category.
- Check answers as a class.

Countable vegetable, cabbage, egg, potato
Uncountable meat, food, fruit, lamb

> **Extra activity: Game**
> Start the game by saying: *I work in the farm shop and I sell eggs*. Then elicit another food item to add to the sentence: *I work in the farm shop and I sell eggs and bread*. Continue around the class, with each student adding a food to the sentence. Remind them to use the plural for countable nouns and the singular for uncountable nouns.

> **Reference and practice 5.1** Workbook page 120
> 1 2 C   3 C   4 U   5 U   6 U   7 U   8 C   9 C   10 U
> 2 2 A; a; some
>   3 a; some
>   4 some; some; a
>   5 a; a
>   6 a; some

Exercise 5 2·02 page 61

- Tell students to look at the nouns in brackets and decide whether they are countable or uncountable.
- Go through the example together: *meat* is uncountable, and so the verb is in the singular form. We use *any* with negatives and questions, and *some* in affirmative sentences.
- Give students two minutes to complete the sentences. Then ask individual students to write the answers on the board. Do not say whether they are correct or incorrect, but ask the rest of the class if they want to make any corrections. This is a good way of finding out how well your students have understood the grammar.
- Play the recording for students to check their answers.
- Check answers as a class.

Audio script
Woman Is there any meat today?
Man Yes, there is. There is some lamb and there are some sausages, but there isn't any beef.
Woman Are there any vegetables?
Man Yes, there are some potatoes, but there isn't any cabbage.
Woman And is there any milk?
Man No, I'm sorry. There isn't any milk today.

1 There is some lamb
2 there are some sausages
3 there isn't any beef
4 Are there any vegetables
5 there are some potatoes
6 there isn't any cabbage
7 is there any milk
8 There isn't any milk

Exercise 6 page 61

- Look at the first sentence together and ask students to find the missing words in the text. Then give them two minutes to complete the sentences.
- Students use the information in the sentences to complete the rules.
- Check answers as a class.

1 many   2 a lot of   3 much   4 many   5 much
a 2   b 1   c 3   d 4

> **Reference and practice 5.2** Workbook page 121
> 1 2 much   6 much
>   3 many; a lot of   7 a lot of
>   4 many   8 much
>   5 a lot of; a lot of
> 2 2 How many people are in your family?
>   3 How much time do you usually spend on your homework?
>   4 How much water do you drink every day?
>   5 How many armchairs have you got in your living room?
>   6 How much chicken do you eat every week?
>   7 How many eggs are in the box?
>   8 How many pets have you got?

Exercise 7 page 61

- Students complete the factfile and then compare answers in pairs.
- With a **weaker class**, read out the noun after each gap and ask: *Countable or uncountable?* Then read out each gapped sentence and ask: *Affirmative, negative or question?* Students use this information to complete the sentences.
- Check answers as a class.

1 much   2 much   3 many   4 many   5 a lot of
6 much   7 a lot of   8 much   9 many   10 a lot of

Exercise 8 2·03 page 61

- Give students one minute to complete the questions.
- Explain to students that they will hear an interview with some students from Oathall School. Remind them that they only need to find the answers to the questions; they do not need to understand every word.
- Check answers as a class.

Audio script
Journalist It's half past seven in the morning here at Oathall Farm, and we are talking to four students who help at the farm. Hello. What are you doing?
Girl 1 I'm giving some food to the animals. We don't give the sheep much food now. It's summer, so there's a lot of grass for them outside. But the pigs and hens are always hungry.
Journalist And what about you? What are you doing?
Boy 1 I'm looking for eggs. We've got eight hens on the farm at the moment. Each hen usually produces one egg every day, but sometimes it's difficult to find them.
Girl 2 And I'm milking one of the cows. Her name's Daisy. One student milks her early in the morning and another student milks her again after school. It's very important to milk the cows at the same times every day, or they don't produce much milk.
Journalist Do you drink the milk?

Unit 5 Food, glorious food

Girl 2 No, we can't drink it because it isn't pasteurized, but the pigs love it.
Journalist Whoa, what's that smell? What are you doing in here?
Boy 2 I'm cleaning the pigs' living area. The smell isn't very nice, but the pigs are great. I spend half an hour with them every day, so I know them quite well. They're very friendly, clever animals.

1 many; four
2 much; no
3 many; eight
4 many; one
5 many; two
6 much; no

Exercise 9 page 61

- Go through the discussion questions together and brainstorm some ideas onto the board. Write two headings on the board, *FARM ANIMALS* and *PLANTS*, and brainstorm words for each heading with the class.
- Provide some extra vocabulary for students to use when discussing farm jobs, e.g. *feed / look after the animals, milk the cows, water the plants, collect the eggs, sell the produce*.
- Circulate and monitor, helping with vocabulary if necessary.

Learning outcome

Ask students: *What have you learned today? What can you do now?* and elicit answers: *I know about a farm school. I can use countable and uncountable nouns with 'some', 'any', 'a lot of', 'much' and 'many'. I can understand an interview about a farm.*

5C Culture, vocabulary and grammar

Traditional food

Lesson summary
Topic: Food from different parts of the UK
Vocabulary: Vocabulary bank: Food quantities
Grammar: *a little / a few*
Reading: Food map of Britain and Ireland
Vocabulary: On the dinner table
Speaking: Describing a traditional dish from your country
Communication worksheet 5A: Party time!

Lead-in

- Write the following names of international dishes on the board and ask students if they can guess where they come from: *paella* (Spain), *tacos* (Mexico), *tandoori chicken* (India), *chow mein* (China), *risotto* (Italy), *sushi* (Japan). If they struggle with this activity, write the country names on the board and ask them to match the food with the country.
- Brainstorm names of other international dishes and ask if students have ever tried them.

Exercise 1 page 62

- With books closed, write the first question on the board: *What traditional dishes does your country have?* In pairs, students write as many traditional dishes from their country as possible. Set a time limit of two minutes. The pair with the longest list write the names on the board.
- Students work in pairs, discussing the dishes on the board.

- Ask students to name traditional dishes from Britain. Write their ideas on the board. Then ask them to open their books and look at the photos to see if their ideas are included.

Exercise 2 page 62

- Go through the strategy together. Explain that even when we look up words in the dictionary, we still need to think about the context; many words in English have more than one meaning.
- Students read the text and underline unknown words. Tell them to underline a maximum of six words, and encourage them to think about which words are vital for them to understand the meaning of the text.

Exercise 3 page 62

- Remind students to identify the key words in the descriptions before they read the text again.
- Check answers as class.

1 barmbrack
2 jellied eels
3 Yorkshire pudding
4 fish and chips
5 –
6 Cornish pasty
7 Devon cream tea
8 haggis

Additional vocabulary
The following words are from the text *Food map of Britain and Ireland*:
- *raisin* /ˈreɪzn/ (n) a dried grape (= a small, sweet fruit)
- *vinegar* /ˈvɪnɪɡə(r)/ (n) a liquid with a strong, sharp taste that is used in cooking
- *lung* /lʌŋ/ (n) one of the two parts inside your body that you use for breathing
- *liver* /ˈlɪvə(r)/ (n) the part inside your body that cleans the blood
- *takeaway* /ˈteɪkəweɪ/ (n) food that you buy from a restaurant that sells hot food that you take out with you to eat somewhere else

Culture notes: British food
Other popular traditional British dishes include:
cottage pie: minced beef with mashed potato on top
bangers and mash: sausages with mashed potato, often served with onion gravy
full English breakfast: fried eggs, bacon, sausage, tomato and mushrooms
black pudding: a type of blood sausage
spotted dick: a steamed suet pudding with dried fruit, served with custard

Exercise 4 page 62

- Students discuss the different dishes in pairs.
- You can hold a class vote to find out the most popular British dish and the least popular.

Extra activity: Further discussion
Ask students to discuss these questions:
Which meal of the day is the most important for you? Why?
Describe your perfect meal.
Do you prefer food from your country or from other countries?
Do you think governments should ban unhealthy food? Why / why not?

70   Unit 5   Food, glorious food

Exercise 5 2·04 page 62

- Students label the objects.
- Play the recording for them to check their answers. Then play it again for them to repeat the words.
- Point out the silent *k* in *knife* /naɪf/, and the /əʊ/ sound in *bowl* /bəʊl/.
- Check answers as a class.

1 cup   2 spoon   3 plate   4 mug   5 fork   6 knife
7 glass   8 bowl   9 jug

Exercise 6 page 63

- Explain that students may need to use more than one word for each answer. For *breakfast*, students' answers will depend on what they eat; if they have toast, they may not use any cutlery, but if they have cereal with milk, they will use a spoon.
- Students ask and answer the questions in pairs.
- Check answers as a class.

1 plate, knife, fork
2 spoon, bowl
3 glass
4 cup or mug
5 spoon, bowl, plate, knife, fork
6 jug

> **Language note:** *a little / a few*
> There is a difference in meaning between *a little* and *little*, and *a few* and *few*.
> *A little* and *a few* mean 'a small amount, but enough'.
> *Little* and *few* mean '**not** enough'. We often use *very* before *little* and *few*.
> *I've got a little money. I want to buy a new dress.*
> *I've got (very) little money. I can't buy a new dress.*

Exercise 7 page 63

- Start reading out the first text (*Barmbrack*) and ask students to put their hands up when they hear *a little* or *a few*. Write *a few surprises* on the board. Ask: *Is 'surprise' countable or uncountable?* (countable)
- Students work individually, finding examples of *a little* and *a few*.
- With a **weaker class**, continue to read out the text, stopping each time there is an example of *a little* and *a few*, and writing it on the board.
- Check the rules as a class.

a uncountable   b countable   c not much   d not many

> **Reference and practice 5.3** Workbook page 121
> 1 2 a few   5 a few
>   3 a little; a few   6 a few
>   4 a little
> 2 2 a little   6 a little
>   3 a little   7 a few
>   4 a few   8 a little
>   5 a few

> **Extra activity: What's in your fridge?**
> Ask **fast finishers** to work in pairs. Each student draws a picture of a fridge with different food items in it, including countable and uncountable nouns. They then take it in turns to ask and answer about the contents of each other's fridge, e.g. *'How much milk is in your fridge?' 'I've got a lot of milk.' 'How many sausages are in your fridge?'*

Exercise 8 page 63

- Focus attention on the photo and ask students what ingredients they think are in this dish. Ask: *Do you want to try it?*
- Students read the text quickly to check their ideas.
- Give them two minutes to complete the dialogue.
- To check answers, ask two students to read out the dialogue and tell the class to call out if they think there are any mistakes.
- Explain that although *cake* is uncountable, we use *a few* because we are talking about *slices* of cake, and *slice* is countable.

1 a little   5 a few
2 a few   6 a little
3 a little   7 a little
4 a little   8 a few

Exercise 9 page 63

- Brainstorm more words for ingredients onto the board. Have dictionaries available for students who want to look up specific words.
- Circulate and monitor, helping with extra vocabulary if necessary.

> **Vocabulary bank: Food quantities** page 130
> 1 1 bread   6 jam
>   2 water   7 sweets
>   3 juice   8 peaches
>   4 pizza   9 apples
>   5 cola   10 oil
> 2 1 a tin of   6 a kilo of
>   2 a loaf of   7 a carton of
>   3 a jar of   8 a slice of
>   4 a bottle of   9 a can of
>   5 a packet of
> 3 Students' own answers

DVD extra Borough Market

Learning outcome Ask students: *What have you learned today? What can you do now?* and elicit answers: *I know about traditional British food. I can use 'a little' and 'a few'. I know words for things on the dinner table. I can talk about traditional food from my own country.*

Unit 5 Food, glorious food   71

5D Listening, speaking and vocabulary

Delicious or disgusting?

Lesson summary
Topic: Unusual food from around the world
Vocabulary: Opinion adjectives
Speaking: Giving opinions; ordering food
Listening: Unusual food
Communication worksheet 5B: What's your opinion?

Lead-in

- Say: *My favourite sandwich is banana and jam.* Ask students if that is *delicious* (smile widely, say 'Yum!' and rub your tummy) or *disgusting* (frown and say 'Yuk!').
- Students work in pairs and create their own unusual sandwiches. Each sandwich must have at least two fillings, and students should think of five different sandwiches.
- When they have finished, ask a few pairs of students to tell you about their sandwiches. The class can vote for the most delicious and most disgusting sandwich.

Exercise 1 page 64

- Focus attention on the photos and ask students: *What do you think? Delicious or disgusting?*
- Point out that three of the words in the list are ingredients and three are countries. You may need to translate the ingredients. If you have a world map in the classroom, show students where the countries are.
- Ask a few students to share their ideas with the class but do not tell them whether they are right or wrong yet.
- Check answers as a class.

A **Dish** caterpillars
  Country South Africa
B **Dish** guinea pigs
  Country Peru
C **Dish** tarantulas
  Country Cambodia

Exercise 2 2·05 page 64

- Play the recording for students to check their answers to exercise 1. With a **stronger class**, students try to complete the table from memory.
- Play the recording again. Students exchange tables with a partner and check their partner's answers.
- Check answers as a class.

Audio script

Speaker Hello, and welcome to *The Food Show*. On the show today, we've got some exciting food from around the world, and three people to taste it. First, we've got Dylan.
Dylan Hi.
Speaker And for you we've got a favourite snack from South Africa – caterpillars! Dylan, are you ready?
Dylan Ew! They're strange! They don't look very nice, but, well, here goes.
Speaker What do you think?
Dylan They're OK … but they aren't great. They taste of salt and … nothing, really. In fact, they've got a boring taste. I prefer sweets as a snack.
Speaker Oh, but sweets are very bad for you, and these caterpillars are very healthy. They've got a lot of protein in them. Well done for trying one, Dylan. … And next, we've got Lauren, and her food today is very popular in Cambodia in Asia – tarantulas!
Lauren Oh no! Spiders are scary. And these tarantulas' legs have got hair on them. They're really disgusting …
Speaker Go on, try one! A lot of people like eating them.
Lauren OK … Wow. It's a really nice taste! It's like … umm … crisps!
Speaker Would you like another?
Lauren Yes, please!
Speaker And now for our last food. Elsa, are you ready for this? It's a popular meat in Peru. It is … guinea pig!
Elsa Oh no! Guinea pigs are lovely pets, but I don't want one for my dinner! Yuk!
Speaker But it's just meat, Elsa. Do you eat beef?
Elsa Yes, sometimes, but that's different.
Speaker Not really. It's all about your culture. The differences around the world are very interesting. In India, people don't eat beef. A lot of Indians think it's wrong to kill a cow.
Elsa Really? Well, I can't eat that guinea pig. No way!
Speaker Oh dear. Lauren, Dylan, would you like some guinea pig meat?
Dylan Yeah, sure.
Lauren OK.
Dylan Yum. It's great. What do you think, Lauren?
Lauren Yes, it's a delicious taste – like chicken.

	Dylan	Lauren	Elsa
Food	caterpillars	tarantulas	guinea pigs
Country	South Africa	Cambodia	Peru
Does he / she like it?	No	Yes	No

Exercise 3 2·05 page 64

- Give students a minute to read the questions. With a **stronger class**, ask students to try to answer the questions from memory before listening to the recording again.
- Play the recording. With a **weaker class**, stop the recording at the following points and give students time to choose the answers: 1: *They're OK … but they aren't great*; 2: *these caterpillars are very healthy*; 3: *It's a really nice taste!* 4: *It's like … um … crisps!* 5: *Guinea pigs are lovely pets*; 6: *A lot of Indians think it's wrong to kill a cow*; 7: *it's a delicious taste – like chicken*.
- Check answers as a class.

1 c   2 a   3 b   4 a   5 a   6 b   7 a

See exercise 2 for audio script

Exercise 4 2·05 page 64

- Students will not know all the adjectives, but explain that they will study their meaning in the next exercise. For this activity, they just have to listen to the recording again and identify what the people are describing.
- Play the recording and then check answers as a class.

1 d   2 c   3 g   4 e   5 h   6 b   7 f   8 a

See exercise 2 for audio script

Exercise 5 2·06 page 65

- Students study the meaning of the adjectives in exercise 4.
- Then ask them to try and complete the sentences. Encourage them to tackle the ones they are certain about first.
- Play the recording for students to check their answers.
- Check answers as a class. Point out that *interesting* has three syllables, not four: /ˈɪntrəstɪŋ/, and focus on the /ʌ/ sound in *lovely*: /ˈlʌvli/.

1 interesting   2 disgusting   3 scary   4 delicious
5 boring   6 lovely   7 strange   8 exciting

Exercise 6 page 65

- Demonstrate the activity for students. Say: *I think fried guinea pig is interesting. Is it disgusting or delicious? I don't know.* Then ask one student: *What do you think?* and elicit their opinion.
- Students work in pairs, giving their opinions. Circulate and monitor, helping with extra vocabulary if necessary.

Extra activity: What do I think?
Ask students to choose five adjectives from exercise 4 and to write them at the top of a piece of paper. Below them, in a different order, they write five nouns, one for each adjective above. They then exchange their papers and try to match their partner's words with the adjectives.

Exercise 7 page 65

- Focus attention on the menu and check that students understand *starter* (the first course of a meal), *main course* and *dessert*.
- Give students two minutes, in pairs, to complete the menu.
- Check answers as a class.

1 bread   2 cheese   3 chips   4 pasta   5 cake
6 strawberry   7 fruit   8 juice

Extra activity: Fast finishers
Ask **fast finishers** to add one more item to each section of the menu. Allow them to use a dictionary.

Exercise 8 2·07 page 65

- Explain to students that they are going to hear a short dialogue in a restaurant. They have to find the items on the menu that the man and woman order.
- Play the recording.
- Check answers as a class.

Audio script
Waiter Hello, are you ready to order?
Man Yes, thank you.
Waiter Would you like a starter?
Woman Yes, please. I'd like some garlic bread.
Waiter What would you like for your starter?
Man I'd like some tomato soup.
Waiter What would you like for your main course?
Woman Can I have a cheese, tomato and mushroom pizza, please?
Man And I'd like the pasta with tomato sauce.
Waiter Would you like anything to drink?
Man Can I have a glass of orange juice, please?
Woman I'd like some lemonade.
Waiter Fine. Thank you.

The man orders tomato soup, pasta with tomato sauce and a glass of orange juice.

The woman orders garlic bread, a cheese, tomato and mushroom pizza and some lemonade.

Exercise 9 2·07 page 65

- Students work in pairs to complete the phrases.
- Play the recording again and then ask individual students to read out the phrases.
- Check answers as a class.

1 ready   2 Would   3 What   4 anything   5 like
6 have

See exercise 8 for audio script

Exercise 10 2·08 page 65

- Go through the phrases together. With a **weaker class**, help students to identify the waiter's phrases and the customers' phrases before they complete the dialogue.
- Play the recording for them to check their answers.
- Check answers as a class.

Audio script
Waiter Would you like a dessert?
Girl Oh, yes. Can we see the menu, please?
Waiter Of course. Here you are.
Girl Great. Can I have some strawberry ice cream, please?
Waiter Any dessert for you, sir?
Boy No, I'm fine, thanks.

1 Can we see the menu
2 Here you are
3 Any dessert for you
4 I'm fine, thanks

Exercise 11 page 65

- Give students a minute to find and underline the phrases in the dialogue.

Can we see the menu, please?
Here you are.
Any … for you?

Exercise 12 page 65

- Students work in pairs to write their own dialogues.
- Circulate and monitor, helping with vocabulary and ideas if necessary.
- Invite a few pairs of students to act out their dialogues for the class.

Learning outcome
Ask students: *What have you learned today? What can you do now?* and elicit answers: *I know opinion adjectives. I can understand a TV programme about unusual food. I can express my opinion about different things. I can order food in a restaurant.*

5E Writing

A description of a festival

> **Lesson summary**
> **Topic:** Guy Fawkes' Night
> **Vocabulary:** Linking words of addition: *too, also*
> **Reading:** A description of Guy Fawkes' Night
> **Writing:** A description of a festival in your country

Lead-in

- Write the following dates and gapped words for festivals on the board:
  1 January, 14 February, 1 May, 31 October, 5 November, 24 December, 26 December
  M _ _ D _ _
  N _ _ Y _ _ _ 's D _ _
  B _ x _ _ g D _ _
  G _ _ F _ w k _ _ N _ _ _ _
  H _ l l _ w _ _ n
  St V _ _ e _ _ i _ _ 's D _ _
  Ch _ _ _ _ m _ s E _ e

- Ask students to complete the names of the festivals and then match them to the appropriate date.

1 January New Year's Day   **14 February** St Valentine's Day
1 May May Day   **31 October** Halloween
5 November Guy Fawkes' Night   **24 December** Christmas Eve
26 December Boxing Day

Exercise 1 page 66

- Write the following words on the board: *toffee apple, bonfire, fireworks.* Then ask students to point to these things in the photos.
- Students discuss the questions in pairs. Elicit their ideas and write them on the board, but do not say if they are correct or incorrect yet.

It's November.
They're watching a fireworks display.

Exercise 2 page 66

- Students read the email quickly to check their ideas from exercise 1 and to find out which festival it is and what happens at this festival.
- Ask **fast finishers** to read the email again and find the answers to the following questions:
  1 *Why is Reece happy?* (Because it's Guy Fawkes' Night, his favourite night of the year.)
  2 *Is Guy Fawkes alive today?* (no)
  3 *What food do people eat on Guy Fawkes' Night?* (sausages, potatoes, parkin and toffee apples)

It's Guy Fawkes' Night.
People make a model of Guy Fawkes and burn it on a bonfire.

Exercise 3 page 66

- Give students two minutes to match the words to the definitions.
- Check answers as a class. Remind students about compound nouns and point out that *toffee apple* is an example of a compound noun.
- With a **stronger class**, ask students to identify four nouns (*celebration, bonfire, plot, toffee*), one adjective (*hard*) and one verb (*blow up*).

1 plot **2** hard **3** bonfires **4** celebration **5** blow up
6 toffee

Exercise 4 page 66

- Students find and underline examples of *too* and *also* in the email and then complete the rules.
- Check answers as a class.

b after; before
c end

Exercise 5 page 66

- Read out the example answer and point out that *and* is used to link the two clauses.
- Students work individually to rewrite the sentences.
- Check answers as a class.

1 Toffee apples are delicious and parkin is also nice.
2 We go to the big bonfire in the park and we have a small bonfire at home too.
3 The fireworks in the park are very beautiful and they are also very noisy.
4 My dog is scared of fireworks and he's also scared of thunder.
5 Guy Fawkes' Night is in November and my birthday is in November too.
6 We usually eat parkin on Guy Fawkes' Night and we also drink hot chocolate.

Exercise 6 page 66

- Go through the strategy together. Explain that knowing the writing goal is important because it affects the *style* of our writing (formal or informal), the *information* we decide to include or leave out, and the *presentation* of the text (e.g. whether to use bullet points or paragraphs).
- Students read the questions and then study Reece's email again to find the answers.
- Check answers as a class.

1 an email
2 a friend
3 to describe his favourite festival
4 facts
5 information about dates, history, activities and food
6 informal style

Writing guide page 67

- Read the **task** together, making sure students understand that they have to write description of a festival similar to the one in Reece's email.
- Give students five to ten minutes to complete the **ideas** stage and **plan** their letter. Circulate and monitor, helping with language and ideas as necessary. Remind students to write notes, not full sentences.

74 Unit 5 Food, glorious food

- Circulate and monitor while students **write** their emails, encouraging them to use the linking words *too* and *also*. Remind them to activate the language they learned earlier in the unit (food vocabulary, countable and uncountable nouns, expressions of quantity).
- When students have finished, they **check** their work. Refer them to the checklist to make sure they have completed the task as well as they can.

> **Extension: Fast finishers**
> Ask **fast finishers** to swap their emails with another student to read and check for mistakes.

> **Additional writing activity**
> Write an email to a friend describing what you usually do on your birthday or on another special family day. Include information about the food you eat, the activities you do and the people you spend time with on the special day.

Learning outcome
Ask students: *What have you learned today? What can you do now?* and elicit answers: *I can read and understand an email about Guy Fawkes' Night. I can use the linking words 'also' and 'too'. I can write a description of a festival in my country.*

Review 5   page 67

1 1 meat   2 bread   3 yoghurt   4 salad   5 tomato
   6 plate   7 knife   8 fork

2 1 fruit salad
   2 ham sandwich
   3 orange juice
   4 ice cream
   5 tomato sauce
   6 olive oil
   7 chocolate cake

3 1 boring   2 lovely   3 disgusting   4 interesting
   5 delicious   6 exciting   7 scary

4 1 You don't need any cucumber.
   2 You don't need any eggs.
   3 You need some garlic.
   4 You need some meat.
   5 You need some onion.
   6 You need some pasta.
   7 You don't need any potatoes.
   8 You don't need any rice.
   9 You need some tomatoes.
   10 You don't need any yoghurt.

5 1 any   8 many
   2 How many   9 an
   3 a few   10 much
   4 some   11 any
   5 How much   12 a little
   6 a lot   13 how much
   7 a

Pronunciation insight 5   Workbook page 134
Answer key: Teacher's book page 154

6 Material world

Map of resources

Section A: Student's Book pages 68–69
Workbook page 52
Vocabulary bank, Shops page 131
Teacher's resource disk, Communication worksheet 6B

Section B: Student's Book pages 70–71
Workbook page 53
Grammar reference and practice 6.1, Workbook page 122
Teacher's resource disk, DVD extra + worksheet, Shopping in London page 71
Teacher's resource disk, Communication worksheet 6A

Section C: Student's Book pages 72–73
Workbook page 54
Grammar reference and practice 6.2, Workbook page 123
Teacher's resource disk, Communication worksheet 6A
Teacher's resource disk, Communication worksheet 6B

Section D: Student's Book pages 74–75
Workbook page 55
Vocabulary bank, Clothes verbs page 131
Teacher's resource disk, Communication worksheet 6B

Section E: Student's Book pages 76–77
Workbook page 58
Teacher's resource disk, Writing bank
Teacher's resource disk, Functional language bank

Review 6 page 77
Pronunciation insight 6, Workbook page 134
Progress check Unit 6, Workbook page 59
Language and skills tests 6A and 6B, Test Bank

Cumulative review Units 1–6 pages 78–79
Literature insight 3, Workbook page 96
Exam insight 3, Workbook page 106

6A Reading and vocabulary

Nearly new

Lesson summary
Topic: Recycling clothes
Vocabulary: Clothes and accessories; shopping and clothes words; negative prefixes; Vocabulary bank: Shops
Reading: Shwopping
Speaking: Discussing clothes and recycling
Communication worksheet 6B: Find the mistake

Lead-in

Write *CLOTHES* in capital letters on the board. Then draw some simple pictures of the following clothes on the board: a T-shirt, a pair of trousers, a pair of shorts, a dress, a pair of boots.

Elicit and write the words for each picture: *T-shirt, trousers, shorts, dress, boots*. Ask students: *How often do you wear a T-shirt?* and demonstrate a possible answer: *I wear a T-shirt every weekend*.

Elicit and write some adverbs of frequency on the board, e.g. *never, every day, rarely, every weekend, sometimes, once or twice a month*. Then ask students to work in pairs, asking and answering about each item of clothing.

Exercise 1   page 68

- Students try to find the things in the photos. Explain that *trousers* and *top* are generic terms, so *jeans* are also *trousers*, and *shirt*, *cardigan* and *jumper* are types of *tops*.
- Ask students to identify the plural nouns (*trousers, jeans, sandals, trainers, socks, boots, tights*) and tell them that we often use *a pair of* before such nouns, e.g. *a pair of tights, a pair of sandals*.
- Check answers as a class.

boots, cap, make-up (in a make-up bag), cardigan, jeans/trousers, jacket, necklace, shirt, skirt, top.

Exercise 2   page 68

- Go through the questions together. Explain, if necessary, that an *accessory* is something that you wear or carry that matches your clothes.
- Students discuss the questions in pairs.
- Circulate and monitor, helping with vocabulary if necessary.
- Check answers as a class.

1 **Clothes**   boots, cardigan, coat, dress, jacket, jeans, jumper, sandals, shirt, shorts, skirt, socks, tights, top, trainers, trousers
  Accessories   cap, hat, necklace, rucksack, scarf
2 **Winter clothes**   boots, cardigan, coat, jumper
  Summer clothes   shorts, sandals

76   Unit 6   Material world

3 **Clothes for women** dress, skirt, tights
Clothes for everyone boots, cap, cardigan, coat, hat, jacket, jeans, jumper, sandals, shirt, shorts, socks, top, trainers, trousers
4 **Not accessory or clothes** make-up
5–8 Students' own answers

Extra activity: Who am I?
Bring some pictures of people wearing different clothes from magazines and newspapers. Lay them out in front of the class and describe one of the photos in the first person, e.g. *I'm wearing black trousers and a long pink top. I've got a black and pink bag. Who am I?* Students listen and try to identify the correct picture. They then take it in turns to describe one of the pictures while the rest of the class listens and guesses.

Exercise 3 page 68

- Go through the strategy together. Remind students that they learned about *skim-reading* for the main ideas in Unit 2. Explain that we often *scan* material in our first language in order to find a specific piece of information, e.g. we scan a train timetable to find the train we want to take; we scan the sports pages of a newspaper to find the results of the team we support.
- Read out the six questions and ask students to underline the key words. They then read the text and try to find the same or similar words.
- Give students three minutes to answer the questions. With a **weaker class**, tell them that the answer to question 1 is in the introduction. For questions 2–5, they should look at the names in the questions; this will help them decide which section of the article to look at.
- Check answers as a class.

1 Shwopping is returning used items to shops when you buy something new.
2 It gives him 5% discount.
3 He receives £5 for every six kilograms of clothes.
4 She sends them to a company in London.
5 It sells them in their shops or sends them to the developing world.
6 She has nine points.

Culture note: Recycling clothes
Several large clothing and shoe companies have launched initiatives in the last decade to encourage consumers to recycle their clothes.
Nike has collected over 28 million pairs of second-hand shoes since 1990. Customers bring their old trainers into stores and leave them in large collection bins. The shoes are recycled and made into new trainers and athletic surfaces.
Marks and Spencer, together with the charity Oxfam, initiated the 'Shwopping' scheme. Customers bring their old Marks and Spencer's clothes into Marks and Spencer's or Oxfam shops and receive a discount voucher for new purchases. There are similar schemes with other clothing companies, such as H&M and Patagonia.
The American company Thredup buys bags of good quality used clothes from consumers and also has a large online used clothes store.

Additional words
The following vocabulary is from the text *Shwopping*:
- *swap* /swɒp/ (v) to give one thing and get another thing for it
- *waste* /weɪst/ (n) things that people throw away because they are not useful
- *advertise* /ˈædvətaɪz/ (v) to put information in a newspaper, on television, on a wall, etc. to make people want to buy something or do something
- *condition* /kənˈdɪʃn/ (n) the state that somebody or something is in

Exercise 4 page 69
- Give students one minute to find the words. Remind them to use the context to help them understand the meaning.
- Students then work in pairs to do the exercise.
- Check answers as a class.

1 material 2 donate 3 recycle 4 scruffy
5 loyalty card 6 fit 7 voucher 8 baggy
9 fashionable 10 expensive

Extra activity: Further discussion
Ask students to discuss these questions in groups:
Is there a difference between 'fashion' and 'style'? What is it?
What do your clothes say about you?
Do you like to look the same as other people your age, or different?
Can you sew? Do you sometimes make your own clothes?
What's your favourite item of clothing?

V insight Negative prefixes
- The negative prefix *un-* usually comes before an adjective, e.g. *unimpressed*, *unkind*, or a verb, e.g. *undo*, *unwrap*.
- The negative prefix *in-* usually comes before an adjective, e.g. *inexpensive*.
- When an adjective begins with *p* or *m*, we often use the prefix *im-*, e.g. *impossible*, *immature*.
- When an adjective begins with *L*, we often use the prefix *il-*, e.g. *illogical*, *illegal*.
- When an adjective begins with *r*, we often use the prefix *ir-*, e.g. *irregular*, *irresponsible*.

Exercise 5 page 69
- Explain that *prefix* means 'a group letters that you add to the beginning of a word to make another word'. Give some examples of prefixes in the students' own language, if these exist. Elicit two examples of negative prefixes from Unit 6 and write them on the board.
- Students work individually to make negative adjectives.
- Check answers as a class.

1 incomplete 2 incorrect 3 inexpensive 4 unfair
5 unfashionable 6 informal 7 unfriendly 8 unhappy
9 unimportant 10 unkind 11 unlucky 12 intolerant

Exercise 6 (page 69)

- Students discuss the questions in groups.
- Circulate and monitor, helping with vocabulary and ideas as necessary.
- Ask a few students to share their group's ideas with the rest of the class.

> **Alternative activity**
> With a **stronger class**, organize a mini debate to discuss the motion: *Fashion is important*. One student speaks in favour and another student opposes the motion. The rest of the class listen and ask questions. At the end of the debate, the class votes for or against the motion.

> **Vocabulary bank: Shops** (page 131)
> 1 1 butcher's   8 department store
>   2 greengrocer's   9 sports shop
>   3 fishmonger's   10 post office
>   4 baker's   11 phone shop
>   5 chemist's   12 bookshop
>   6 sandwich shop   13 clothes shop
>   7 market   14 newsagents
> 2 1 baker's   8 greengrocer's
>   2 butcher's   9 phone shop
>   3 sports shop   10 post office
>   4 clothes shop   11 chemist's
>   5 market   12 newsagent's
>   6 sandwich shop   13 bookshop
>   7 fishmonger's   14 department store
> 3 Students' own answers

Learning outcome

Ask students: *What have you learned today? What can you do now?* and elicit answers: *I can talk about clothes and shopping. I can read and understand a text about 'shwopping'. I can use negative prefixes 'un-' and 'in-'. I can discuss fashion and clothes recycling.*

6B Grammar and listening

Cyber Monday

> **Lesson summary**
> **Topic:** Online shopping
> **Grammar:** Comparatives
> **Listening:** Online shopping
> **Reading:** A shopping blog
> **Speaking:** Discussing the difference between shopping on the high street and shopping online
> **Communication worksheet 6A:** The more the better!

Lead-in

- Write *SHOPPING* in capital letters on the board. Then ask students in their own language: *What have you bought recently?* Encourage them to give simple answers in English, e.g. *a book, a pair of jeans*. Write their answers on the board.

- Then write the following questions for students to discuss in pairs:
How often do you go shopping?
Do you prefer shopping for clothes, food or gadgets?
What's your favourite shop? Why?

Exercise 1 (page 70)

- Focus attention on the photos. Ask students to work in pairs and point to the photos illustrating the words.
- They then discuss where they buy the different things. Encourage them to use the names for different shops in the Vocabulary bank on page 131.

(Possible answers)
food baker's, butcher's, fishmonger's, greengrocer's, market, sandwich shop, supermarket
clothes clothes shop, department store, market, sports shop, supermarket
shower gel and shampoo chemist's, department store, market, supermarket
books and music bookshop, department store
gadgets department store, market, phone shop, supermarket

Exercise 2 (page 70)

- Ask students to look at the headings and identify the key words. Then give them two minutes to match the headings to the paragraphs. Remind them that they should *skim* – reading quickly to understand the main ideas.
- Students compare answers in pairs.
- Check answers as a class.

A After the weekend …
B It's fast and easy
C The busy hours
D Spend, spend, spend

> **Language note: Comparative adjectives**
> - We use the comparative form of an adjective to compare two things. We often use *than* after the adjective.
>   *My homework is more difficult than yours.*
>   *Your bike is newer than mine.*
> - We can also use the comparative form with *and* to describe how something changes.
>   *My little sister is getting bigger and bigger.*

Exercise 3 (page 27)

- Use objects in the classroom to demonstrate comparative adjectives. Hold up two books, one big and one small, and say, e.g. *The blue book is bigger than the black book. The black book is smaller than the blue book.*
- Tell students to read the blog post again and underline the comparative adjectives. They then put the comparative forms into the correct place in the table.
- Check answers as a class.

1 cheaper   2 quicker   3 safer   4 larger   5 bigger
6 wetter   7 busier   8 easier   9 noisier
10 more convenient   11 more expensive   12 better

Extra activity: Game

Elicit and write some adjectives on the board, e.g. *beautiful*, *scary*, *delicious*, *disgusting*, *exciting*, *boring*, *big*, *small*. Start the game by choosing one of the adjectives and making a sentence with *I've got*, e.g. *I've got a beautiful jacket*. Elicit the response from a student: *My jacket is more beautiful than yours*. The same student then makes a sentence using a different adjective from the board, e.g. *I've got a delicious sandwich*, and chooses another student to reply with the comparative sentence: *My sandwich is more delicious than yours*. Continue around the class with different students making sentences.

Exercise 4 page 71

- Give students two minutes to complete the rules.
- Students compare answers in pairs.
- Check answers as a class.

a quicker; cheaper
b safer; larger
c bigger; wetter
d busier; easier, noisier
e more convenient; more expensive
g better

Reference and practice 6.1 Workbook page 122

1 2 closer
   3 friendlier / more friendly; more intelligent
   4 better; worse
   5 more important
   6 sadder
   7 quieter
   8 later

2 2 Jim's dog is thinner than Hal's dog.
   3 Your house is larger than our house.
   4 Pete's exam results are worse than Jay's exam results.
   5 Today is wetter than yesterday.
   6 Your dress is prettier than my dress.
   7 These jeans are cheaper than those jeans.
   8 The supermarket is more convenient than the shops on the high street.
   9 The film is more exciting than the book.
   10 I think maths is easier than geography.

3 2 younger   3 earlier   4 smaller   5 better
   6 nicer   7 more expensive   8 further / farther

Exercise 5 page 71

- Students write the comparative forms of the adjectives.
- With a **weaker class**, go through each adjective in turn and help students to match it with a rule in exercise 4 (*thin* – rule c; *busy* – rule d; *exciting* – rule e; *important* – rule e; *bad* – rule g; *small* – rule a).
- To check answers, ask different students to write their answers on the board and get the class to vote on whether they are correct or incorrect.

1 thinner   2 busier   3 more exciting   4 more important
5 worse   6 smaller

Exercise 6 page 71

- Elicit the comparative form of *interesting* (*more interesting*). Then tell students to complete the rest of the text.
- Check answers as a class.

1 more interesting
2 more fashionable
3 bigger
4 better
5 friendlier / more friendly
6 smaller
7 smarter
8 easier
9 more traditional
10 lower

Exercise 7 2·09 page 71

- Tell students that this is a long listening, but they only need to find the answers to four simple questions. Go through the questions together and ask students to predict the answers. This prediction exercise will help them to focus on the type of information they should listen for.
- Play the recording once and then let students compare answers in pairs.
- Check answers as a class.

Audio script

Reporter Recent statistics show that online shopping is becoming more popular in Britain. Seventy per cent of British adults now use the internet to buy clothes, food, holidays or music. Why is that? Today, we're talking to listeners to find out why. Good morning, Anna. You're an online shopper, is that right?
Woman Morning. Yes, that's right. I do my food shopping online once a week. It's easier than going to the supermarket. And I think it's also quicker. It takes about fifteen minutes – I sit down with my laptop, add items to my basket, pay for my order at the checkout, and then wait for the delivery. It's great. Going to the supermarket takes longer and it's noisier, too.
Reporter So you think shopping online is the best way to shop?
Woman Well, for some things, yes. I don't buy clothes online. I like trying on clothes first. My sister buys all her clothes online, but it's more difficult to return clothes you don't like or don't fit.
Reporter Good point. Thank you, Anna. Next, we have Steve. So, Steve, how about you? Do you buy a lot of things online?
Man Yes, I buy all my books and music online.
Reporter And why is that?
Man I live in a small town. The music shops here don't have new music or the bands I like, and I like more unusual rock bands. But when I shop online, I find what I'm looking for. I can listen to a track and then download it. I buy a lot of books online, too. Online bookshops are cheaper than high street bookshops. And there is often a better choice of books.
Reporter OK. And what about other things?
Man Well, I'm thinking about going on a city break with my friends. We're looking at different hotels online. It's more useful than visiting a travel agent because people post reviews and photos. The reviews are very helpful. For example, you can see which hotels have friendlier staff.
Reporter Thank you, Steve. That's very interesting. Now, we're going to talk about …

1 70%
2 food
3 clothes
4 books and music (and hotels)

Exercise 8 2·09 page 71

- With a **stronger class**, ask students to try and complete the sentences before they listen. Play the recording again for students to write their answers. With a **weaker class**, go through each adjective and elicit the comparative form, e.g. *quick, quicker*. Be prepared to play the recording again for less confident students.
- Check answers as a class.

1 more popular
2 easier, quicker
3 longer, noisier
4 more difficult
5 cheaper
6 better
7 more useful
8 friendlier

See exercise 7 for audio script

Exercise 9 page 71

- Discuss the first question with the class. Ask students to vote on which they prefer: shopping in high street shops or shopping online. Then ask a few students to give reasons for their preference.
- Students discuss the other two questions in pairs.
- Circulate and monitor, helping with vocabulary and ideas if necessary.

DVD extra Shopping in London

Learning outcome

Ask students: *What have you learned today? What can you do now?* and elicit answers: *I can use comparative adjectives. I can read an article about online shopping. I can understand an interview with people about online shopping. I can discuss my shopping preferences.*

6C Culture, vocabulary and grammar

Black Friday

Lesson summary
Topic: Spending money
Vocabulary: Shopping
Grammar: Superlative adjectives
Reading: Black Friday or Buy Nothing Day?
Speaking: Spending habits
Communication worksheet 6A: The more the better!
Communication worksheet 6B: Find the mistake

Lead-in

- Write the following phrases on the board: *50% off! Sale: everything must go! Fantastic bargains!* Do not translate the phrases, but ask students if they can guess where they might see them.

- Once they have given the correct answer (in a shop window), ask them to discuss the following questions in pairs:
Do you often buy things in sales? Why / why not?
Do you wait for a sale before you buy something?
- When they have finished, ask a few pairs to share their ideas with the class.

Exercise 1 page 72

- Focus attention on the photos and ask students to say what they can see, e.g. *lines of people, shopping trolleys, TVs, tablet computers*. Write their ideas on the board. Then ask: *What is happening? Where are the people?* Accept all suggestions for the time being and tell students that they will be able to check their ideas later.
- Ask students to guess what time of year it is.

Exercise 2 page 72

- Give students one minute to skim-read the newspaper article and check their ideas.
- Ask questions to check general comprehension:
When is Black Friday? (the day after Thanksgiving)
Who loves Black Friday? (Chantelle)
Who doesn't like Black Friday? (Brad)

Exercise 3 page 72

- Go through the questions together and remind students to identify the key words to help them find the answers.
- With a **weaker class**, tell students that the answers to questions 1 and 2 are in paragraph 1, the answers to questions 3 and 4 are in paragraph 2 and the answers to questions 5 and 6 are in paragraph 3.
- Check answers as a class.

1 They prepare and eat special food with their families.
2 Because people don't return to work after the Thanksgiving holiday and because they decide to start their Christmas shopping on this day.
3 Because she can get the best bargains.
4 She leaves Macy's at 6.30 a.m. She buys two mobile phones and some designer clothes.
5 He doesn't want to buy anything because he thinks that North Americans buy unnecessary things.
6 They are talking to people about 'Buy Nothing Day'.

> **Culture notes: Black Friday and Buy Nothing Day**
>
> The term **'Black Friday'** originally came from Philadelphia, USA. It was used to describe the crowds and heavy traffic on the roads on the day after Thanksgiving (which is celebrated on the last Thursday of November).
>
> Many stores in the USA now compete with earlier and earlier opening hours on Black Friday, and some stores, for example Walmart and Toys R Us, even open on the evening of Thanksgiving.
>
> In 2012 a total of $59.1 billion was spent on Black Friday.
>
> **Buy Nothing Day** is a relatively recent development which was first organized in Canada in 1992. Protesters use various ways of publicizing the campaign: they cut up credit cards, hold free non-commercial street parties and push empty trolleys around supermarkets.

Extra activity: Roleplay

Ask students to work in groups of four or five. They should imagine that they are in a large store on Black Friday. Half the students in the group are Brad and his friends. The other students are customers in the store. They prepare and perform a roleplay, with Brad and his friends talking to the customers about Buy Nothing Day. Each group can decide if the customers will agree or argue with Brad.

Additional vocabulary

The following vocabulary is from the article *Black Friday*:

- *calendar* /ˈkælɪndə(r)/ (n) a list of the days, weeks and months of one year
- *queue* /kjuː/ (n) a line of people who are waiting to do something
- *immediately* /ɪˈmiːdiətli/ (adv) now or very soon
- *celebrate* /ˈselɪbreɪt/ (v) to do something special to show that you are happy for a special reason or because it is a special day
- *crazy* /ˈkreɪzi/ (adj) stupid; not sensible

Exercise 4   page 73

- Ask students to brainstorm different places where they can read English. Write suggestions on the board and then ask them to look at the strategy and see if their ideas are included. Emphasize that they do not need to read long, difficult texts in order to improve their English; reading short texts two or three times a week is more effective than reading one long text a month.
- Explain that the shopping words are all in the newspaper article. Encourage students to find them and read them in context before they do the exercise.
- Students compare answers in pairs.
- Check answers as a class.

1 sale	5 bargains, discount
2 half price	6 debt
3 wallet	7 Consumers
4 credit card	8 purchases

Language note: Superlative adjectives

- We use superlative adjectives when we compare three or more people or things.
- Superlative adjectives are often followed by phrases like *in the class, in the world, of the year*.
  She's the funniest girl in my class.
  He's the strongest man in the world.
  Today is the hottest day of the year.

Exercise 5   page 73

- Draw three boxes on the board in ascending order of size. Then say: *Box 1 is the smallest box. Box 2 is bigger than Box 1 and it's smaller than Box 3. Box 3 is the biggest box.* Explain that we use superlatives to compare three or more things.
- Tell students to underline the superlative forms in the text and match them with the adjectives in exercise 5.
- Check answers as a class.

1 the most important
2 the busiest
3 the longest
4 the best
5 the biggest
6 the fastest

Extra activity

Put students into three or four teams. Write the following prompts on the board:
Who / be / tall / student in the class?
Who / be / short / student / in the class?
Which student / have got / long / hair?
Which student / have got / curly / hair?
Which student / be / old /in the class?
Which student / be / young / in the class?

Students make questions using the prompts and the superlative form of the adjectives. They then answer the questions.

Set this up as a competition between teams and award points for correctly formed questions as well as correct answers.

Who is the tallest student in the class?
Who is the shortest student in the class?
Which student has got the longest hair?
Which student has got the curliest hair?
Which student is the oldest in the class?
Which student is the youngest in the class?

Students' own answers

Reference and practice 6.2   Workbook page 123

1 2 rainier; the rainiest
  3 more delicious; the most delicious
  4 farther / further; the farthest / the furthest
  5 more famous; the most famous
  6 more traditional; the most traditional
  7 smarter; the smartest
  8 better; the best
  9 baggier; the baggiest
  10 fatter; the fattest
  11 safer; the safest
  12 nicer; the nicest

2 2 the hottest
  3 the friendliest / the most friendly
  4 the richest; the most popular
  5 the strangest
  6 the biggest
  7 best
  8 the most interesting

3 3 the most expensive
  4 the oldest
  5 older than
  6 faster than
  7 the fastest
  8 the longest
  9 shorter than
  10 the shortest

Exercise 6 (page 73)

- Give students two minutes to complete the rules. Tell them to use the superlative forms in exercise 5 as a reference.
- Students compare answers in pairs.
- Check answers as a class.

a est **b** st **c** double **d** i **e** most **f** the

Exercise 7 (page 73)

- Explain that the factfile has some interesting facts about shopping and shopping malls.
- Students do the exercise on their own.
- Check answers as a class.

1 largest **2** emptiest **3** most expensive **4** wettest
5 biggest

Exercise 8 (page 73)

- Students discuss the questions in pairs.
- Circulate and monitor, helping with vocabulary and ideas if necessary.
- Ask a few pairs to share their ideas with the class.

> **Extra activity: Further discussion**
>
> Ask students to discuss these questions in groups:
>
> *When you go shopping, do you usually buy a few expensive things or a lot or cheap things?*
>
> *Do you go to lots of different shops to compare prices or do you always go to one or two favourite shops?*
>
> *Your favourite shop has a big sale. Are you happy to wait for a long time in a queue outside the shop? How long?*

Learning outcome

Ask students: *What have you learned today? What can you do now?* and elicit answers: *I know shopping vocabulary. I can use superlative adjectives. I know about Black Friday. I can talk about shopping in my country and my own shopping habits.*

6D Listening, speaking and vocabulary

Can't live without it

Lesson summary
Topic: Technology
Vocabulary: Gadgets; Vocabulary bank: Clothes verbs
Speaking: Buying clothes
Writing: A dialogue in a clothes shop
Communication worksheet 6B: Find the mistake

Lead-in

- Begin by saying *I am a gadget. What gadget am I? Guess.* If necessary, translate *gadget* and tell students to ask *yes/no* questions to find out what kind of gadget you are, e.g. *Can I make phone calls on this gadget? Can I watch TV on this gadget? Can I play games on this gadget?*
- Tell students they can only ask three questions before they guess. If their guesses are wrong, you have won the game.

Exercise 1 (page 74)

- Go through the gadgets and check that students understand all the words. Ask:
  Which gadgets can you see in the photo? (tablet, laptop, smartphone)
  How many gadgets are in our classroom today?
  Remind students that if they have a smartphone, then they probably also have a camera, an e-reader and an MP3 player, as these gadgets are incorporated into most smartphones nowadays.
- Students discuss the questions in pairs.
- Go round the class, asking about the most and least important gadget for each student.

> **Extra activity: Desert island**
>
> Tell students to imagine they are going to live on a desert island for a year. They can take one gadget with them. (This desert island has a solar powered generator!) Which gadget will they choose and why? Students discuss their ideas. Then ask a few students to present their decision to the class.

Exercise 2 2•10 (page 74)

- Explain to students that they are going to listen to a very short introduction to a TV programme. Focus attention on the gapped sentences and ask: *What kind of information goes in the gaps?* (numbers)
- Play the recording.
- Check answers as a class.

Audio script

In a recent survey, 84% of people say they can't live without their smartphones for one day. Fifty per cent say that they sleep with their phones by their bed, and 20% say that they check their phones every ten minutes. What about you? This week's experiment is: Can you live without technology for a week?

1 84 **2** 50 **3** 20

Exercise 3 2•11 (page 74)

- Check that students understand what the TV programme is about. Ask:
  What are Bella and Tony doing for one week? (living without their gadgets)
  Do you think it is difficult or easy for them?
- Play the recording.
- To check answers, ask different students to write the gadgets on the board.

Audio script

Speaker Can you live without technology for a week? Tony and Bella are trying to live without their gadgets. Tony, which gadgets do you usually use every day?
Tony Well, my smartphone, of course! I send about twenty or thirty texts every day. And I use my phone to go online and check Facebook.
Speaker What about a computer or a laptop?
Tony Yes, I use a laptop at home for my homework, and I watch TV in the evenings or play on my games console.
Speaker So, Tony, this is the last day of your week without technology. What's it like?

82 Unit 6 Material world

Tony It's really strange. I don't like it! I don't know what my friends are saying. My friends discuss everything on Facebook. I can't see their photos …
Speaker Yes, but you see your friends every day at school.
Tony I know, but it's not the same.
Speaker And what do you do in the evenings?
Tony Well, I read magazines and I play football with my friends.
Speaker Are you enjoying your time with no technology?
Tony No, I'm not! My phone is my social life!
Speaker But there is one advantage: you are doing more sport … you're getting healthier …
Tony Yeah, OK, that's true.
Speaker Now let's talk to Bella. Are you enjoying your week without technology?
Bella It's fine. I'm reading lots of books, I'm going out with my friends …
Speaker What about your college work? Is it more difficult to do your college work without a laptop?
Bella Well, I go to the library every afternoon and study there. It's OK. It's really quiet and I do a lot of work. When I work at home on the laptop, I often stop and look at other websites, or check Facebook, but with no computer, I finish my college work really quickly! The hardest problem is life without music. I listen to my MP3 player all the time.
Speaker So … now … do you want your gadgets, Bella? Or do you prefer your life without technology?
Bella Oh, no! I want my gadgets, please. I need my phone and my laptop, and I want to listen to music again!

Tony smartphone, laptop, TV, games console
Bella laptop, MP3 player, phone

Exercise 4 2•11 page 74

- Give students one minute to read the sentence halves. With a **stronger class**, ask students to try to match the sentence halves before they listen to the recording again.
- Play the recording again.
- Students compare answers in pairs.
- Check answers as a class.

1 c   2 d   3 f   4 a   5 e   6 b

See exercise 3 for audio script

Exercise 5 page 74

- Write two headings on the board: *Without internet & gadgets* and *With internet & gadgets*. Then elicit some ideas and write them under the relevant heading, e.g.
Without: more sport, go out more, can't communicate with friends in other places
With: less active, easier to do homework.
- Students discuss the questions in pairs. Circulate and monitor, noting any common errors.

Exercise 6 page 75

- Focus attention on the photo and elicit the answers to the questions. Ask students if they think the man works there or is a customer. Accept either answer but ask for reasons, e.g. *I think he works there because he's tidying the clothes. I think he's a customer because he's looking at the clothes.*
- Ask: *Do you go into shops like these? Do you like trying on clothes?*
- Check answers as a class.

Students' own answers

Exercise 7 2•12 page 75

- Tell students that they are going to listen to a conversation in a clothes shop between a sales assistant and a customer.
- Play the recording and check the answer. If students say: *He wants to buy some jeans*, ask *What colour?* (black)
- With a **stronger class**, ask students: *Does the man buy the jeans?* (no) *Why not?* (They're too small.)

Audio script

Sales assistant Hello. Do you need any help?
Man Oh, yes. I'm looking for some black jeans.
Sales assistant What size are you?
Man Size 32.
Sales assistant Well, we've got these ones here.
Man They're nice. How much are they?
Sales assistant These jeans are £26.
Man OK. Can I try them on, please?
Sales assistant Yes, of course. The changing room's over there.
…
How are they?
Man They're too small. Have you got a bigger size?
Sales assistant I'm afraid not.
Man Oh, well, never mind then.

He wants to buy some black jeans.

Exercise 8 2•12 page 75

- Go through the gapped phrases together. Explain what a *changing room* is.
- Play the recording for students to complete the phrases.
- With a **weaker class**, pause the recording after each phrase to give students time to write their answers.
- Check answers as a class.

1 need any help   6 looking for
2 size are   7 much
3 's (over) there   8 try them
4 are they   9 too small
5 afraid   10 bigger size

See exercise 7 for audio script

Exercise 9 2•13 page 75

- Ask students to read the dialogue quickly. Then ask: *What does the woman want to buy?* (a pink scarf) *How much does it cost?* (£12)
- Give students one minute to put the dialogue in the correct order.
- With a **weaker class**, identify the final sentence in the dialogue for students.

Audio script

Sales assistant Hello, can I help you?
Woman Yes, please. Does this scarf come in a different colour?
Sales assistant Yes, it does. We have it in blue, green or pink.
Woman Could I see the pink one, please?
Sales assistant Here you are.
Woman Thank you. It's lovely. How much does it cost?
Sales assistant Well, it's half price this week. So it's only £12.
Woman Great. I'll take it.

Exercise 10 page 75

- Give students two minutes to work in pairs and underline more phrases.
- Write the following headings on the board: *Sales assistant* and *Customer*. Then ask different students to write the phrases on the board under the correct heading.

Sales assistant Can I help you? We have it in blue, green or pink. Here you are.
Customer Does this scarf come in a different colour? Could I see the pink one, please? How much does it cost? I'll take it.

Exercise 11 page 75

- Divide the class into customers and sales assistants. Customers discuss their answers to the bullet points together, and sales assistants can do the same.
- When they have finished, tell students to work in customer–sales assistant pairs and write their dialogues. Circulate and monitor, helping with vocabulary if necessary.
- Invite a few pairs to perform their dialogue for the class.

Vocabulary bank: Clothes verbs page 131

1
1 put on, take off
2 zip up, unzip
3 try on
4 take back
5 hang up
6 take out, put awayt
7 do up
8 look for
9 undo

2
1 take off
2 take back
3 do up
4 take out
5 hang up
6 zip up
7 look for
8 try on

3 Students' own answers

Learning outcome

Ask students: *What have you learned today? What can you do now?* and elicit answers: *I know the names of different gadgets. I can understand an interview about living without technology. I can use language for buying clothes.*

6E Writing

A review of a gadget

Lesson summary
Topic: Reviews
Vocabulary: Positive and negative adjectives
Reading: A review of an e-reader
Writing: A review of a gadget

Lead-in

Write *E-READER* on the board in capital letters and ask if any students have an e-reader or have ever used one.

- Write the following questions on the board:
  Do you like reading? When and where do you read? What kind of books do you like? Do you think e-readers encourage people to read? Do you read paper books?
- Students discuss the questions in pairs.

Exercise 1 page 76

- Say: *You've got £500. You want to buy a new laptop or tablet. How do you decide what to get?* Elicit ideas.
- Find out how many students read reviews. Ask: *Where do you read reviews? In online shops? In specialist magazines? In newspapers?*
- Students then discuss the questions in pairs.

Exercise 2 page 76

- Focus attention on the diagram and ask: *What is this gadget?* (an e-reader)
- Give students one minute to label the diagram.
- Check answers as a class.

1 clip-on light
2 screen
3 keyboard
4 page forward button
5 home button
6 page back button

Exercise 3 page 76

- Focus attention on the title and check that they understand the reviewer has given the e-slate three out of five stars.
- Students match the sections to the descriptions.
- Check answers as a class.

1 B   2 A   3 C   4 D

Exercise 4 page 76

- Go through the questions together and encourage students to underline the key words before they look for the information in the text.
- Ask different students to read out their answers to the questions and tell the rest of the class to put their hands up if they think the answer is wrong. This will encourage students to listen carefully to the answers.

1 £65
2 3,500
3 big screen, easy to read the text, clear keyboard, easy to use, light
4 The page buttons are on the right side.
5 words
6 pictures and photos

Exercise 5 page 76

- Tell students to underline the adjectives in the review. This will help them to understand the meaning in context. Remind them that paragraph B focuses on the positive points and paragraph C focuses on the negative points.
- Check answers as a class and explain that we use *clear* and *fuzzy* to talk about the appearance of something, e.g. text, a photo.

Positive clear, excellent, perfect
Negative fuzzy, inconvenient, unattractive

Exercise 6 page 76

- Students work in pairs to complete the sentences.
- Check answers as a class.

1 clear   2 unattractive   3 perfect   4 excellent
5 inconvenient   6 fuzzy

Exercise 7 page 76

- Go through the strategy together. Remind students that when they record new words in their notebooks, they should also write the word in a sentence so that they have an example of context.
- Students use bilingual dictionaries to find the words for the pictures.
- Check answers as a class. Emphasize that most bilingual dictionaries have pronunciation guides, and make sure students pronounce the words correctly when they give their answers.

a speakers /ˈspiːkəz/
b (camera) lens /lenz/
c battery /ˈbæt(ə)ri/
d headphones /ˈhedfəʊnz/ (or earphones /ˈɪəfəʊnz/)

Writing guide page 77

- Read the **task** together, making sure students are clear that they have to write a review similar to the review of the e-slate.
- Give students five to ten minutes to complete the **ideas** stage and **plan** their review. Circulate and monitor, helping with language and ideas as necessary. Remind students to write notes, not full sentences.
- Circulate and monitor while students **write** their reviews, encouraging them to use positive and negative adjectives. Remind them to activate the language they learned earlier in the unit (vocabulary for gadgets, comparative and superlative adjectives).
- When students have finished, they **check** their work. Refer them to the checklist to make sure they have completed the task as well as they can.

Extension: Fast finishers

Ask **fast finishers** to swap reviews with another student to read and check for mistakes.

Additional writing activity

Write a review of a local shop. Include information about products (what the shop sells), service (how good the shop assistants are), location (where the shop is) and price (how cheap / expensive the products are).

Learning outcome

Ask students: *What have you learned today? What can you do now?* and elicit answers: *I can read and understand a review of an e-reader. I can use positive and negative adjectives. I can write a review of a gadget.*

Review 6 page 77

1 1 calculator   2 scarves   3 e-reader   4 necklace
5 games console   6 tights   7 DVD player   8 shirts

2 1 inexpensive   2 incorrect   3 unhappy
4 incomplete   5 unfashionable   6 unfriendly
7 unimportant

3 1 bargain   2 discount   3 half price   4 credit card
5 dollars   6 purchases   7 debts

4 1 scruffier than   5 noisier than
2 heavier than   6 better than
3 safe than   7 smaller than
4 cheaper than   8 wetter than

5 1 the largest   6 the most expensive
2 the most beautiful   7 The worst
3 the longest   8 the most dangerous
4 the fastest   9 the oldest
5 the most famous

6 1 most   2 best   3 the   4 in   5 more   6 than

Pronunciation insight 6 Workbook page 134
Answer key: Teacher's book page 155

Unit 6 Material world 85

Cumulative review Units 1–6

pages 78–79

1 🔘 2•14

Audio script

1 Boy I've got some new trainers and I love them! They're black with orange and white stripes down the side, and I think they're really cool. I wear them everywhere: when I go to school, when I'm out with my friends and when I do things with my family. But I don't wear them when I do sport – I've got an old pair for that. My new ones cost a lot of money, so I need to look after them.

2 Girl My sister buys a lot of clothes because she has her own money – she's a nurse at the local hospital. She often gives me things when she doesn't want them any more, but they're usually a bit big for me. But now I've got one of her tops, and I love it! It was too small for her, so it's perfect for me. It's black and white, and it looks great with my new shorts. I wear it all the time.

3 Boy My mum isn't very happy about the clothes I wear. She says I look a mess. And she doesn't really like my favourite pair of jeans. They're quite new, actually, but they don't look it. They're quite loose and they're really comfortable, so I wear them a lot. Most of my friends wear the same kind of clothes as me, and they don't have any problems with their parents!

4 Girl I'm really excited because it's my birthday next week, and I've got the perfect dress for my party. I'm a bit bored of wearing the same clothes every day and this dress is a bit different – I'm sure none of my friends has anything the same. It's short and it's quite colourful: half of it is black and the other half is pink. I've got some high black shoes and some black tights to wear with it.

Speaker 1 D
Speaker 2 A
Speaker 3 E
Speaker 4 B

2 Students' own answers

3 1 E 2 D 3 F 4 C 5 A

4 1 a 2 a 3 a 4 b 5 b

5 1 c 2 b 3 a 4 c 5 a 6 a 7 b 8 a 9 b 10 c

6 Students' own answers

Additional materials
Literature insight 3 Workbook page 96 Answer key: Teacher's book page 152
Exam insight 3 Workbook page 106 Answer key: See website

7 It's tough!

Map of resources

Section A: Student's Book pages 80–81
Workbook page 60
Teacher's resource disk, Communication worksheet 7A

Section B: Student's Book pages 82–83
Workbook page 61
Grammar reference and practice 7.1, Workbook page 123
Vocabulary bank, Housework page 132
Teacher's resource disk, DVD extra + worksheet, Cleaning beaches page 83
Teacher's resource disk, Communication worksheet 7B

Section C: Student's Book pages 84–85
Workbook page 62
Grammar reference and practice 7.2, Workbook page 125

Section D: Student's Book pages 86–87
Workbook page 63
Vocabulary bank, Health problems page 132

Section E: Student's Book pages 88–89
Workbook page 66
Teacher's resource disk, Writing bank
Teacher's resource disk, Functional language bank
Teacher's resource disk, Communication worksheet 7B

Review 7 page 89
Pronunciation insight 7, Workbook page 135
Progress check Unit 7, Workbook page 67
Language and skills tests 7A and 7B, Test Bank

7A Reading and vocabulary

Different shapes

Lesson summary
Topic: Different body types and extreme events
Vocabulary: Parts of the body; noun suffixes: -er / -or
Reading: The world's toughest
Speaking: Organizing a tough sports event
Communication worksheet 7A: Who does what?

Lead-in

- Write *How many?* at the top of the board. Below this write the following words: *eyes, teeth, bones, fingers, muscles.* Translate them if necessary, or draw small cartoon pictures next to each word to illustrate the meaning.
- Ask students to work in pairs and discuss how many we have of each of the body parts on the board. Give students two minutes for this. Then ask a few students to write their guess next to the words on the word.
- Finally reveal the correct answers: two eyes, thirty-two teeth, 206 bones, ten fingers, 640 muscles.

Exercise 1 page 80

- Model and drill the words, especially *elbow* /ˈelbəʊ/, *knee* /niː/, *wrist* /rɪst/ and *stomach* /ˈstʌmək/.
- Students match the words to the body parts in the illustrations.
- Check answers as a class.

1 head   2 face   3 neck   4 shoulder   5 back   6 chest
7 arm   8 elbow   9 hand   10 wrist   11 finger
12 stomach   13 hip   14 leg   15 knee   16 ankle
17 foot   18 toe

Exercise 2 page 80

- Write the following on the board: *Below the hips*, *Above the hips but below the shoulders*, *Above the shoulders*.
- Say *knee* and ask a student to write the word under the correct heading.
- Students then work in pairs, testing each other.
- Check answers by asking different students to write the words under the correct heading on the board.

Below the hips ankle, foot, knee, leg, toe
Above the hips arm, back, chest, elbow, finger, hand, stomach, wrist
Above the shoulders face, head, neck

Exercise 3 page 80

- Go through the questions and check that students understand *marathon runner* (a person who runs a marathon – a 42 km race) and *weight lifter* (a person who lifts heavy weights).

- Students look at the diagrams in exercise 1 and discuss, in pairs, which body type is best for which sport.
- Give students two minutes to read the text quickly and check their ideas.
- Check answers as a class.

1 3   **2** 2   **3** 1

Exercise 4 page 80
- Ask students to scan the text to find the three words and then match them to the body types.
- Check answers as a class.

Body type 1 endomorph
Body type 2 ectomorph
Body type 3 mesomorph

Exercise 5 page 80
- Tell students to read the questions and identify the key words.
- With a **weaker class**, tell students that sentences 1 and 2 are about the first text, sentences 3 and 4 are about the second, and sentences 5 and 6 are about the last.
- Check answers as a class.

1 It is an endurance race.
2 They're slimmer and taller than swimmers, with longer legs and arms.
3 an ectomorph
4 weight lifting and wrestling
5 in winter
6 70 km per hour

> **Additional vocabulary**
> The following words are from the article *The world's toughest*:
> - *slim* /slɪm/ (adj) thin, but not too thin
> - *narrow* /ˈnærəʊ/ (adj) not far from one side to another
> - *block* /blɒk/ (n) a big heavy piece of something, with flat sides
> - *broad* /brɔːd/ (adj) large from one side to the other
> - *turn* /tɜːn/ (n) a change of direction

Culture notes: Endurance events
The **Marathon des Sables** takes place every year in southern Morocco, in the Sahara desert. The first event took place in 1986. It is considered to be the toughest footrace in the world. The winners usually complete the race in just over twenty hours.
The **World's Strongest Man** competition is held in different locations at the end of December each year. There are ten men in the final competition. The competition features a number of different events, including carrying two fridges for a certain distance; throwing a five-metre long log and carrying a 182 kg stone on the chest.
The **Crashed Ice Championship** is a touring downhill ice skating event. Competitors use ice skates to race down a 535-metre urban ice track. The course usually takes about twenty days to build and uses 25,000 gallons of water. The finals take place in March.

Exercise 6 page 80
- Go through the strategy together. Explain that there are different ways of using context to understand unknown words; context can include the illustrations and headings as well as the text itself.
- Give students three minutes to find the highlighted words and guess their meanings before they check their answers in a dictionary. Remind them to write the new words in their vocabulary notebooks and include an example sentence for each word.

> **Extra activity: Further discussion**
> Ask students to discuss these questions in groups:
> *Do you think endurance sports are good or bad for health?*
> *Imagine you want to compete in an endurance event. Which event do you choose? Why?*
> *What is your favourite sport? What do you think is the ideal body type for this sport?*

> **V insight Noun suffixes -er / -or**
> A suffix is letters that you add to the end of a word to make another word. The suffix usually changes the type of word, e.g. from a noun to an adjective or from a verb to a noun.
> The *-er* or *-or* suffix usually changes a verb to a noun, and it is particularly common when describing a person who does something. The *-er* suffix is much more common than *-or*.

Exercise 7 page 81
- Explain to students that the verbs can be changed into nouns by adding *-er* or *-or*. Students find and underline the noun forms of the verbs in the text. With a **stronger class**, ask students to form the nouns first and then check their answers in the text.
- To check answers, ask different students to write the nouns on the board. Point out the spelling changes:
  - one-syllable verbs with one vowel + one consonant: double the final consonant
  - verbs ending in *e*: add *-r*, not *-er*
- Focus attention on *competitor*, which involves a more complex change.

1 competitor   **2** swimmer   **3** rujnner   **4** skater
5 player   **6** sprinter

Exercise 8 page 81
- Give students two minutes to complete the sentences.
- With a **weaker class**, tell students that *visit* and *direct* are the only two verbs which take *-or*.
- Students exchange answers with a partner and then check their partner's answers in a dictionary.
- Check answers as a class.

1 reporter   **2** driver   **3** fighter   **4** visitors   **5** jogger
6 director   **7** rider   **8** designer

88   Unit 7 It's tough!

Exercise 9 page 81
- Students complete the definitions. Emphasize that they will not need to use two of the words.
- With a **stronger class**, ask students to write definitions for *rider* and *fighter*.
- Check answers as a class.

1 jogger 2 driver 3 designer 4 reporter 5 visitor
6 director

> **Extra activity: Internet research**
> Ask students to research one of these endurance events:
> *Dakar Motor Rally*
> *Vendée Globe*
> *Iditarod Trail Sled Dog Race*
> They then create a factfile with at least four facts about the event.

Exercise 10 page 81
- Students work in pairs to plan their own new 'tough' sports events.
- Circulate and monitor, helping with vocabulary if necessary.
- Ask a few pairs of students to present their ideas to the rest of the class.

Learning outcome
Ask students: *What have you learned today? What can you do now?* and elicit answers: *I know the names of parts of the body. I can understand a text about extreme endurance events. I can make nouns from verbs with the suffixes '-er' and '-or'. I can create and plan my own 'tough' sports event.*

7B Grammar and listening

Keep it clean!

Lesson summary
Topic: Unusual jobs
Vocabulary: Vocabulary bank: Housework
Grammar: *have to* and *should*
Listening: After school club rules
Reading: Behind the scenes: Cleaning the UK's favourite tourist attractions
Speaking: Creating rules for an after-school club
Communication worksheet 7B: What should I do?

Lead-in
Write CLEAN on the board in capital letters and mime the meaning, e.g. mime polishing your desk, sweeping the floor, cleaning the window.
Then ask students to add a suffix to the verb and form the noun: *cleaner*. Ask them to work in pairs and think of places where cleaners work, e.g. *schools, offices, shops*.
Finally, ask students to open their books and check to see if their ideas are included in the photos on page 82.

Exercise 1 page 82
- Focus attention on the two photos. Ask:
  What's strange about the photo on the left? (The buildings are all very small.)
  What's the link between the two photos? (The first photo shows a model of the building in the second photo.)
- Students discuss the questions in pairs.

Exercise 2 page 82
- Ask students to read the article quickly and check their answers to exercise 1. Challenge them to find the names of the two places in the photos as quickly as possible. (Legoland and Big Ben) If necessary, explain that Legoland is a theme park in which everything is made out of Lego. Find out if any students have visited Legoland or any similar 'model' towns.
- Check answers as a class.

The people are cleaning the model of Big Ben and the actual clock face of the real Big Ben.

Exercise 3 page 82
- Focus attention on the questions. Tell students to look at the question words and think about what kind of answers these you expect, e.g. numbers, dates, names.
- Give students three minutes to read the article again and answer the questions. With a **stronger class**, ask students to write full sentences. With a **weaker class**, allow students to give one- or two-word answers.
- Check answers as a class.

1 more than 800   4 every five years
2 760   5 80 million
3 312   6 two days

> **Culture notes: UK tourist attractions**
> **Buckingham Palace** is situated in the centre of London. It was built in 1705, but it did not become the official royal residence until Queen Victoria came to the throne in 1837. Many rooms in Buckingham Palace are open to the public in August and September every year. They contain paintings by artists such as Rembrandt, Van Dyck and Vermeer, antique furniture, nineteenth-century porcelain, and many other art treasures.
> **Big Ben** is part of the clock tower of the Palace of Westminster. The Palace of Westminster holds the two houses of Parliament that govern the UK. Many people refer to the clock and the clock tower as Big Ben, although in fact Big Ben actually refers only to the bell in the clock tower. The tower was built in 1858. It was originally called the Clock Tower but was renamed the Elizabeth Tower in 2012, to celebrate Queen Elizabeth II's Diamond Jubilee.
> **Legoland** is a chain of Lego-themed theme parks. There are six Legolands around the world. The UK Legoland is in Windsor. It has over fifty-five interactive rides, live shows and Lego-building workshops.

Language note: *have to* and *should*

We use *have to* to express obligation, usually from an external source.
I have to get to school early today.
We have to pay for our hotel room.

In British English we can sometimes use *have got to* in place of *have to*. Both forms are correct, but *have to* is more common in written English.

Don't have to is used to express a lack of obligation. It must not be confused with *mustn't*, which is used to talk about prohibition.

We also use *should* to express obligation, but it is not as strong as *have to*.

Exercise 4 page 82

- Students work individually to do the exercise.
- To check answers, ask students to read out the sentences. Model and drill the pronunciation of *have to*, and make sure they pronounce *to* correctly: /ˈhæv tə/.

1 have to
2 don't have to
3 have to
4 should
5 shouldn't
6 don't have to

Exercise 5 page 83

- Students study the example sentences in exercise 4 and complete the rules.
- Check answers as a class.

a should   b shouldn't   c have to   d don't have to

Reference and practice 7.1 Workbook page 123

1 2 They have to empty the bins after breakfast.
3 Do you have to do your homework on Friday night?
4 We have to make our beds in the morning.
5 My friends don't have to wear school uniform.
6 Julie and I have to walk home every afternoon.
7 I don't have to go to school at the weekend.
8 My dog has to sleep in the kitchen.

2 2 have to wear
3 doesn't have to do
4 have to do
5 doesn't have to be
6 have to be
7 has to eat
8 don't have to eat
9 doesn't have to tidy
10 don't have to tidy

3 2 shouldn't; should   3 should   4 should
5 shouldn't   6 shouldn't   7 should   8 should

4 2 They shouldn't work so late.
3 I should drink more water.
4 You should go to the doctor.
5 He shouldn't buy that expensive computer.
6 Should I phone my sister?

Exercise 6 page 83

- Ask students to read the problems. Then elicit some advice, e.g. *buy some new flowers; talk to your parents*. Accept phrases and do not expect students to form sentences with *should* and *shouldn't* yet. Write these ideas on the board for the **fast finisher** activity below.
- Give students two minutes to match the problems to the advice. They then compare answers in pairs.
- Check answers as a class.

1 d   2 e   3 a   4 b   5 c

Extra activity: Fast finishers

Fast finishers use some of the ideas on the board to write an extra piece of advice for each problem in exercise 6. Tell them to write full sentences with *should* and *shouldn't*.

Exercise 7 page 83

- Explain that Tracy is an *agony aunt* (a person who writes in a newspaper or magazine giving advice in reply to people's letters about their personal problems). Find out if anyone in your class reads such columns.
- Give students one minute to read the two letters quickly and ask: *Which letter complains about housework?* (Hannah's) *Which letter gives advice?* (Tracy's)
- Students work individually to complete the letters.
- Check answers as a class.

1 have to walk
2 has to take out
3 have to tidy
4 doesn't have to do
5 have to do
6 should make
7 shouldn't get
8 should stay

Exercise 8 2·15 page 83

- Explain to students that they are going to listen to a teacher talking about an after-school club. Ask: *What after-school clubs are there at this school? Who goes to an after-school club? Are there any rules at the club?*
- Play the recording for students to identify the club.

Audio script
Teacher Right, OK. Now, please listen before we start. This isn't a lesson, it is a club, but everyone still has to follow some important rules. All right? … You don't have to wear school uniform, but you should wear an apron, and of course you have to clean your hands before we start.
Girl Do we have to buy food for the club?
Teacher No, you don't. We've got all the food here. You have to pay your club fee – that's £20 per term – but you don't have to buy any food. So, today, we're making chocolate biscuits. … Shush! You should listen to me, please. I don't want to shout! Now, there are some bags of flour on this table. You need 100 g of flour per person. You shouldn't take more than 100 g. Please weigh your flour carefully. Now, next you need …
Good. So, your biscuits are now ready, and you can take them out of the oven.
Boy Do we have to use oven gloves?
Teacher Yes, you do! Take the biscuits out of the oven. Great! Now, the most important part. You should always try your food. So … let's have a biscuit!

b a cooking club

Exercise 9 2•15 page 83

- Focus attention on the pictures of the apron /ˈeɪprən/ and the oven gloves /ˈʌvn glʌvz/ and model and drill the pronunciation.
- Give students a minute to read the gapped sentences. With a **stronger class**, ask students to complete them before listening.
- Play the recording again for students to complete the sentences or check their answers.
- Check answers as a class.

1 don't have to	5 have to
2 should	6 shouldn't
3 have to	7 have to
4 don't have to	8 should

See exercise 8 for audio script

Exercise 10 page 83

- Go through the after-school clubs and then elicit and write any further suggestions on the board.
- Students work in pairs to decide on their club's rules. Circulate and monitor, checking that they use *have to*, *don't have to*, *should* and *shouldn't* correctly.
- Ask each pair to make a presentation about their club to the class. The class then votes on the best club.

Vocabulary bank: Housework page 132

1
 1 do the ironing
 2 load / unload the dishwasher
 3 hoover the floor
 4 take out the rubbish
 5 wash the car
 6 lay the table
 7 help with the cooking
 8 do the shopping
 9 load / unload the washing machine
 10 do the washing up
 11 make the bed
 12 tidy your bedroom
 13 hang out / bring in the washing
 14 walk the dog
 15 clear the table

2 1 do the shopping
 2 walk the dog
 3 take out the rubbish
 4 do the ironing
 5 do the washing up / load the dishwasher
 6 load the washing machine
 7 lay the table
 8 make the bed
 9 wash the car
 10 do the washing up

3 Students' own answers

DVD extra Cleaning beaches

Learning outcome

Ask students: *What have you learned today? What can you do now?* and elicit answers: *I can understand an article about unusual cleaning jobs. I can use 'have to' and 'should'. I can understand the rules of an after-school club. I can create and talk about rules for my own after-school club.*

7C Culture, vocabulary and grammar

The first Thanksgiving

Lesson summary
Topic: The history of Thanksgiving
Vocabulary: Opposite adjectives
Grammar: Past simple: *be*; past simple: *can*
Reading: The diary of Constance Hopkins, aged 14
Writing: Writing a diary entry about a journey to a new place

Lead-in

- Write THANKSGIVING on the board in capital letters. Explain that Thanksgiving is an important national holiday in the USA.
- Then ask students to discuss the following questions in groups:
 Which is the most important holiday in your country?
 What do you do on this day?
 What do you usually eat on this day?
 Which day of the year do you like best? Why?
- Ask a few students to share their group's ideas with the class.

Exercise 1 page 84

- Focus attention on the picture. Revise clothes vocabulary by asking students to call out the words for the clothes they can see, e.g. *hat, dress, apron, boots*.
- Ask:
 What is the woman doing with the food? (She is giving it to the Indians.)
 Do the people look happy or sad? (happy)
- Students work in pairs to discuss what the people are doing and where they are.

Students' own answers

Exercise 2 page 84

- Read out the introduction and elicit answers to the questions.
- Explain that for many Americans in the USA, Thanksgiving is the most important holiday of the year and the one time when families try to be together.

They usually have roast turkey and pumpkin pie.

Because the food reminds them about the first Thanksgiving celebration in 1621.

Exercise 3 page 84

- Make sure students understand the meaning of *diary* (a book where you write what you have done each day). Explain that Constance's diary includes a description of her journey from England to America and her life as a settler in America.
- Give students two minutes to do the exercise.
- Check answers as a class. Students can give their answers using the present tense as they have not yet learned the past simple.

1 102
2 sixty-six days
3 Because they don't have a house.
4 Because it is difficult to build houses in the cold weather.
5 Because they want advice about the land.
6 three days

Culture notes: The *Mayflower* crossing

Constance Hopkins is the actual name of one of the *Mayflower* pilgrims. She was fourteen years old at the time of the *Mayflower* crossing. Her father, Stephen, was one of the ambassadors who made the first contact with the Native Americans. You can see a photograph of Constance's hat on the *Mayflower* history website: mayflowerhistory.com/hopkins-constance

Not all Americans celebrate Thanksgiving. Some Native Americans and their supporters believe it is wrong to celebrate the invasion of their country by Europeans. They call this day a Day of Mourning and remember the slaughter of millions of Native Americans and the loss of their rights and property.

The text refers to the **Wampanoag Indians**, which was the name given to them by the settlers, but it is now considered to be incorrect to use the term 'Indians' for the native people of the USA. The preferred term is 'Native Americans'.

Additional vocabulary

The following words are from *The Diary of Constance Hopkins*:

- *on board* /ɒn 'bɔːd/ on a ship or in a plane
- *amazed* /ə'meɪzd/ (adj) very surprised
- *advice* /əd'vaɪs/ (n) words that you say to help somebody decide what to do
- *harvest* /'hɑːvɪst/ (n) all the grain, fruit, or vegetables that are cut or picked
- *final* /'faɪnl/ (adj) not followed by any others

Extra activity: Further discussion

Ask students to discuss these questions:

Constance talks about the cold, sickness, missing friends and being poor. Which of these problems do you think is the worst? Why?

Do you keep a diary? If you do, what kind of things do you write about? If you don't, why don't you?

Why do people leave their home country and move to a new place? Think of at least three reasons.

Exercise 4 page 84

- Remind students that we often record words with their *antonyms* or *opposites*.
- With a **weaker class**, ask students to underline the adjectives in the text first.
- Students do the exercise.
- Check answers as a class.

1 dangerous   2 well   3 poor   4 happy   5 lazy

Exercise 5 page 84

- Students complete the sentences.
- Check answers as a class.

1 rich   2 ill   3 hard-working   4 dangerous
5 safe / happy

Exercise 6 page 85

- Give students one minute to complete the sentences.
- To check answers, write the gapped sentences on the board and then ask a few students to read out their completed sentences so that you can fill in the gaps. Use this as an opportunity to model the pronunciation of *could* /kʊd/ and *couldn't* /'kʊdnt/.

1 was; couldn't   3 wasn't; was
2 weren't; weren't   4 were; could

Exercise 7 page 85

- Students use the sentences in exercise 6 as a reference to complete the tables.
- Check answers as a class.

1 was   2 weren't   3 could   4 couldn't

Reference and practice 7.2 Workbook page 125

1 2 were   3 were   4 were   5 was; were
   6 Were; was   7 were   8 were

2 2 She was at school.
   3 A: Were you a student?
      B: No, I wasn't. I was a teacher!
   4 A: Was your sister in her bedroom?
      B: Yes, she was.
   5 We weren't very rich, but we were happy.
   6 They were at the station.

3 2 My friends couldn't hear the music at the concert.
   3 I couldn't swim when I was a child.
   4 Could you play the violin when you were younger?
   5 We could remember the teacher's name.
   6 Could they climb up the ladder?

4 2 Orla couldn't speak two languages.
   3 I couldn't play the trumpet.
   4 I could swim when I was five.
   5 We could understand English films.
   6 Maya could visit her grandparents.

Exercise 8 page 85

- Give students two minutes to complete the text.
- With a **weaker class**, help students to identify the sentences about ability (2, 5, 6) and tell them to complete these first with *could* or *couldn't*.
- Check answers as a class.

1 was   2 could   3 was   4 was   5 couldn't   6 could
7 was   8 was   9 weren't   10 were

> **Extra activity: Find someone who …**
> Write the following phrases on the board:
> ride a horse ride a bike read write
> sing a song play the piano speak English
> Ask a student: *Could you ride a horse when you were five?* Elicit a reply (*Yes, I could. / No, I couldn't.*). Then tell students to ask and answer questions about the activities on the board and try to find someone who could do each of these things when he / she was five years old.

Exercise 9 page 85

- Go through the strategy together. Remind students of the strategies they have covered so far for learning new vocabulary: recording antonyms and synonyms, using word webs and writing words in context, and emphasize that actually using new words is the most effective way of remembering them.
- Students complete the questions and then ask and answer in pairs.

1 happy   2 safe   3 rich   4 lazy   5 ill

Exercise 10 page 85

- Students write the diary entry. Remind them to use the past simple of *be* and *can*.
- Ask a few students to read their diary entries to the class.

Learning outcome

Ask students: *What have you learned today? What can you do now?* and elicit answers: *I know about the history of Thanksgiving. I can use 'be' and 'can' in the past tense. I can write a diary entry in the past tense.*

7D Listening, speaking and vocabulary

What's wrong?

Lesson summary
Topic: Health and illness
Vocabulary: Health; Vocabulary bank: Health problems
Listening: Health facts and myths
Speaking: Talking about illness
Writing: A dialogue asking for and giving advice

Lead-in

Say: *I feel ill today*. Then point to your head and say: *I've got a headache*. Point to your stomach and say: *And I've got a stomach ache*. Sneeze and say: *And I've got a cold. What should I do?* Write on the board: *You should …* and then get students to brainstorm advice for you. If they do not know the words in English, allow them to say them in their own language but translate them and write them in English on the board.

Exercise 1 page 86

- If necessary, explain that *treatment* means 'the things that a doctor does to make a sick person well again'.
- Read out the first word, *antibiotics,* and ask: *Problem or treatment?* (treatment)
- Students do the exercise in pairs or small groups.
- Check answers as a class.

Problem broken leg, burn, cold, cough, cut, dizzy, flu, headache, sneeze, sore throat
Treatment antibiotics, bandage, injection, medicine, painkiller, plaster

Exercise 2 page 86

- Students look at the picture and try to find some of the things in exercise 1. With a **weaker class**, tell them that there are five problems and three treatments.
- Students compare answers in pairs.
- Check answers as a class.

bandage, broken leg, cold, cut, headache, medicine, plaster, sore throat

> **Extra activity**
> Students work in pairs. Give them one minute to study the picture. Then one student in each pair closes the book and tries to describe the picture from memory. The other student can ask questions for their partner to answer, e.g. *What colour T-shirt has the woman got?*

Exercise 3 page 86

- Focus attention on the title and explain that a *myth* is a story or belief that is not true.
- Give students two minutes to discuss the statements in pairs.
- Hold a class vote. Read out each statement and ask a student to count how many people vote *true* and how many vote *false*. Write the results on the board, e.g. *sentence 1 – true: 6; false: 13*.

Exercise 4 2•16 page 86

- Tell students to listen just to check their answers; they do not need to understand every word.
- Play the recording. Stop after each piece of information and ask: *True or false?* Write the correct answer on the board next to the class vote results.

Audio script

Speaker Hello, today we're talking about some of the most common health facts and myths. In the studio with me, I have Dr Priya Kapoor. Dr Kapoor, let's start with water. You should drink eight glasses of water every day. True or false?
Dr Kapoor Well, this one is false. Most people can get enough liquid from tea, coffee, juice and milk, and also from their food, especially fruit and vegetables. In fact, sometimes it's dangerous to drink a lot of water. The general rule is, drink water when you feel thirsty.

Unit 7 It's tough! 93

Speaker OK, let's move on to flu. Can we treat flu with antibiotics?
Dr Kapoor No, we can't. Antibiotics are for infections. Flu is a virus. You can't treat flu with antibiotics. Of course, sometimes, when you have flu, you also have other problems, like a chest infection. Then you can treat the chest infection with antibiotics. But, please, don't take antibiotics for a cold or for flu.
Speaker Right, so now, you say we shouldn't take antibiotics for a cold. But what about chicken soup? Now this is something that my grandmother always says: chicken soup can help when you have a cold. Is that true?
Dr Kapoor Does your grandmother make chicken soup for you when you have a cold?
Speaker Well, actually, yes, she does!
Dr Kapoor So, she's absolutely right! Chicken soup is really good for you. We don't understand exactly why, but yes, chicken soup has got lots of good ingredients and can really help with a cough and a sore throat.
Speaker That's very interesting. My grandmother's always right! So, chicken soup is also good for a sore throat. Now, is it true that you shouldn't have cold drinks when you have a sore throat?
Dr Kapoor No, this isn't true. You can drink cold drinks, warm drinks, hot drinks when you have a sore throat. The temperature of the drink isn't important. But don't have a lot of sweet fizzy drinks.
Speaker Are they bad for sore throats?
Dr Kapoor No, but they're very bad for your teeth!
Speaker Ah, yes. Now, finally. Is it dangerous to go swimming immediately after a meal?
Dr Kapoor No, it isn't. It's quite safe to go swimming after a meal. Of course, you probably don't want to go swimming when you have a full stomach. But it's not dangerous.

1 F: Most people can get enough liquid from tea, coffee, juice and milk.
2 F: You can't treat flu with antibiotics. Antibiotics are for infections. Flu is a virus.
3 T
4 F: You can drink cold, warm and hot drinks when you have a sore throat.
5 T

Exercise 5 2•16 page 86

- Students work individually to do the exercise.
- Play the recording for them to check their answers.
- Check answers as a class.

1 tea
2 juice
3 fruit
4 an infection / a chest infection
5 flu
6 good
7 cough
8 temperature
9 sweet
10 safe

See exercise 4 for audio script

Exercise 6 page 86

- Go through the sentences together and explain any difficult vocabulary.
- Students discuss the facts in groups.
- Hold another class vote to find out how many people think each sentence is false and how many think it is true.
- Finally, reveal the answers.

1 T
2 F: The tongue is the strongest muscle in the body.
3 F: You use 100 muscles to take one step.
4 T
5 T
6 F: A sneeze travels at 160 km per hour.

Exercise 7 page 87

- Make sure students understand what they have to do. Match the first problem with a picture and with the advice as an example.
- Students do the exercise individually or in pairs.
- Check answers as a class.

1 I've got a headache. – d
2 I feel dizzy. – e
3 I've got a cough and sore throat. – c
4 I can't sleep. – b
5 I've got a bad cut. – a

> **Vocabulary bank: Health problems** page 132
>
> 1 1 a (high) temperature   9 toothache
>   2 ill/unwell   10 a blocked nose
>   3 sick   11 a sore throat
>   4 stomach ache   12 a sprained ankle
>   5 shivery   13 a bruise
>   6 hay fever   14 flu
>   7 weak   15 a rash
>   8 a nosebleed   16 a broken arm
>
> 2 **I'm feeling** ill/unwell, shivery, sick, weak
>   **I've got** a blocked nose, a broken arm, a bruise, flu, hay fever, a nosebleed, a rash, a sore throat, a sprained ankle, stomach ache, a (high) temperature, toothache
>
> 3 1 I feel sick.
>   2 He's got toothache.
>   3 You've got a (high) temperature.
>   4 She's feeling shivery.
>   5 They're feeling weak.
>   6 I feel ill / unwell.
>   7 She's got a broken arm.
>   8 You've got hay fever.
>   9 I've got a blocked nose.
>   10 You've got a bruise.
>
> 4 Students' own answers

Exercise 8 2•17 page 87

- Explain to students that they are going to listen to a dialogue at a doctor's surgery.
- Play the recording for students to identify James' problems.
- Check answers as a class.

Audio script

Doctor Hello, James. Now, what's the problem?
James I've got a really bad headache.
Doctor Hmm. Do you often get headaches?
James No, I don't. This is very unusual.
Doctor I see.
James And I can't sleep at night.
Doctor Are you worried about anything?
James Well, I've got my exams next week …
Doctor That's probably the problem. Try to relax. You should have a bath and listen to some music before you go to bed. Read a funny book or a magazine. Don't think about school work or exams before bedtime.
James Yes, OK. Thanks very much.

He's got a headache and he can't sleep.

Exercise 9 2·17 page 87

- Students work individually or in pairs to complete the phrases.
- Play the recording for them to check their answers.
- Check answers as a class.

1 problem	4 can't sleep
2 worried	5 relax
3 've got	6 Don't think

See exercise 8 for audio script

Exercise 10 2·18 page 87

- Go through the phrases in the list together. Ask students to identify the phrases that ask about health (2 and 5), those that describe problems (4), and those which give advice (1 and 3).
- Give them one minute to complete the dialogue.
- Play the recording for them to check their answers.
- Check answers as a class.

Audio script

Rick Hello, Martha. You don't look very well. Are you OK?
Martha No, I'm not. I feel really dizzy.
Rick Oh dear. You should sit down. And you should raise your feet.
Martha Why?
Rick It makes the blood go to your brain.
Martha Oh, OK, thanks.
Rick Do you feel sick?
Martha No, I don't. But I've got a bad sore throat.
Rick I think you should see a doctor.
Martha Yes, maybe you're right.

1 Are you OK
2 I feel really dizzy
3 you should raise your feet
4 Do you feel sick
5 I think you should see a doctor

Exercise 11 page 87

- Give students one minute to underline more phrases.
- Write two headings on the board: *Describing problems* and *Giving advice*. Then ask different students to write the phrases on the board under the correct heading.

Describing problems I've got a bad sore throat.
Giving advice You should sit down.

Exercise 12 page 87

- Divide the class into patients and doctors. Patients can discuss their symptoms together, and doctors can think about what questions they might ask and what advice they might give.
- Then put students in patient–doctor pairs and ask them to prepare their dialogues.
- Circulate and monitor, helping with vocabulary if necessary.
- When they have finished, ask a few pairs to act out their dialogue for the class.

Learning outcome

Ask students: *What have you learned today? What can you do now?* and elicit answers: *I know the names of problems and treatments. I can understand a description of health facts and myths. I can describe health problems and give advice.*

7E Writing

A letter of advice

Lesson summary
Topic: Problems and advice
Vocabulary: Making suggestions and giving advice
Reading: Letters describing problems and letters giving advice
Writing: A letter of advice
Communcation worksheet 7B: What should I do?

Lead-in

Write AGONY AUNT in capital letters on the board. Ask students if they remember this word. If not, remind them that an *agony aunt* is a person who writes in a newspaper or magazine giving advice in reply to people's letters about their personal problems. Brainstorm suggestions for the kinds of problems that appear in agony aunt columns, e.g. *I don't have many friends. I have lots of arguments with my parents. My friends have got more expensive clothes than me.*

Exercise 1 page 88

- Students discuss the questions in pairs.
- Ask a few pairs to share their ideas with the class.

Exercise 2 page 88

- Tell students to read letters 1–3 and underline the key information. This should help them to match the letters to the replies. With a **weaker class**, ask students to identify the key words.
- Students work individually to do the exercise.
- Check answers as a class.

1 b   2 c   3 a

Exercise 3 page 88

- Ask the first question and encourage students to mention other typical problems at their school. You can also refer to the ideas from the lead-in activity.
- Students then discuss questions 2 and 3 in pairs.

Unit 7 It's tough!   95

Exercise 4 (page 88)

- Give students two minutes to read letters a–c again and complete the sentences. Explain that these are all ways of making suggestions.

1 Why don't you
2 You could
3 You should
4 Perhaps you can

Exercise 5 (page 88)

- Read out the first problem and elicit advice from a student.
- Students then practise giving advice in pairs. Circulate and monitor, making sure that they use full sentences.

Exercise 6 (page 88)

- Go through the strategy together. Point out to students that they already do a lot of brainstorming in their English classes. Emphasize the importance of writing down all the ideas they think of. They can 'edit' their ideas later.
- Give students two minutes to read the problem and brainstorm ideas.
- They then compare ideas in pairs or in small groups.

Writing guide (page 89)

- Read the **task** together, making sure students are clear that they have to choose one of the problems and write a letter of advice. They do not have to write a letter about the problem.
- Give students five to ten minutes to complete the **ideas** stage and **plan** their letters. Circulate and monitor, helping with language and ideas as necessary. Remind students to use expressions for making suggestions.
- Circulate and monitor while students **write** their letters. Remind them to activate the language they learned earlier in the unit (*should* for advice, vocabulary for health problems).
- When students have finished, they **check** their work. Refer them to the checklist to make sure they have completed the task as well as they can.

> **Extension: Fast finishers**
> Ask **fast finishers** to swap letters with another student to read and check for mistakes.

> **Additional writing activity**
> It is 1621 and you are living in England. Your good friend Constance Hopkins writes to you from the Plymouth Colony in America. She is lonely and her life is hard. Write her a letter of advice.

Learning outcome

Ask students: *What have you learned today? What can you do now?* and elicit answers: *I can read and understand a letter of advice. I can make suggestions. I can brainstorm ideas. I can write a letter of advice.*

Review 7 (page 89)

1 1 neck 2 shoulder 3 elbow 4 wrist 5 hip
   6 knee 7 ankle

2 1 swimmers 2 director 3 players 4 reporter
   5 designer 6 drivers 7 visitor 8 riders

3 1 sneeze 2 sore throat 3 headache 4 dizzy
   5 antibiotics 6 painkillers 7 medicine

4 1 Do (you) have to do
   2 Should (you) help
   3 don't have to do
   4 have to make
   5 should take
   6 has to leave
   7 doesn't have to walk
   8 have to run
   9 should get up
   10 shouldn't be

5 1 was 2 was 3 could 4 was 5 were 6 could
   7 was 8 weren't 9 was 10 was 11 was
   12 was 13 was

> **Pronunciation insight 7** Workbook page 135
> **Answer key:** Teacher's book page 155

96 Unit 7 It's tough!

8 Life story

Map of resources

Section A: Student's Book pages 90–91
Workbook page 68
Vocabulary bank, Jobs page 133

Section B: Student's Book pages 92–93
Workbook page 69
Grammar reference and practice 8.1, Workbook page 126
Grammar reference and practice 8.2, Workbook page 126
Vocabulary bank, Past time expressions page 133
Teacher's resource disk, Communication worksheet 8B

Section C: Student's Book pages 94–95
Workbook page 70
Grammar reference and practice 8.3, Workbook page 127
Teacher's resource disk, DVD extra + worksheet, The magic of Roald Dahl page 95
Teacher's resource disk, Communication worksheet 8B

Section D: Student's Book pages 96–97
Workbook page 71
Teacher's resource disk, Communication worksheet 8A

Section E: Student's Book pages 98–99
Workbook page 74
Teacher's resource disk, Writing bank
Teacher's resource disk, Functional language bank

Review 8 page 99
Pronunciation insight 8, Workbook page 135
Progress check Unit 8, Workbook page 75
Language and skills tests 8A and 8B, Test Bank

Cumulative review Units 1–8 pages 100–101
Literature insight 4, Workbook page 98
Exam insight 4, Workbook page 108

8A Reading and vocabulary

Life's ups and downs

Lesson summary
Topic: Success stories
Vocabulary: Life stages; adjective suffixes: *-ful* and *-al*; Vocabulary bank: Jobs
Reading: Music: the road to success
Speaking: Discussing people and their jobs

Lead-in

- Write the names of the following famous people on the board: *Johnny Depp, Gwyneth Paltrow, Nelson Mandela, Barack Obama, JK Rowling*. Explain in students' own language that these people all had ordinary jobs before they became famous. Then write the following jobs on the board: *university teacher*, *pen salesperson*, *secretary*, *lawyer*, *waiter / waitress*. Ask: *Can you match the people to the jobs?*
- Students work in pairs to discuss their ideas. After two minutes, model a sentence using the past tense of *be*, e.g. *I think Nelson Mandela was a university teacher.* Ask different pairs for their suggestions.

Johnny Depp pen salesperson   **Gwyneth Paltrow** waitress
Barack Obama university teacher   **Nelson Mandela** lawyer
JK Rowling secretary

Exercise 1 page 90

- Go through the words and phrases together. Explain that *a long life* means that you live for a long time – you do not die when you are young.
- Give students two minutes to work in pairs to rank the different things.
- Write the things on the board and go round the class, asking each pair to report back on their ranking. Write the numbers, building up a class score for each thing. The thing with the lowest score is the most important, and the thing with the highest score is the least important.

Exercise 2 2•19 page 90

- Focus attention on the pictures at the top of the page. Elicit the answer for the first picture (*be born*).
- Students work individually to do the exercise.
- Play the recording for them to check their answers.
- Play the recording again for them to repeat the phrases.
- Check answers as a class.

1 be born
2 grow up
3 go to university
4 get a job
5 fall in love
6 get married
7 have a baby
8 get divorced
9 retire
10 die

Exercise 3 2·20 page 90

- Students work in pairs to complete the sentences.
- Play the recording for students to check their answers.
- Check answers as a class. Ask: *Are these facts surprising? Which fact is the most surprising? Which is the least surprising?*

1 are born; die
2 retire
3 has a baby; grows up
4 get a job
5 go to university
6 falls in love; gets married; get divorced

Extra activity: Internet research
Ask students to do some internet research to find out the answers to the following questions:
How old is the average woman in your country when she has a baby?
What is the average number of children in a family in your country?
What percentage of people go to university in your country?
Students write sentences about the results of their research.

Exercise 4 page 90

- Students work in pairs to label the photos. Then ask them to use the photos to make predictions about the two texts.
- Ask a few pairs for their predictions (they can give these in their own language), and then tell them to read the texts quickly to check their ideas.
- Check answers as a class.

1 singer songwriter
2 builder
3 opera singer
4 American football player

Exercise 5 page 91

- Remind students to read the sentences carefully and underline the key words. They then scan the text to check the facts. Point out that questions 1–5 are about Sixto Rodriguez and questions 6–10 are about Keith Miller.
- Check answers as a class.

1 T
2 F: Sixto's music was more famous in South Africa than Elvis Presley's.
3 F: There weren't many visitors to South Africa in the 1970s and 1980s.
4 F: No money from his record sales in South Africa reached him.
5 T
6 F: He had no interest in music.
7 T
8 F: They hated opera.
9 F: They thought he was stupid because he couldn't read music very well.
10 T

Culture notes: Sixto Rodriguez and Keith Miller
Sixto Rodriguez' first name refers to the fact that he was the sixth child in his family. He came from a working class background and many of his political songs are about the problems of poor people in inner cities. In 2012 a successful documentary, *Searching for Sugar Man*, was made about Sixto Rodriguez and his fans in South Africa. Since the release of the documentary Rodriguez has become popular again in the USA.

Keith Miller was a professional American football player for five years before he started his career as an opera singer. He carried the Olympic torch at the Olympic Games in Atlanta in 1996, and played for European and Arena Football leagues. He studied at Philadelphia's Academy of Vocal Arts from 2002–2006 and got his first part in Puccini's opera *Madame Butterfly* just a few days after graduating. He has developed a physical training programme for opera singers, known as 'puissance training'. (*Puissance* is a French word meaning 'power'.)

Additional vocabulary
The following words are from the text *Music: the road to success*:

- *situation* /ˌsɪtʃuˈeɪʃn/ (n) the things that are happening in a certain place or at a certain time
- *believe* /bɪˈliːv/ (v) to feel sure that something is true
- *discover* /dɪˈskʌvə(r)/ (v) to find or learn something for the first time
- *wonderful* /ˈwʌndəfl/ (adj) very good
- *in private* /ɪn ˈpraɪvət/ alone; without other people there
- *audition* /ɔːˈdɪʃn/ (v) to sing, act, dance, etc. for someone so that they can find out if a person is good enough to be in a play, show, etc.

V insight Adjective suffixes: *-ful* and *-al*
We can add the suffix *-ful* (meaning 'full of') to some nouns to make adjectives, e.g. *careful*.
We can add the suffix *-al* (meaning 'relating to' or 'about') to some nouns to make adjectives, e.g. *natural*.

Exercise 6 page 91

- Read out the nouns in the table and give students one minute to find the adjective forms in the text.
- Students compare answers in pairs. They then complete the gapped text.
- Check answers as a class.

success successful   nature natural   profession professional
beauty beautiful   music musical   peace peaceful
wonder wonderful   power powerful   politics political

1 professional   2 successful   3 beautiful   4 political
5 wonderful   6 peaceful   7 powerful   8 natural

Exercise 7 page 91

- Students discuss the questions in pairs.
- Circulate and monitor, helping with vocabulary and ideas if necessary.
- Ask a few pairs to share their ideas with the class.

Extra activity: Fast finishers

Ask **fast finishers** to work in pairs and describe the life of a family member whom they respect. Tell them to talk about what this person does and why they respect them.

Vocabulary bank: Jobs (page 133)

1
1	lawyer	9	office worker
2	builder	10	accountant
3	teacher	11	shop assistant
4	vet	12	engineer
5	electrician	13	nurse
6	plumber	14	scientist
7	doctor	15	architect
8	waiter	16	factory worker

2
1	a scientist	6	a plumber
2	a vet	7	an engineer
3	a doctor / a nurse	8	a factory worker
4	a lawyer	9	a doctor / a nurse
5	an accountant	10	an architect

3 Students' own answers

Extra activity: Further discussion

Ask students to discuss these questions in groups:

You can choose a job you love with a low salary or a job you hate with a high salary. Which one do you choose? Why?

Do you think you need a good education to get a good job? Why / why not?

Do you know anyone with an interesting job? What do they do?

Do you think that money and fame = success? Why / why not?

Learning outcome

Ask students: *What have you learned today? What can you do now?* and elicit answers: *I can talk about life events. I can read and understand a text about two people's careers. I can use the suffixes '-ful' and '-al' to make adjectives. I can describe the life of a person I respect.*

8B Grammar and listening

The human story

Lesson summary
Topic: Human ancestors
Grammar: Past simple affirmative: regular verbs; past simple affirmative: irregular verbs
Listening: Neanderthals
Reading: Out of Africa
Speaking: Describing an important event from human history
Communication worksheet 8B: That's life!

Lead-in

Write the following events from human prehistory on the board:

*Humans … built the first city   used fire   farmed land
               used tools   wrote words*

Elicit or explain the meaning of *tools*: write *tools* on the board and draw pictures of a *hammer* and *saw* next to it.

Ask students to work in groups and put the events in chronological order, starting with the earliest. When they have finished, write the dates:

*Humans …   used tools: 2,000,000 BC
            used fire: 700,000 BC
            farmed land: 10,000 BC
            built the first city: 8,000 BC
            wrote words: 3,500 BC*

Exercise 1 (page 92)

- Go through the sentences together. If necessary, explain that *ancestors* are people in your family who lived a very long time ago.
- Students discuss the answers to the questions in pairs.
- They then read the text to check their answers.
- Check answers as a class.

1 Africa   2 45,000   3 were   4 could

Language note: Past simple affirmative: regular verbs
We use the past simple to describe an event that took place at a specific time in the past. We often use past time expressions with the past simple, e.g. *yesterday, five years ago, in the Ice Age*.

Exercise 2 (page 92)

- Students look at the verbs in a–d and work out the spelling rules.
- When they have finished, they compare answers in pairs. They then match the highlighted verbs in the text to the rules.
- Check answers as a class.

a 1: disappeared, tested, covered, seemed, started
b 4: died, continued
c 2: tried
d 3: travelled

Unit 8 Life story   99

Extra activity: Memory game

Ask students to work in pairs. Give them two minutes to read the text again and memorize the main facts. Then ask one student in each pair to close the book. The other student reads out a sentence from the text. They can choose either to read the sentence exactly as it appears in the text, or to change one important piece of information, e.g. *About 65,000 years ago, one tribe left **Europe**.* The first student listens and decides if the sentence is true or false.

Reference and practice 8.1 Workbook page 126

1 1 looked 2 chatted 3 used 4 invented
      5 tried 6 wanted

2 2 stayed   6 liked
      3 copied   7 studied
      4 waited   8 hated
      5 started; finished

Exercise 3 2·21 page 92

- Tell students to use the rules in exercise 2 to help them complete the text.
- With a **weaker class**, go through each verb in brackets and ask the students to match the verb to a rule.
- Play the recording for students to check their answers.
- Check answers as a class.

1 hunted   2 looked   3 travelled   4 carried
5 invented 6 changed   7 planted   8 laughed
9 waited   10 noticed 11 produced 12 chatted
13 copied 14 stopped 15 lived   16 started

Language note: Past simple affirmative: irregular verbs

Encourage students to keep a list of irregular verbs and to use different strategies to learn and revise them, e.g.:
- Make flashcards with the base form on one side and the irregular past simple form on the other side.
- Write sentences with past simple forms in them.
- Write short stories including many irregular past simple forms.
- Make a chart of the most common irregular past simple forms and stick it on your wall or above your desk at home.

Exercise 4 page 93

- Students look at the text on page 92 again and find the irregular past simple forms of the verbs in the list.
- They then exchange their answers with a partner and use the irregular verbs list on page 126 of the Workbook to check their partner's answers.

1 became 2 had 3 made 4 left 5 grew 6 went
7 came

Reference and practice 8.2 Workbook page 126

1 2 We bought a new armchair last weekend.
      3 I wore a beautiful green dress at my friend's party.
      4 Jude and Max went to Australia in 2013.
      5 My sister made a cheese and mushroom pizza and I ate it.
      6 We wrote a letter to the President of the USA last year.
      7 My friends gave me a wonderful present for my birthday.
      8 Gemma left her homework in her bag.

2 1 wrote 2 found 3 had 4 put 5 went
      6 heard 7 left 8 ran

Exercise 5 page 93

- Tell students to read the timeline quickly before they complete it.
- Circulate and monitor, helping with any comprehension queries if necessary.
- Check answers as a class.

1 sang   2 made   3 went   4 saw   5 had   6 wore
7 wrote 8 heard 9 left   10 became

Exercise 6 2·22 page 93

- Go through the strategy together. Point out that listening for gist is similar to *skim-reading* when we read – it is a strategy that we use to get a general idea of the meaning. Similarly, listening for detail is like *scanning* when we read – we want to find out specific information.
- Read out the three options and then play the recording. Ask students to vote for the correct answer.

Audio script

Journalist Today, I'm with scientist Lucas Jones, and he's here to tell us about Neanderthals. Lucas, who exactly were Neanderthals?
Scientist Neanderthals were very like modern humans, and started living in Europe and the west of Asia a long time before *Homo sapiens* arrived. They had bigger heads and chests than us, longer noses and shorter arms and legs. They were stronger than us, too, and they were better at living in cold climates.
Journalist What else do we know about them?
Scientist They used tools, and we think they had a language – or probably a lot of different languages – and lived in tribes. They were hunters, and they cooked vegetables, too.
Journalist So they could use fire?
Scientist Yes, they could. And they also made homes from animal bones.
Journalist Why aren't there any Neanderthals today?
Scientist We can't be sure. The last Neanderthals probably died about 25,000 years ago. Some scientists think that modern humans came to live in Neanderthal areas. Because modern humans were better hunters, the Neanderthals couldn't find much food. Some people even think that modern humans hunted and killed the Neanderthals. But there are other possible reasons, too.
Journalist For example?

Scientist Well, there were a lot of climate changes in the years before they disappeared. Perhaps the hotter weather killed a lot of them. And maybe some of them joined tribes of modern humans and had babies with them. Perhaps there is some Neanderthal in the people of today!

c

Exercise 7 2·22 page 93

- Remind students that they should listen for detail. Give them time to read the sentences. With a **stronger class**, ask students to choose the correct words from memory.
- Play the recording again for students to check their answers.
- Check answers as a class.

1 Europe   2 heads   3 cold   4 used tools   5 homes
6 25,000   7 killed   8 climate change

See exercise 6 for audio script

Exercise 8 page 93

- Students may need extra time to do some research for this presentation. If you know what they are studying in history, encourage them use resources from these classes to help in their research.
- Remind them to include information about *when* and *where* the event took place and *why* it was important.
- Ask students to write and design a factsheet about their event.

Vocabulary bank: Past time expressions page 133

1 2 yesterday evening
   3 yesterday afternoon
   4 yesterday morning
   5 the day before yesterday
   6 three days ago
   7 last weekend
   8 last week
   9 two weeks ago
   10 last month
   11 four months ago
   12 last year
   13 last summer
   14 five years ago

2 **ago** four months, three days, five years, two weeks, a decade
   last night, week, weekend, month, year, summer
   yesterday morning, evening, afternoon, the day before yesterday

3 1 g   2 f   3 l   4 j   5 h   6 d   7 k   8 i   9 e
   10 b   11 a   12 c
   We use *in* with years and centuries.
   We use *at* with *the beginning of …* and *the end of …* a period of time.

4 Students' own answers

Learning outcome

Ask students: *What have you learned today? What can you do now?* and elicit answers: *I can use the past simple affirmative form of regular and irregular verbs. I know about our earliest human ancestors. I can understand a description of Neanderthal life. I can describe an important event in history.*

8C Culture, vocabulary and grammar

Great writers

Lesson summary
Topic: Famous writers
Vocabulary: Types of writing
Grammar: Past simple: negative, questions and short answers
Reading: Mary Shelley and Emily Dickinson
Speaking: Asking and answering about a famous person in the past
Communication worksheet 8B: That's life!

Lead-in

- Write GREAT WRITERS on the board in capital letters. Give students two minutes to work in groups and brainstorm the names of as many English language writers as possible.
- When they have finished, ask students to open their books and see if their ideas are in the list of names in exercise 1.

Exercise 1 page 94

- Focus attention on the portraits and ask students to identify William Shakespeare. Then give them one minute to match the other names to the portraits.
- Then ask students to put the writers in chronological order (William Shakespeare (1564?–1616); Jane Austen (1775–1817); Charles Dickens (1812–1870); Mark Twain (1835–1910); Agatha Christie (1890–1976); Roald Dahl (1916–1990)).
- Check answers as a class.

1 Charles Dickens   4 Jane Austen
2 Agatha Christie   5 Roald Dahl
3 William Shakespeare   6 Mark Twain

Exercise 2 page 94

- Ask students to identify Shakespeare's work. They then work in pairs to match the other writers to their novels.
- Check answers as a class.

Charlie and the Chocolate Factory: Roald Dahl
Hamlet: William Shakespeare
Murder on the Orient Express: Agatha Christie
Oliver Twist: Charles Dickens
Pride and Prejudice: Jane Austen
The Adventures of Tom Sawyer: Mark Twain

Exercise 3 page 94

- Remind students that this is a skim-reading activity, so they do not need to understand every word in order to answer the questions.
- Students compare answers in pairs.
- Check answers as a class.

1 Mary Shelley
2 Emily Dickinson
3 Mary Shelley

Unit 8 Life story   101

Exercise 4 page 94

- Students work individually to answer the questions. With a **weaker class**, go through the questions together and encourage students to underline key words that will help them find the answers in the text.
- Check answers as a class.

1 women
2 had a wife in London
3 died in a sailing accident
4 *Frankenstein*
5 Massachusetts, the USA
6 mother
7 unusual
8 published her poems

Culture notes: Mary Shelley and Emily Dickinson

Mary Shelley wrote her famous novel *Frankenstein* while she was on a summer holiday in Geneva with Percy Shelley, the poet Lord Byron and John William Polidori. One night Byron suggested that they each write a horror story and Mary was inspired by a dream that she had recently had.

Emily Dickinson's poems were very unconventional for their time. They rarely had titles and did not use many capital letters or much punctuation. For this reason, the few poems that were published during her life were heavily edited by the publisher.

Additional words

The following words are from the text *Mary Shelley and Emily Dickinson*:

- *campaign* /kæmˈpeɪn/ (v) to take part in planned activities in order to get a special result
- *accident* /ˈæksɪdənt/ (n) something bad that happens by chance
- *science fiction* /ˌsaɪəns ˈfɪkʃn/ (n) stories about things like travel in space, life on other planets or life in the future
- *gardening* /ˈɡɑːdnɪŋ/ (n) the work that you do in a garden to keep it looking attractive
- *in print* /ˌɪn ˈprɪnt/ (used about a book) still available from the company that published it

Exercise 5 page 94

- Give students one minute to find the past simple forms of the verbs. Remind them to keep a list of these irregular past simple forms and to revise and practise them regularly.
- Check answers as a class.

do did   fall fell   find found   get got   run ran
write wrote

Extra activity: Further discussion

Ask students to discuss these questions in groups:

'Frankenstein' is a book that has been made into a film many times. Should you read a book before you see the film?
Can you name any other films based on books?
Do you read poetry in your own language?
Do you write poetry?

Exercise 6 page 95

- Explain to students that the words are different types of writing. Give them two minutes to match the words to the definitions.
- Check answers as a class.

1 novel   2 poem   3 script   4 play   5 article
6 short story   7 non-fiction   8 fiction

Exercise 7 page 95

- Students discuss the questions in pairs.
- Circulate and monitor, helping with ideas and vocabulary if necessary.

Language note: Past simple: negative

The past simple negative form is the same for both regular and irregular verbs. We nearly always use the contracted form *didn't* unless we want to emphasize the negative or contradict a previous statement, e.g. 'You went to the party last night.' 'I did **not** go to the party! I stayed at home and did my homework.'

Exercise 8 page 95

- Students find the sentences and then complete the rules.
- Remind students how we form the present simple negative. Say *I like cats* and elicit *I don't like dogs*. Then say *She likes cats* and elicit *She doesn't like dogs*. Write the two negative sentences on the board and underline the auxiliary verbs *don't* and *doesn't*. Then elicit and write the past simple version of these two sentences: *I didn't like dogs. She didn't like dogs.* and underline the auxiliary verb *didn't*. Emphasize that in the past simple, *didn't* remains the same for all persons.
- Check answers as a class.

didn't finish   didn't like
a infinitive   b doesn't change

Reference and practice 8.3 Workbook page 127

1 2 We didn't see a cat in the road.
3 My cousins didn't write a book about Spanish history.
4 Ned didn't play tennis with his friend, James.
5 I didn't plant a tree in our garden.
6 The children didn't wait for their friends.
7 I didn't buy a new pair of jeans yesterday.
8 The dog didn't eat all the biscuits on the table.

Exercise 9 page 95

- If anyone in the class knows the original *Frankenstein* story, elicit a summary of the plot in the students' own language.
- Students work individually to complete the text.
- They then compare answers in pairs.
- Check answers as a class.

1 didn't talk   5 didn't give
2 didn't sleep   6 didn't meet
3 didn't like   7 didn't want
4 didn't understand

102   Unit 8 Life story

Exercise 10 page 95

- Students find and underline the questions and short answers in the text and then complete the rules. With a **weaker class**, tell students that the headings for each paragraph are all past simple questions, and the short answers are in the first line of each paragraph.
- Check answers as a class.

a did   b did   c didn't

Reference and practice 8.3   Workbook page 127

2 2 Where did your sister find her phone?
   3 Did she like the ice cream?
   4 What did Tom put on the table?
   5 How did you get here?
   6 Did you remember your book?
   7 Did he read my magazine?
   8 Did we see this film last year?

3 a 2   b 4   c –   d 8   e 6   f –   g 3   h 5
   i 1   j 7

Extra activity: Internet research

Ask students to find out about one of the great writers mentioned in exercise 1 and to write a short biography.

Exercise 11 2·23 page 95

- Go through the example together. Students then write questions 2–5.
- They then ask and answer in pairs before listening to check their ideas.
- Check answers as a class.

1 Did Steven Spielberg make *Star Wars*? No, he didn't. George Lucas made it.
2 Did Sherlock Holmes and Doctor Watson live in Paris? No, they didn't. They lived in London.
3 Did the Brontë sisters write novels? Yes, they did. Charlotte Brontë wrote *Jane Eyre*, Emily Brontë wrote *Wuthering Heights* and Anne Brontë wrote *Agnes Grey*.
4 Did Homer tell stories about the Trojan War? Yes, he did. The stories were in two long poems, *The Iliad* and *The Odyssey*.
5 Did JK Rowling write *The Hobbit*? No, she didn't. She wrote the Harry Potter novels.

Exercise 12 page 95

- Students work in pairs. One student thinks of a famous person and the other student tries to guess who the person is by asking *yes/no* questions. Remind them that they cannot use *Wh-* questions; they can only make questions beginning *Did … ?*
- Circulate and monitor, helping with vocabulary if necessary.

DVD extra   The magic of Roald Dahl

Learning outcome

Ask students: *What have you learned today? What can you do now?* and elicit answers: *I know about two famous writers. I can use the past simple negative and question forms. I know about the story of 'Frankenstein'. I can talk about famous people from the past.*

8D Listening, speaking and vocabulary

Moments to remember

Lesson summary
Topic: Memorable life events
Vocabulary: Life stages; collocations with *take*
Speaking: Talking about your weekend
Listening: What's the best moment of your life?
Communication worksheet 8A: Good weekend, bad weekend

Lead-in

- Revise the past simple and prepare for the topic by eliciting some past simple irregular verbs and writing them on the board, e.g. *ate, bought, came, drank, got, had, heard, left, made, met, sang, saw, took, went, wore, wrote.*
- Point to one of the verbs and begin the long sentence, e.g. *I ate a delicious breakfast yesterday.* Then point to another verb and elicit the next part of the sentence from a student, e.g. *I ate a delicious breakfast and wrote an email to my friend.* Continue around the class, with each student adding another part and choosing a verb for the next person.

Exercise 1 page 96

- Focus attention on the photos at the top of the page and ask students to call out ideas for what the people are doing. Write their ideas on the board but do not say if they are right or wrong yet.
- Students work in pairs to discuss whether they want to do these things in the future.
- Ask a few pairs to share their ideas with the class.

Exercise 2 2·24 page 96

- Remind students that they need to listen for gist, so they do not need to understand every word.
- Play the recording for students to do the exercise.
- With a **weaker class**, stop the recording after each speaker and ask students to point to the correct photo.
- Check answers as a class.

Audio script

1
Interviewer What's the best moment of your life so far?
Mark The best moment of my life? That's easy! It was when my daughter was born three years ago. Those little fingers and toes – she was the most beautiful thing in the world! I took about a thousand photos of her in that first week. Now my wife and I take turns to stay at home and take care of her during the day. She's growing up fast and she's more fun now. But those first moments with her were amazing.

2
Interviewer What's the best moment of your life so far?
Jenny It was when I passed my driving test last summer. When I took the test the first time, I didn't pass. I was really sad. But the second time, I passed! It was a fantastic feeling. Finally I could drive without my mum in the car. I was free!

3
Interviewer What's the best moment of your life so far?
Peter Well, one of the best was definitely when I got my job. When I left university, there weren't many jobs. I went to a lot of interviews, but everyone said no. It was really difficult. Then I heard from a TV company, and they wanted me to join them as a journalist! Yay! I was so excited! I started work the next week, and it's a brilliant job.

4
Interviewer What's the best moment of your life so far?
Isobel Probably the best moment was when I retired from my job last year. I didn't hate my job. In fact, I really liked it. But now I've got a lot of free time, and I can take a break when I want. I can go on long holidays to interesting places. Life really is fun when you get older!

[Ed: Check answer order against corrected SB when available]

1 A   2 B   3 C   4 D

Exercise 3 2•24 page 96

- Play the recording again for students to complete the sentences.
- With a **weaker class**, write the missing words in jumbled order on the board; students choose the correct word for each gap.
- Check answers as a class.

1 daughter's   2 photos   3 fun   4 sad   5 drive
6 interviews   7 week   8 retired   9 liked   10 life

See exercise 2 for audio script

> **Extra activity: Stronger students**
>
> Ask **stronger students** to work in pairs and discuss the best moment in their life so far. Brainstorm some ideas on the board, e.g. *learned to ride a bike, met my best friend, went on holiday, won a competition, passed an important exam*. Then invite a few students to tell the class about the best moment in their life.

Exercise 4 page 96

- Go through the strategy together. Remind students that they have already learned sport collocations with *go, play* and *do*, e.g. *go swimming, play tennis, do athletics*.
- Do the first sentence together and then give students two minutes to complete the rest of the sentences.
- Check answers as a class.

1 control   2 part   3 care   4 a break   5 photos
6 turns   7 a test   8 place

Exercise 5 page 97

- Students discuss the questions in pairs. Circulate and monitor, helping with ideas or vocabulary as necessary.
- Ask a few students to tell the class about their partner. Tell the partner to listen carefully and check that all the facts are correct.

Exercise 6 page 97

- Focus attention on the pictures and ask students to say what each one shows.
- Demonstrate the activity by asking one student: *What did you do at the weekend? Where did you go? Did you enjoy it?*
- Students then ask and answer about their weekend in pairs. This is a warm-up, so set a time limit of two minutes.

Exercise 7 2•25 page 97

- Remind students that they just need to listen for gist.
- Play the recording for students to write their answers.
- Check answers as a class.

Audio script
Ned Hi, Jasmine. How was your weekend?
Jasmine It was fantastic, thanks. I went to a party at Martha's house on Saturday night.
Ned That sounds fun.
Jasmine Yes, it was great. And then on Sunday my brother and I went to a football match – Liverpool against Manchester United. It was brilliant.
Ned Wow! Lucky you!
Jasmine What about your weekend, Ned? Did you have a good time?
Ned No, it was a disaster!
Jasmine Bad luck! What was the problem?
Ned Well, I wanted to see that new Frankenstein film at the cinema on Saturday, but when I got there, there weren't any tickets.
Jasmine Oh no! Poor you!
Ned And then on Sunday, we went to see my grandmother. It was a two-hour drive, but when we got to her house, she wasn't there.
Jasmine Really? Where was she?
Ned At a friend's house. My mum wrote the wrong date in her diary, so we have to go again next weekend!

Jasmine went to a party and a football match. Yes, she had fun.

Ned went to the cinema and to his grandmother's house. No, he didn't have fun.

Exercise 8 2•25 page 97

- Students work in pairs to complete the phrases.
- When they have finished, play the recording again so they can check their answers.
- To check answers as a class, ask individual students to read out the phrases.

1 was   2 about   3 time   4 thanks   5 it was   6 fun
7 you   8 Bad   9 no

See exercise 7 for audio script

Exercise 9 2•26 page 97

- Ask students to read the dialogue quickly. Then elicit the phrase that completes the first gap.
- Student work individually to complete the dialogue.
- Play the recording for students to check their answers.
- **Fast finishers** practise acting out the dialogue in pairs. Tell them that to sound more fluent and empathetic, they should stress key words like *disaster*, *a shame*, *fantastic* and *poor*.

104   Unit 8 Life story

- Check answers as a class.

1 your weekend	4 What about
2 a disaster	5 Did you have
3 Poor you	6 it was fantastic

Exercise 10 (page 97)

- Give students one minute to read the dialogue again and find more ways of expressing interest and sympathy.
- Write two headings on the board: *Expressing interest* and *Expressing sympathy*. Then ask two students to write the correct phrase under each heading.

Expressing interest How brilliant!
Expressing sympathy That's a shame.

Exercise 11 (page 97)

- Go through the situations together and brainstorm some more ideas for weekend activities. Encourage students to be inventive, e.g. win the lottery, set the house on fire.
- Circulate and monitor, helping with vocabulary if necessary and noting any common errors.
- When they have finished, ask a few pairs to act out their dialogue for the class.

> **Alternative activity**
> Students can use similar expressions to talk about their last holiday. Provide some prompts: *spend a week in New York, go to an amazing beach, lose my passport, get sick.*

Learning outcome

Ask students: *What have you learned today? What can you do now?* and elicit answers: *I can understand people describing the best moment of their life. I can use collocations with 'take'. I can ask and answer about my weekend. I can use expressions to show interest and sympathy.*

8E Writing

A narrative

> **Lesson summary**
> **Topic:** A charity cycle ride
> **Vocabulary:** Narrative adverbs
> **Reading:** A memorable day
> **Writing:** A narrative about a memorable day

Lead-in

- Write *Sponsored bike ride* on the board and explain or elicit that a sponsored event is when we ask people to pay us money to do something difficult, like ride a long distance on a bike or swim 100 lengths of a swimming pool. We then donate the money to a charity.
- Write the following questions on the board for students to discuss in small groups:
  Do you sometimes do sponsored events? Which ones?
  Do you support any charities? Which ones?
  Can you name any famous sponsored events in your country?

Exercise 1 (page 98)

- Write the following gist questions on the board:
  Where did the writer ride to? (Brighton)
  How long did it take? (six hours)
  Did the writer enjoy the ride? (yes)
- Tell students to read the text quickly to find the answers.

Exercise 2 (page 98)

- Remind students that they have already studied adverbs of frequency, which answer the question *How often … ?*, and adverbs of manner which answer the question *How … ?* They will now learn about narrative adverbs, which answer the question *When … ?*
- Ask students to find the adverbs in the text and read them in context. This will help them to understand their meaning.
- They then match the adverbs to the definitions.
- Check answers as a class.

1 d   2 a   3 c   4 e   5 b

Exercise 3 (page 98)

- Students work in pairs to complete the paragraph.
- Check understanding of the text by asking:
  What is the text about? (someone's first day at school)
  Who was nice to the writer? (Melissa)
  When was the writer happy? (when it was time to go home)
- Check answers as a class.

1 at first   2 Soon   3 immediately   4 Suddenly
5 at last

Exercise 4 (page 98)

- Go through the strategy together and explain that it is particularly important to make writing interesting when we are telling a story, whether a true story or a piece of fiction.
- Students read the text in exercise 1 again to identify the different ways that the writer has made it interesting.
- Check answers as a class.

(Possible answers)
1 When I got up that morning, I was worried because the cycle ride was very long – from London to Brighton. There were hundreds of people of all ages and most of them weren't cyclists.
My friends and I chatted to a lot of nice people as we rode and at first it was a lovely sunny day.
Soon we were really cold and wet because we didn't have rain jackets.
2 It was a fantastic day.
Suddenly it started to rain.
3 Positive adjectives: better, nice, lovely, sunny, happy, easy, great, fun
Negative adjectives: worried, (long,) cold, wet, horrible, tired, difficult
4 Could I get to the end?
5 Sometimes the most difficult things in life are the most fun!

Unit 8 Life story

Writing guide (page 99)

- Read the **task** together, making sure students understand that they have to write a narrative similar to the narrative about the sponsored bike ride.
- Give students five to ten minutes to complete the **ideas** stage and **plan** their narrative. Circulate and monitor, helping with language and ideas as necessary. Remind them to write notes, not full sentences.
- Circulate and monitor while students **write** their narratives and encourage them to use narrative adverbs, e.g. *at first*, *soon*, *suddenly*, *immediately*, *at last*, and to use the strategies to make their writing interesting. Remind them to activate the language they learned earlier in the unit (past simple, collocations with *take*).
- When students have finished, they **check** their work. Refer them to the checklist to make sure they have completed the task as well as they can.

Extension: Fast finishers
Ask **fast finishers** to swap narratives with another student to read and check for mistakes.

Additional writing activity
Choose one of your favourite fictional characters. Write a narrative about a day in the character's life, including information about where they were, what they did, who they were with and why they enjoyed / did not enjoy that day.

Learning outcome
Ask students: *What have you learned today? What can you do now?* and elicit answers: *I can read and understand a narrative about a memorable day. I can use narrative adverbs. I can make my writing interesting. I can write a narrative about a memorable day.*

Review 8 (page 99)

1
1 was born
2 grew up
3 went to university
4 fell in love
5 got married
6 had a baby
7 got divorced
8 died

2 1 successful 2 natural 3 powerful 4 peaceful
5 musical 6 political 7 professional

3 1 a break 2 part 3 a test 4 photos / a photo
5 place 6 care 7 turns

4
1 got on
2 were
3 didn't have
4 didn't arrive
5 took
6 woke up
7 spoke
8 didn't sleep
9 asked
10 left
11 went
12 heard
13 opened
14 didn't see
15 was

5
1 When did Maurice Sendak write the book?
2 How old was Max?
3 Where did his mother send him?
4 Where did Max go?
5 How many monsters were there?
6 What did the monsters do?
7 Why did Max go home?
8 What did he find in his room?

Pronunciation insight 8 Workbook page 135
Answer key: Teacher's book page 155

106 Unit 8 Life story

Cumulative review Units 1–8

pages 100–101

1 2·27

Audio script

Man Hello, and welcome to *Celebrity Watch*. Now, some people think that famous people have an easy life, but that isn't necessarily true. Magazine editor Ruth Philips is in the studio with us today, and she's going to tell us about some of the stars who had a difficult start. Ruth, who's your first celebrity?
Ruth Well, I'm going to start with one of the richest men in the world: Bill Gates. Did you know that Bill Gates didn't finish university?
Man Really?
Ruth Yeah, he went to one of the best universities in the USA, Harvard, but then he left to set up a company before he got his degree. But his first company was a failure, and he didn't make much money. It wasn't until he started Microsoft that Bill Gates became successful.
Man How interesting! I didn't know that. Who have you got next for us?
Ruth Film director, Steven Spielberg.
Man But he's one of the most successful directors in Hollywood!
Ruth That's right, but it wasn't always that way. When he applied for film school, the school said that they didn't want him. This happened three times, and so he had to go to a different one. But he didn't stay until the end of the course because he left to become a director. Thirty-five years later, in 2002, he went back and finished his degree.
Man Wow. I never knew. Who's next on your list?
Ruth Well, our next person is also a Stephen: Stephen King.
Man The novelist?
Ruth Yes. Now, when Stephen King started writing his first novel, he decided that he didn't like it, so he threw it away. Fortunately, his wife found it. She read it and told him she thought it was a great story, so he finished it. The novel was *Carrie*, and it went on to sell over four million copies.
Man Wow! That's a lot of books! Ruth, we've got time for one more. Who is it?
Ruth The greatest basketball player of all time: Michael Jordan. Jordan was only one metre eighty tall when he was sixteen, so he was too short to play for the school team. But he trained hard every night, and he grew ten centimetres that summer, so the following year, the coach gave him a place. By the time he was twenty-one, he was playing for the NBA.
Man That's incredible! Ruth Philips, thanks for joining us.
Ruth You're welcome.

1 F: He went to Harvard but didn't finish his degree.
2 T
3 T
4 F: He got his university degree in 2002.
5 T
6 F: His wife told him to finish it.
7 T
8 F: He started playing professional basketball when he was twenty-one.

2 Students' own answers
3 1 a 2 c 3 d 4 b 5 b 6 c
4 1 c 2 b 3 b 4 a 5 b 6 a 7 c 8 c 9 b
   10 a
5 Students' own answers

Additional materials			
Literature insight 4	Workbook page 98	Answer key:	Teacher's book page 153
Exam insight 4	Workbook page 108	Answer key:	See website

9 Changes

Map of resources

Section A: Student's Book pages 102–103
Workbook page 76
Teacher's resource disk, Communication worksheet 9A
Vocabulary bank, Materials page 134

Section B: Student's Book pages 104–105
Workbook page 77
Grammar reference and practice 9.1, Workbook page 128
Teacher's resource disk, Communication worksheet 9B

Section C: Student's Book pages 106–107
Workbook page 78
Grammar reference and practice 9.2, Workbook page 128

Section D: Student's Book pages 108–109
Workbook page 79
Vocabulary bank, On the phone: phrasal verbs page 134
Teacher's resource disk, DVD extra + worksheet, i-mag: 'zine for teens page 108

Section E: Student's Book pages 110–111
Workbook page 82
Teacher's resource disk, Writing bank
Teacher's resource disk, Functional language bank

Review 9 page 111
Pronunciation insight 9, Workbook page 136
Progress check Unit 9, Workbook page 83
Language and skills tests 9A and 9B, Test Bank

9A Reading and vocabulary

A new model

Lesson summary
Topic: Making a waxwork model
Vocabulary: Describing people; different uses of *like*; Vocabulary bank: Materials
Reading: It's a model job!
Speaking: Describing people's appearance; discussing sculptures
Communication worksheet 9A: Tell me about your …

Lead-in

- Bring in some photos of people from magazines. Include different sizes, ethnicity and appearance. Lay the pictures out in front of the class, and give each picture a number.
- Write the following adjectives on the board: *tall*, *short*, *attractive*, *interesting*, *funny*, *intelligent*, *unusual*. Point to the pictures and say: *Who is the tallest person?* Students respond, e.g. *Number 5 is the tallest person*.
- Students work in groups to ask and answer about the pictures, giving their opinions and forming the superlative of the adjectives on the board.
- When they have finished, ask a few students to share their group's ideas with the class. Emphasize that while height is objective, they may have different opinions about the other adjectives on the board.

Exercise 1 page 102

- Focus attention on the table and make sure that students understand the meaning of *height* and *size*. Ask: *How tall are you?* and move your hand vertically up to indicate height. Ask: *How big are you?* and move your hand vertically and horizontally to indicate size.
- Students put the words in the correct place in the table.
- Check answers as a class, making sure students understand the new words. Where possible, use students to provide examples of hair colour, style, etc. You could also use the magazine pictures from the lead-in activity.

Height medium height
Weight medium weight, overweight, thin
Hair colour blonde
Hair style curly, dyed
Other features beard, freckles, glasses, moustache, tanned

Exercise 2 page 102

- Students read the description and match it to the correct photo.
- Read out the description and ask students to put their hands up when you come to a verb. Explain that we use *be* to describe height and weight and we also use it with *bald* and *tanned*, e.g. *He is bald and tanned*. We use *have*

got to describe eye and hair colour and hair style, and we also use it with *beard, moustache, freckles* and *dyed hair*, e.g. *He's got a beard, freckles and dyed hair*. We use *wear* with clothes and *glasses*.
- Check answers as a class.

Picture 1
The three verbs are *is, has got* and *wears*.

Exercise 3 page 102
- Students work in pairs to write their descriptions.
- Ask a few pairs to read out their descriptions to the class.
- Check answers as a class.

(Possible answers)
She's tall and slim. She's got long, straight blonde / fair hair.
He's medium-height and slim. He's got brown / red hair and a beard.

Extra activity: Fast finishers
Fast finishers write descriptions of the people in the magazine pictures from the lead-in activity. They then swap descriptions with a partner and try to identify the picture in their partner's description.

Exercise 4 page 102
- Demonstrate the activity. Say: *He's tall and slim. He's got curly black hair. His eyes are brown. He doesn't wear glasses.* (Barack Obama) You could then give more clues, e.g. *His wife is also tall. He's got two daughters.*
- Students work in pairs, describing a famous person to their partner. Circulate and monitor, helping with vocabulary if necessary.

Exercise 5 page 102
- Go through the strategy together. Ask students where they might read a summary of a text in their own language, e.g. in a book description in an online bookshop, in an article about a long speech.
- Give students three or four minutes to read the text and choose the best summary.
- Then ask students what is wrong with the other two summaries.

b
Summary a does not include enough important information. Summary c includes the writer's opinion of the text.

Culture note: Marie Tussaud
Marie Tussaud began her career as a wax model maker when she was sixteen years old. She learned the art of wax modelling from her mother's employer, Dr Philippe Curtis, in Switzerland. She developed her skill during the French Revolution, when she made wax models of recently decapitated prisoners. She moved to London in 1804 and exhibited her models at the Lyceum Theatre in London. She opened her first museum in London in 1835, when she was seventy-four years old. There are now eighteen branches of Madame Tussauds Waxworks Museum around the world.

Additional vocabulary
The following words are from the text *It's a model job!*:
- *process* /ˈprəʊses/ (n) a number of actions, one after the other, for doing or making something
- *series* /ˈsɪəriːz/ (n) a number of things of the same kind that come one after another
- *skeleton* /ˈskelɪtn/ (n) the bones of a whole animal or person
- *mould* /məʊld/ (n) a container that you pour a liquid into. The liquid then becomes hard and takes the shape of the container.
- *ceremony* /ˈserəməni/ (n) a formal public or religious event

Exercise 6 page 103
- Remind students to read the questions carefully and underline the key words. These will help them to find the relevant information in the text.
- Students ask and answer the questions in pairs.
- Check answers as a class.

1 They measure the person's body and take photographs.
2 What does this person look like? What's this person like?
3 They can change the position of the model's body.
4 ten to twelve weeks
5 Because they add one hair at a time.
6 Celebrities often donate their own clothes.

Extra activity: Further discussion
Ask students to discuss these questions in groups:
Do you like visiting places like Madame Tussauds? Why / why not?
Madame Tussauds' waxwork models came before television or film. Do you think the idea is now old fashioned? Why / why not?
Do you think the job of sculptor for Madame Tussauds is interesting? Why / why not?

V insight *like*
Be like is often used to talk about personality.
'What's she like?' 'She's friendly but she gets angry quickly.'
Look like is used to ask about appearance. It can also mean 'similar to'.
'What does your sister look like?' 'She looks like me!'
Like means 'enjoy'. It can be followed by a noun, the infinitive of a verb with *to*, or the *-ing* form of a verb.
I like sport. I like playing tennis.
I like to get up in the morning and go for a swim.

Exercise 7 page 103
- Refer students back to their answer to question 2 in exercise 6. Ask:
Which question is about appearance?
Which question is about personality?
- Students match the examples with *like* to the descriptions.
- Check answers as a class.

1 c 2 a 3 b

Unit 9 Changes 109

Exercise 8 page 103
- Students complete the sentences.
- Check answers as a class.

1 does (Jade) look like
2 Do (you) like
3 is (Rick) like
4 'm not like
5 like; don't like
6 look like

Exercise 9 page 103
- Focus attention on the sculptures. Point to the first photo and ask: *What is the subject of the sculpture?* Ask different students for their ideas and then get the class to vote on whether they like it or not.
- Students discuss the other photo in pairs.

> **Culture note: Two sculptures**
> The first sculpture is *Madame Cactus*, a bronze figure made by the Catalan sculptor Julio González in 1939. González taught Picasso techniques of welding in iron, and was in turn influenced by Picasso's ideas. Together with its partner work *Monsieur Cactus*, *Madame Cactus* reflects González's emotional reaction to the events of the Spanish Civil War.
> The second picture is an 1881 bronze casting of a work by the French artist and sculptor Edgar Degas: *La Petite Danseuse de Quatorze Ans* (Little Dancer Aged Fourteen). Originally sculpted in wax, twenty-eight bronze castings were made after Degas' death and can be seen in museums and galleries around the world. The tutus and hair ribbons are made from fabric, and vary from museum to museum.

Exercise 10 page 103
- Ask students to find out about a piece of art by an artist from their country. Alternatively, brainstorm famous pieces of art and write them on the board. Students choose one of these or they can use their own ideas.
- Give an example answer for each question, e.g. *The painting is called* Bedroom in Arles. *Vincent van Gogh painted it. Its subject is van Gogh's bedroom at 2, Place Lamartine in Arles in France. It's an oil painting. It's now in the Van Gogh Museum in Amsterdam. I like it because it is simple and because the artist used beautiful colours.*
- You could collate the students' research into an art factfile for classroom display.

> **Vocabulary bank: Materials** page 134
> 1 1 leather 2 paper 3 wood 4 clay 5 wax
>   6 cardboard 7 glass 8 stone 9 marble
>   10 foam 11 metal 12 plastic
> 2 1 wood 2 foam 3 stone 4 glass 5 plastic
>   6 clay 7 metal 8 leather 9 cardboard
>   10 marble 11 wax 12 paper
> 3 Students' own answers

Learning outcome
Ask students: *What have you learned today? What can you do now?* and elicit answers: *I can describe people's appearance. I know how sculptors make waxwork models at Madame Tussauds. I can identify a summary. I can use 'be like', 'look like' and 'like'. I can discuss famous pieces of art.*

9B Grammar and listening
A new life

> **Lesson summary**
> **Topic:** Life changes
> **Grammar:** *going to*: plans
> **Listening:** People taking about their plans
> **Reading:** Everything's going to be different!
> **Speaking:** Discussing life as a volunteer in another country
> **Communication worksheet 9B:** What are you going to do?

Lead-in
- Introduce the subject by asking students in their own language to think of one significant event that has changed in their life in the last four or five years. Write the following questions on the board:
  What happened?
  Name one good thing about the change.
  Name one bad thing about the change.
- Give an example: *Last year I moved to a new flat. I like my new flat because it's bigger than my old flat and it's closer to school. But I miss the beautiful park near my old flat.*
- Students work in groups or pairs to discuss the significant changes in their lives.

Exercise 1 page 104
- Look at the four different life events together. Explain that a *volunteer* is someone who works to help other people but does not get paid. Ask students to think of examples of volunteer jobs, e.g. working in a charity shop, picking up litter in a public place, helping at a elderly people's home.
- Students work in pairs to discuss the events and decide which is the best, the worst, the biggest and the scariest.
- When they have finished, ask a few pairs to share their ideas with the class.

Exercise 2 page 104
- Focus attention on the title of the text and ask students to predict what it is about.
- Give them two minutes to read the text quickly and match the people to the sentences. Remind them that they do not need to understand every word in order to do this task.
- Check answers as a class.

1 c 2 a 3 b

> **Language note: *going to*: plans**
> We use *going to* to describe plans and intentions for the future. The nearness of the future is not important; more important is the fact that it is planned.
> *I'm going to meet my friends in the park tomorrow.*
> *We're going to buy a new car next year.*
> We rarely use *going to* with *go*; we usually use the present continuous for future instead.
> *I'm going to go to the supermarket this afternoon.* ✗
> *I'm going to the supermarket this afternoon.* ✓

110 Unit 9 Changes

Exercise 3 page 105

- Make sure students understand that the text is about the teenagers' plans for the future. Ask:
  Is Marnie in Ghana now? (no)
  Was she in Ghana in the past? (no)
- Give students two minutes to find and underline examples of *going to* in the text.
- Make sure students understand what an *infinitive* and a *present participle* are. Write *infinitive without 'to'* and *present participle* on the board. Then write *talk* under *infinitive without 'to'* and elicit *talking* for the *present participle* heading. Ask students to write more examples on the board (e.g. *play, playing*) before they complete the rules.
- Check answers as a class.

a plans   b be   c infinitive without *to*

Reference and practice 9.1   Workbook page 128

1 3 's going to find
   4 isn't going to do
   5 isn't going to watch
   6 's going to drive
   7 isn't going to play
   8 's going to fly

2 1 'm going to play
   2 isn't going to buy; 's going to save
   3 Are you going to make
   4 are they going to stay
   5 aren't going to have
   6 A: Is he going to tidy
      B: isn't; 's going to visit
   7 are going to join
   8 're going to start

Exercise 4 page 105

- Go through the example together. Students then work individually to write questions and answers.
- When they have finished, they work in pairs to ask and answer their questions. Circulate and monitor, noting any common errors.
- Check answers as a class.

2 Is Fred going to move away from home? No, he isn't going to move away from home. He's going to stay at home.
3 Are the apprentices going to teach video production? No, they aren't going to teach video production. They're going to learn about video production.
4 Are they going to start the first project immediately? No, they aren't going to start the first project immediately. They're going to have twelve weeks of training.
5 Is Fred going to earn a lot of money? No, he isn't going to earn a lot of money. He's going to learn a lot about web design.

Exercise 5 page 105

- Remind students that Isabelle is going to move to Sydney, Australia. Ask them to read her email quickly and find out: *When is her dad going to fly to Australia?* (tomorrow) *When are they going to have a big party?* (on Tuesday night) *When is she going to meet Yasmin and Tarek?* (Saturday morning)

- Give students two minutes to complete the email.
- Check answers as a class.

2 is going to fly
3 aren't going to leave
4 're going to have
5 're going to say
6 're going to clean
7 isn't going to be
8 's going to make
9 Are you going to come
10 are you going to do
11 'm going to meet
12 're going to play

Exercise 6 2·28 page 105

- Ask students to read the text about Marnie again very quickly. Ask:
  Where is Marnie going to go? (Ghana)
  What is she going to do there? (work as a volunteer)
- Play the recording for students to answer the question.
- Check the answer as a class.

Audio script
Marnie Hello?
Mum Hello, Marnie. Can you hear me?
Marnie Hi, Mum. Yes, I can hear you fine!
Mum How are you?
Marnie I'm great. It's really hot here, and I'm very busy, but I'm having a really good time.
Mum So, what's the orphanage like?
Marnie Well, there are about thirty children here, all aged between six and fifteen. They're really friendly, and they want to know all about my life in England. Tomorrow I'm going to show them some photos of my school … and of you and Dad.
Mum And where are you staying?
Marnie I'm staying with a lovely family. I've got my own room, and I eat with the family. This evening their son, Kojo, is going to prepare a typical Ghanaian meal of beans and rice. He's only twelve, but he's a great cook. And at the weekend, I'm going to go to the capital city, Accra.
Mum How are you going to get there?
Marnie Everyone here travels by tro-tro. It's like a minibus.
Mum And what are you going to do in Accra?
Marnie I'm going to go shopping. I want to buy some sports equipment for the children at the orphanage. They're all crazy about football.
Mum And have you got plans to visit any other places in Ghana?
Marnie Yes, I have. My friend Olly and I are going to visit Kakum National Park next month. There's a hotel by the water there, and you can see lots of crocodiles!
Mum Oh! Not my idea of fun.

She's in Ghana.

Exercise 7 2·28 page 105

- Focus on the phrase *by tro-tro* and ask: *What is a tro-tro?* Students may remember from the first listening that it is a kind of minibus. Students complete the sentences.
- Play the recording again for students to check their answers.
- Check answers as a class.

1 is going to show photos of her school
2 is going to prepare a typical Ghanaian meal
3 is going by tro-tro
4 's going to buy sports equipment
5 are going to visit Kakum National Park

See exercise 6 for audio script

Unit 9 Changes   111

Extra activity: Listening for detail

Write the following questions on the board:
1 How many children are at the orphanage?
2 How old is Kojo?
3 What sport do the children at the orphanage like?
4 Where is Marnie going to stay at Kakum National Park?
5 What animals can you see there?

Ask students to listen to the dialogue again and write the answers. Then let students compare answers in pairs. Check answers as a class.

1 thirty **2** twelve **3** football
4 at a hotel by the water **5** crocodiles

Exercise 8 page 105

- Ask students to prepare for this activity by doing some internet research. Websites like www.unitedplanet.org and www.workingabroad.com have information about volunteering opportunities in countries around the world.
- If your students do not have the time or resources to do the internet research, write the following ideas on the board and tell them that they can use them or their own ideas:
  Working on a farm in Guatemala
  Looking after children at a day centre in Quito
  Helping nurses in Indonesia
  Sorting library books in Togo
- Circulate and monitor, helping with vocabulary and ideas if necessary.

Learning outcome

Ask students: *What have you learned today? What can you do now?* and elicit answers: *I can use 'going to' to talk about plans. I can understand a phone conversation about future plans. I know about volunteering abroad. I can discuss my future plans.*

9C Culture, vocabulary and grammar

A new year

Lesson summary
Topic: New Year celebrations in different countries
Vocabulary: Noun suffixes: *-ion* and *-ment*
Grammar: Predictions with *will*
Reading: Let's celebrate!
Speaking: Making predictions and resolutions for the new year

Lead-in

- Play hangman with the phrase *Happy New Year*. Draw a dash on the board for each letter of the phrase:
  _ _ _ _ _ / _ _ _ / _ _ _ _ . Students take it in turns to call out a letter. If the letter is in the phrase, write it on the corresponding dash. If the letter occurs more than once in the phrase, write it wherever it occurs. Insist that students say the letters correctly. If a letter is not in the phrase, write it on the board and then start drawing the hangman. If you draw the complete picture before the students guess the phrase, you win the game.

Exercise 1 page 106

- Focus attention on the photos and ask students to match them with the countries.
- Ask: *Do you know how people celebrate New Year in these countries?* Write students' ideas on the board but do not say if they are correct or incorrect yet.

Exercise 2 page 106

- Give students one minute to read the text and check their answers to exercise 1.
- Point to students' ideas on the board and ask: *Did you find any of your ideas in the texts?*
- Check answers as a class.

1 Japan **2** Mexico **3** Scotland

Culture note

Buddhist temples in **Japan** ring their bells 108 times in order to symbolize the 108 human sins in Buddhist belief. On New Year's Day, Japanese people often give children money in a small colourful envelope called a *pochibukuro*. Sunrise is very important in Japanese culture, and many Japanese people like to travel to a special place, for example, the coast or a mountain, to watch the first sunrise of the New Year.

In **Mexico**, there are a number of New Year traditions and superstitions. People who want to travel in the New Year often put their suitcases outside and go for a walk at midnight. On New Year's Eve, many Mexicans clean the house and take a bath before midnight so that everything is clean for the New Year. The tradition of eating twelve grapes is also common in Spain and in other Spanish-speaking countries in America.

In **Scotland** there is a special word for the last day of the year: *Hogmanay* /ˈhɒgməneɪ/. There is a superstition that if the first person to enter your house on New Year's Day is a tall dark man – this person is known as a first footer – he will bring you luck, so some people arrange for this to happen. The footer traditionally brings coal (to symbolize warmth in the house), whisky and cake or shortbread (a type of Scottish biscuit). Historians believe that the tradition of the tall dark first footer dates back to Viking times, when Scottish people wanted to be sure that their visitors were not (fair-haired) Vikings.

Additional vocabulary

The following words are from the text *Let's celebrate!*:
- *remove* /rɪˈmuːv/ (v) to take somebody or something off or away from somebody or something
- *prayer* /preə(r)/ (n) words that you speak to God or a god
- *symbolize* /ˈsɪmbəlaɪz/ (v) to represent something
- *make a wish* /ˌmeɪk ə ˈwɪʃ/ (v) to try to make something happen by saying you want it to happen or hoping that it will happen

Exercise 3 page 106

- Tell students to identify the key words in each question and then look for these, or for synonyms, in the text.

Unit 9 Changes

- With a **stronger class**, students write one more '*find out where people …*' clue for each country and then swap their clues with a partner. Their partner tries to guess the country without reading the text.
- Check answers as a class.

1 Scotland 2 Japan, Mexico 3 Mexico 4 Scotland
5 Japan, Mexico 6 Japan 7 Scotland 8 Mexico

Exercise 4 page 106

- Demonstrate the activity. Say: *I'd like to celebrate New Year in Scotland because I like dancing and street parties.* Students discuss their preferences in pairs.
- They then describe how they celebrate New Year in their country.

Exercise 5 page 106

- Remind students that they have learned adjectives that end with -y in Unit 4 (e.g. *rainy, sunny*) and adjectives that end with -*ful* and -*al* in Unit 8 (e.g. *peaceful, musical*). Now they will study suffixes that change verbs into nouns.
- Give students two minutes to find the noun forms in the text.
- To check answers, go round the class asking students to read out the words. Point out that the stress is on the penultimate syllable – the syllable before the suffix.

1 achievement 2 attraction 3 celebration
4 decoration 5 disappointment 6 enjoyment
7 entertainment 8 prediction

Exercise 6 page 107

- Tell students to find the noun forms in the text and use the context to work out the meanings.
- They then work in pairs to complete the sentences. Point out that they will need to make some of the nouns plural.
- With a **weaker class**, tell students that *enjoyment* and *celebration* are not needed.
- Check answers as a class.

1 predictions 2 entertainment 3 disappointment
4 achievement 5 decorations 6 attractions

Exercise 7 page 107

- Tell students that there are no rules for whether a verb will take -*ion* or -*ment*, so they have to learn and keep a record of the noun forms. Point out that when we add -*ion* to verbs which end in -*e*, e.g. *celebrate* and *decorate*, we drop the -*e*: *celebration, decoration*.
- Students work individually to do the exercise.
- Check answers as a class.

1 education 2 government 3 information
4 donation 5 amusement 6 payment

> **Language note: *will***
> We use *will* to make predictions about the future. We often use it with verbs like *think, believe, promise* and *hope*. These verbs show that we are not entirely certain about the future. We also often use the adverbs *probably, maybe* or *possibly* with *will*, again to show uncertainty.
> When we are more sure about our future plans we use the present continuous or *going to*.

Exercise 8 page 107

- Students look for the sentences in the text and complete them. Point out that we often use the contracted form of *will*.
- Check answers as a class.

1 will bring 2 will deliver 3 Will (we) find 4 won't be

Exercise 9 page 107

- Give students two minutes to study the sentences and complete the rules. Remind them that we use *going to* for plans and compare this use with *will* for predictions.
- Check answers as a class.

a predictions b without

> **Reference and practice 9.2** Workbook page 128
> 1 2 will win
>   3 won't get married
>   4 will be
>   5 Will it be
>   6 will move
>   7 won't go; will earn
>   8 will sell
> 2 2 Many people will take holidays on the moon.
>   3 Families will probably live in smaller houses.
>   4 People won't eat meat.
>   5 We'll grow plants in space.
>   6 I think there won't be any wars.
>   7 It won't rain very often.
>   8 We probably won't use desktop computers.
> 3 2 's going to
>   3 aren't going to; 're going to
>   4 won't
>   5 'm going to
>   6 wil

Exercise 10 page 107

- Ask:
  Where is Alejandro from? (Mexico)
  What colours do people wear to symbolize love (red), *money* (green) *and work* (yellow)?
- Then explain that the sentences are Alejandro's predictions for the New Year. Ask: *Are these definite plans?* (no)
- Students work in pairs to complete the predictions.
- Check answers as a class.

1 will sell; will ride; will take
2 will get; won't leave
3 will do
4 won't stay; 'll get
5 will visit; won't travel

> **Extra activity: Fast finishers**
> Ask **fast finishers** to imagine that they are either Kyoko from Japan or Alistair from Scotland and write four predictions. They then read each other's predictions and decide which ones they agree with.

Unit 9 Changes 113

Exercise 11 page 107

- Go through the strategy together. Remind students of the importance of frequent revision and tell them that revising in small, manageable chunks (little and often) is usually more achievable and more effective than trying to revise many weeks' worth of material in one long session.
- Go through the different ideas and ask students how many of these they have actually tried.
- Tell them to choose five words from exercise 1 on page 102 and exercise 5 on page 106. They can use dictionaries to write their definitions or they can draw pictures.
- Students work in pairs, testing each other on the new vocabulary.

Exercise 12 page 107

- Demonstrate the activity. Make some predictions about your life, e.g. *I will teach a new class next year. I will buy some new furniture for my living room. My brother will learn to drive.*
- Students discuss and compare their predictions in pairs or in small groups. Circulate and monitor, helping with vocabulary and ideas if necessary.

> **Extra activity: Further discussion**
>
> Ask students to discuss these questions in groups:
> *What's your favourite way to celebrate the New Year? With family or friends? At home or in a public place?*
> *Do you make New Year's resolutions? Why / why not?*
> *Do you always stay up until midnight on New Year's Eve?*
> *What are your hopes for next year? What are you disappointed about this year?*

Learning outcome

Ask students: *What have you learned today? What can you do now?* and elicit answers: *I know how people celebrate the New Year in Mexico, Japan and Scotland. I can form nouns from verbs with the suffixes '-ment' and '-ion'. I can use 'will' to make predictions about the future.*

9D Listening, speaking and vocabulary

A new business

Lesson summary
Topic: Starting a new business
Vocabulary: Phrasal verbs; Vocabulary bank: On the phone: phrasal verbs
Listening: Young Enterprise
Speaking: Discussing a business idea; talking on the phone
Writing: A dialogue between two friends

Lead-in

- Write *Young Enterprise* on the board. Explain that *Young Enterprise* is a business and education charity. It teaches young people in schools how to run a business. Local businesses volunteer to help and advise the young people. Write the following questions on the board:

Is there a similar scheme in your school?
Do you think this is a good idea? Why / why not?
Do you know any students who run a business?
What kinds of businesses do students run?

- Give students a few minutes to answer the questions in pairs or groups. Then ask them to open their books and look at the ideas on the website.

Exercise 1 page 108

- Explain that the website is for an after-school Young Enterprise club. Ask different students to read out the five ideas on the website. Make sure they understand what a *memory stick* is; show an example, if possible.
- Students discuss the ideas in pairs. Then ask the class to vote for the most and least popular ideas.

Exercise 2 2·29 page 108

- Tell students that Abi is a student who has taken part in the Young Enterprise Club.
- Play the recording for students to match Abi's idea with the correct idea on the Young Enterprise website.
- Check the answer as a class.

Audio script

Interviewer So, today we're talking to people about their big achievements and I've got Abi Tomlin from North Park Secondary School with me. Abi, what was your big achievement of the year?
Abi Well, I took part in an after-school club called 'Young Enterprise' at my school. The idea is that students come up with an original idea and then they set up and manage a business together.
Interviewer So, what was your idea?
Abi We decided to set up a web design company. I'm really good at computer studies – it's my favourite subject – and my friend Jade is really artistic. So we had the right skills. First we did some research. We wanted to find out about prices.
Interviewer How did you do your research?
Abi We talked to local small businesses. We listened to lots of opinions, and then we decided on the best price for our website design services.
Interviewer OK, so you did your research, you worked out the best price … and then what?
Abi Well, we then talked to our mentor. A mentor is an expert who gives you advice and help. We were really lucky because we got loads of useful advice from Pepe Dubois. He runs a web design company. So he showed us some of his most popular website designs, and he also gave us advice about marketing and advertising.
Interviewer Right. Very useful. And then what did you do?
Abi We put together some sample website designs and we showed them to local businesses.
Interviewer And?
Abi Oh, they were terrible! No one liked them.
Interviewer Oh no!
Abi But we didn't give up! We looked for different design ideas online and then we went ahead and designed free websites for four local companies. We made a Facebook page to advertise our website designs.
Interviewer And these new designs were more popular?
Abi Yes. We had a lot of interest from local businesses and from people at school who wanted their own personal blogs. And now, at the end of the year, we've got a profit of £200.

Interviewer Wow! I'm impressed! Are you going to buy something exciting with the money?
Abi Yes, I'm going to do a course on website design!

'I want to design websites.'

Exercise 3 2·29 page 108

- Play the recording again for students to put the events into the correct order.
- With a **weaker class**, pause the recording after each event to give students time to make a note of the order. You could also tell them that sentence 7 is the final sentence.
- Check answers as a class.

1 They did some research to discover the best price.
2 They talked to their mentor.
3 They made sample website designs and showed them to local businesses.
4 Local businesses didn't like their designs.
5 They searched for different designs online.
6 They designed free websites for local businesses.
7 They made a Facebook page to advertise their designs.
8 They sold their website designs to local businesses and people at school.

See exercise 2 for audio script

DVD extra i-mag – 'zine for teens

Language note: Phrasal verbs

A phrasal verb is a verb + preposition or a verb + adverb. The preposition or adverb changes the meaning of the verb.

Some phrasal verbs are followed by an object:
We put together a plan.

Other phrasal verbs are intransitive, i.e. they are not followed by an object:
She didn't give up.

Some phrasal verbs can be separated by the object:
The teacher told us off.

Other phrasal verbs cannot be separated:
They looked for a new idea.

Exercise 4 2·29 page 108

- Go through the description of phrasal verbs together. Tell students that they probably already know some basic phrasal verbs, e.g. *get up*, *go out*.
- Give them a minute to read the sentences and then play the recording again. Pause the recording after each sentence to give students time to write their answers.
- Check answers as a class.

1 up with   2 up   3 out   4 out   5 together   6 up
7 for   8 ahead

See exercise 2 for audio script

Exercise 5 page 108

- Remind students that reading the phrasal verbs in context in the sentences in exercise 4 will help them to understand the meaning.
- Students do the exercise in pairs. They then check their answers in a dictionary if possible.
- Check answers as a class.

1 set up   2 go ahead   3 work out   4 find out
5 put together   6 give up   7 come up with   8 look for

Exercise 6 page 108

- Brainstorm some more business ideas together, e.g. design and make mobile phone covers, make jewellery, make school band CDs, design and sell T-shirts.
- Students discuss their business plans in pairs. Circulate and monitor, helping with vocabulary if necessary.

Extra activity: Dragons' Den

Ask four or five **stronger students** to imagine they are wealthy entrepreneurs (known as 'dragons'). They want to invest some money in an exciting new business. Then ask pairs of students to present their business ideas to the dragons. The dragons have to ask questions about the ideas and decide which business they will invest in.

Exercise 7 page 109

- Give students two minutes to ask and answer the questions in pairs.
- When they have finished, ask a few students to tell the class about their partner. Their partner listens and corrects any mistakes they hear.

Exercise 8 2·30 page 109

- Tell students they are going to listen to a short dialogue on the phone. They have to decide if it is formal or informal. Elicit some situations when you would use formal language, e.g. when making a business call, when talking to your bank, and some situations when you would use informal language, e.g. when chatting to a friend, when talking to your brother or sister.
- Play the recording for students.
- Check the answer as a class.

Audio script
Woman Hello.
Jack Hello. Is that Sarah?
Woman No, this is her mum. Who's calling, please?
Jack It's Jack. Can I speak to Sarah, please?
Woman I'm sorry, Jack, she's not here at the moment. Do you want to leave a message?
Jack No, it's OK. It's not important. I'll call back later.
Woman I'll tell her you called.
Jack Thank you. Goodbye.
Woman Bye.

The conversation is informal.

Exercise 9 2·30 page 109

- Read out the four headings and make sure students understand *apologize* (to say that you are sorry).
- Play the recording for students to complete the phrases.
- To check answers, ask different students to read out the phrases.

1 Is that   4 I'm sorry
2 It's   5 Do you want
3 speak to   6 I'll tell

See exercise 8 for audio script

Unit 9 Changes   115

Exercise 10 ♪ 2•31 page 109

- Ask students to read the dialogue quickly. Ask: *Is this dialogue formal or informal?* (formal)
- Students work individually to put the dialogue into the correct order.
- Check answers by asking two students to at out the dialogue.

Audio script
Receptionist Good morning, Golden Sands Activity Centre.
Tessa Hello, could you put me through to Mr Harris, please?
Receptionist Who's calling, please?
Tessa This is Tessa Grey.
Receptionist Just a moment, Ms Grey. I'm afraid Mr Harris isn't at his desk. Can I take a message?
Tessa Yes, please. Could you ask him to call me on 01227 847522?
Receptionist 01227 847522. Yes, no problem, I'll give him the message.
Tessa Thank you.
Receptionist Goodbye.

Exercise 11 page 109

- Give students two minutes to read the dialogue again and find more phrases.
- Write the following headings on the board: *Giving / Asking for your name, Asking to speak to someone, Apologizing, Offering to give a message*. Ask different students to write the relevant phrases under the correct headings.

Giving / Asking for your name This is Tessa Grey. Who's calling, please?
Asking to speak to someone Could you put me through to Mr Harris, please?
Apologizing I'm afraid Mr Harris isn't at his desk.
Offering to give a message Can I take a message? Yes, no problem, I'll give him the message.

Exercise 12 page 109

- Circulate and monitor as students prepare their dialogues, helping with vocabulary if necessary.
- Ask a few pairs to act out their dialogue for the class.

Vocabulary bank: On the phone: phrasal verbs
page 134

1 look up (line 2), pick up (line 4), hang up (line 8), call back (line 8), hold on (line 9), get off (line 9), put through (line 10), get through (line 11), speak up (line 12), cut off (line 13)

2
1 hang up
2 speak up
3 get through
4 call back
5 put through
6 cut off
7 look up
8 hold on
9 pick up
10 get off

3
1 get through
2 speak up
3 call back
4 hang up
5 put (me) through
6 look up
7 pick up
8 get off
9 hold on
10 cut (me) off

4 Students' own answers

Learning outcome
Ask students: *What have you learned today? What can you do now?* and elicit answers: *I can understand an interview about a new business. I can use phrasal verbs. I can use phone language. I can ask for people and leave messages on the phone.*

9E Writing

An informal email

Lesson summary
Topic: Holiday plans
Vocabulary: Informal language for emails
Reading: An informal email to a friend
Writing: An informal email about future plans

Lead-in

- To introduce the topic of summer holidays, get students to make up a story about a summer holiday by playing 'Fortunately / Unfortunately'. Begin the game by saying: *Last year, I went on holiday to the beach.* Then choose a student to continue the story, beginning with the word *unfortunately*. Explain that *unfortunately* introduces a sentence with bad news, so the sentence must be about an unfortunate event, e.g. *Unfortunately, I forgot my sunscreen*. This student then chooses another student to continue the story, this time beginning with the word *fortunately*. Explain that *fortunately* introduces a sentence with good news, so the sentence must be about a fortunate event, e.g. *Fortunately, there was a supermarket at the beach, so I bought some there.*
- Students continue making sentences, alternately beginning with *unfortunately* or *fortunately*.

Exercise 1 page 110

- Demonstrate the activity to students. Ask one student: *What are you going to do this summer? Are you going away on holiday?* Tell them about some of your holiday plans, e.g. *I'm going to drive to my friend's house in Łódź.*
- Students ask and answer questions in pairs.

Exercise 2 page 110

- Remind students to read the questions and identify the key words.
- Give them two minutes to answer the questions.
- Check answers as a class.

1 Tom
2 Chelsea
3 Hong Kong
4 Jade and her friend Sally
5 Paris
6 She's going to teach tennis at a summer camp at the sports centre.

Exercise 3 page 110

- Go through the questions together. Make sure students understand *sympathy* (feeling sorry for someone).
- Elicit the answer for question 1. Students then work in pairs to find the answers.
- Check answers as a class.

116 Unit 9 Changes

1 I was really sorry to hear about your broken leg.
2 How are you now?
3 Your holiday plans sound fantastic!
4 I can't wait!
5 Write again soon!
6 PS Don't forget to take lots of photos in Hong Kong!

Exercise 4 page 110

- Go through the strategy together. Explain that adding extra details with personal information makes writing more interesting. It is also important to ask questions about the person you are writing to; this show that you are thinking about them.
- Students use the points in the strategy to help them add more information to Tom's email.

(Possible answers)

Did you enjoy your trip to Paris? / How was your job at the sports centre? Did you like teaching tennis?

We saw the new James Bond film. It was amazing! / It was very exciting and the special effects were really good.

We're going to take the train there and then we're going to stay at a small hotel near their apartment. We're going to visit Edinburgh Castle and take a trip to Loch Ness.

Exercise 5 page 110

- Students exchange emails and compare their ideas with their partner's ideas.
- Ask a few students to read out their emails.

Writing guide page 111

- Read the **task** together, making sure students are clear that they have to write an email similar to Jade's email.
- Give students five to ten minutes to complete the **ideas** stage and **plan** their email. Circulate and monitor, helping with language and ideas as necessary. Remind students to write notes, not full sentences.
- Circulate and monitor while students **write** their emails, encouraging them to use informal language and to make their writing personal. Remind them to activate the language they learned earlier in the unit (*going to* for plans, *will* for predictions, phrasal verbs).
- When students have finished, they **check** their work. Refer them to the checklist to make sure they have completed the task as well as they can.

> **Extension: Fast finishers**
> Ask **fast finishers** to swap emails with another student to read and check for mistakes.

> **Additional writing activity**
> Imagine you are going to start your first job. Write an informal email to a friend about your plans. Think about these questions:
> What is the job?
> Where is the job?
> How are you going to travel to work?
> Are you going to do any training in the job?
> How do you feel about it?

Learning outcome

Ask students: *What have you learned today? What can you do now?* and elicit answers: *I can read and understand an email about holiday plans. I can use informal language in emails. I can make my writing more personal. I can write an informal letter about my plans for the future.*

Review 9 page 111

1 1 curly 2 glasses 3 freckles 4 tanned
  5 dyed hair 6 bald 7 overweight 8 beard

2 1 donations 2 disappointment 3 predictions
  4 achievement 5 attraction 6 government

3 1 find 2 work 3 come 4 Give 5 look 6 set
  7 put 8 go

4 1 's going to retire
  2 isn't going to swim
  3 is (she) going to do
  4 's going to work
  5 are going to teach
  6 isn't going to be
  7 isn't / aren't going to stop

5 1 will fly
  2 won't stay
  3 will do
  4 will build
  5 won't be
  6 will live
  7 won't have
  8 will open

6 1 are you going to
  2 I'll
  3 I won't
  4 I'm going to
  5 I'm not going to
  6 are you going to
  7 I'm going to
  8 I won't

> **Pronunciation insight 9** Workbook page 136
> **Answer key:** Teacher's book page 155

10 Explore

Map of resources

Section A: Student's Book pages 112–113
Workbook page 84
Vocabulary bank, Types of holidays page 135
Teacher's resource disk, DVD extra + worksheet, Venice at risk page 113
Teacher's resource disk, Communication worksheet 10B

Section B: Student's Book pages 114–115
Workbook page 85
Grammar reference and practice 10.1, Workbook page 129
Irregular verb list, Workbook page 126
Teacher's resource disk, Communication worksheet 10A

Section C: Student's Book pages 116–117
Workbook page 86
Grammar reference and practice 10.2, Workbook page 130
Grammar reference and practice 10.3, Workbook page 131
Teacher's resource disk, Communication worksheet 10A

Section D: Student's Book pages 118–119
Workbook page 87
Vocabulary bank, Holidays: phrasal verbs page 135

Section E: Student's Book pages 120–121
Workbook page 90
Teacher's resource disk, Writing bank
Teacher's resource disk, Functional language bank

Review 10 page 121
Pronunciation insight 10, Workbook page 136
Progress check Unit 10, Workbook page 91
Language and skills tests 10A and 10B, Test Bank

Cumulative review Units 1–10 pages 122–123
Literature insight 5, Workbook page 100
Exam insight 5, Workbook page 110
Cumulative language and skills tests 1–10A and 1–10B, Test Bank

10A Reading and vocabulary

Tourists … Who wants them?

Lesson summary
Topic: Tourism
Vocabulary: Holiday places; prepositions of place: *in*, *on*, and *at*; Vocabulary bank: Types of holidays
Reading: Tourism – the pros and cons
Speaking: Discussing the pros and cons of tourism in your own country
Communication worksheet 10B: Have a nice holiday!

Lead-in

- Ask students to imagine that a friend or relative from another country is visiting their home town. If students live in a village or small town, they can think about their nearest large town. Students work in groups and decide what they are going to do and see with their visitors. Write the following prompts on the board to help them: *shopping, interesting buildings / museums / art galleries, sports and outdoor activities, good cafés or restaurants*.

- Give an example: *On Tuesday morning we're going to visit the library. This is an interesting old building and it's got lots of great books. Then we're going to have lunch at the Jubilee Café on the High Street. After lunch, …*

- Give students three minutes to discuss their ideas. Then ask a few students to share their ideas with the class.

Exercise 1   page 112

- Brainstorm different types of holiday on the board, e.g. *beach, sightseeing, walking, camping*.
- Tell students about the kind of holiday you enjoy, e.g. *I usually go to the mountains on holiday. I go walking with friends and sometimes we visit the villages in the area. I love the beautiful views from the mountains.*
- Students work in pairs, discussing their holiday activities.

Exercise 2   2•32   page 112

- Give students two minutes to match the places to the pictures.
- Play the recording for them to check their answers and repeat the words. Point out the different pronunciations of *ea*: /e/ in *breakfast* /ˈbrekfəst/ and /iː/ in *beach* /biːtʃ/. Also point out the silent *s* in *island* /ˈaɪlənd/.

1 theme park
2 lake
3 tower
4 coast
5 harbour
6 campsite
7 island
8 bed and breakfast
9 temple
10 beach
11 volcano
12 ski resort
13 river
14 caravan
15 camper van
16 waterfall

Exercise 3 page 112

- Focus attention on the categories and elicit or give one example for each: *historical monument: temple; natural place: beach; place to stay: ski resort; place in my town: bed and breakfast.*
- Students put some of the places in exercise 2 into the correct category.
- Check answers as a class.

1 temple, tower
2 beach, coast, harbour, island, lake, river, volcano, waterfall
3 bed and breakfast, camper van, campsite, caravan, ski resort, (theme park)
4 Students' own answers

Extra activity: Game
Demonstrate the game. Say: *I can swim here, it's very hot and most people are lying on the ground. Where am I?* (beach) Students play the game in small groups. They choose one of the places in exercise 2 and describe it in one or two sentences. The other students guess the place.

Exercise 4 2·33 page 112

- Explain that this is a general knowledge quiz about places around the world. Students do the quiz on their own.
- Play the recording for them to check their answers.
- Check answers as a class.

1 theme park; the USA
2 coast; Egypt
3 Harbour; Australia
4 volcano; Italy
5 Venezuela; waterfall
6 temple; Greece
7 island; India
8 Tower; France

Exercise 5 page 112

- With a **weaker class**, focus attention on the photos and ask students what they can see, e.g. *temple, boats, water, beach, forest, orangutan* (or *animal / monkey*, if they do not know *orangutan*). They then look for these words in the texts. Remind students to skim the text to get the general gist and not try to understand every word. Give them two minutes to do the exercise.
- Check answers as a class.

A Lama Pasang   B Mahfoud   C May   D Lia

Culture notes: Tourism
Ban Talae Nok is a small Thai village by the sea. It was founded in the early twentieth century, when people came to the area in order to find tin. Tin supplies have now run out, and most of the men in the village earn their living from the sea while many of the women make soap and batik prints. Ban Talae Nok was hit by the Boxing Day Tsunami in 2004. Forty-six villagers were killed, including sixteen children, and many houses were destroyed.

Zanzibar is made up of several islands in the Indian Ocean, off the coast of Tanzania. The capital of Zanzibar is Zanzibar City, and the old part of this city, Stone Town, is a World Heritage Site. Zanzibar is famous for its spices, especially cloves, nutmeg, cinnamon and black pepper.

The Himalayas are a mountain range in Asia with over 250 peaks, including Mount Everest, the highest mountain in the world. Many of the Himalayan peaks have great religious significance for both Buddhists and Hindus. The Himalayas extend 2,400 kilometres across five countries: Nepal, India, Bhutan, Pakistan and China.

Bukit Lawang is a small tourist village on the banks of the Bahorok River in Sumatra, Indonesia. Many people come to Bukit Lawang in order to visit the Gunung Leuser National Park, one of only two remaining natural habitats for the Sumatran orangutan. The Bohorok Orangutan Sanctuary in Bukit Lawang is also popular and offers tourists an opportunity see semi-wild orangutans.

Additional vocabulary
The following words are from the text *Tourism – the pros and cons*:

- *fish* /fɪʃ/ (v) to try to catch fish
- *batik* /bəˈtiːk/ (n) a piece of cloth printed with a pattern using wax
- *cruise* /kruːz/ (n) a holiday when you travel on a ship and visit a lot of different places
- *trek* /trek/ (n) a long hard walk, lasting several days or weeks, usually in the mountains
- *respect* /rɪˈspekt/ (v) to have a good opinion of somebody or something
- *conservation* /ˌkɒnsəˈveɪʃn/ (n) taking good care of the world and its forests, lakes, plants, and animals

Extra activity: Further discussion
Ask students to discuss these questions in groups:
Which would you prefer to do: travel around your own country or visit another country?
Do you think you would like to have tourists staying in your home? Why / why not?
Which of the four tourist destinations in the text would you like to visit? Why?

Exercise 6 page 113

- If necessary, explain that *pros* are advantages and *cons* are disadvantages. Then focus attention on the examples and ask students which text they come from (use money for educational and environmental projects: Ban Talae Nok; hotels use a lot of fresh water: Zanzibar).
- Students work in pairs to make lists of pros and cons. They then compare their lists with other pairs.

Pros use their money for education and environmental projects; tourists spend money in the restaurants and the market; tourism protects the rainforest better than conservation laws can

Cons villagers have lost their traditional way of life; hotels use a lot of fresh water; people get dangerous diseases from dirty water; tourists leave a lot of rubbish on the mountains; tourists don't respect traditions; tourists use a lot of firewood

Unit 10 Explore   119

> **V insight** Prepositions of place: *in, on* and *at*
>
> In general we use:
> - *in* with enclosed spaces, e.g. *in my pocket, in a car*
> - *at* for a point, e.g. *at the gate, at the bus stop*
> - *on* for a surface, e.g. *on the floor, on a page*
>
> There are also standard expressions which students have to learn, e.g. *at home, on Green Street, on a bicycle*.

Exercise 7 page 113

- Give students two minutes to find the highlighted words in the text and add them to the correct list. Encourage them to keep a list of expressions with *in, on* and *at* in their vocabulary notebook and to add to it whenever they come across a new expression.
- Check answers as a class. Point out that we use *in* with place names and countries.

in Ban Talae Nok, the world, Indonesia, the west, my restaurant, the village
on the coast, our beautiful beach, holiday, our island, the planet
at home, the harbour, the market

Exercise 8 page 113

- Focus attention on the photo. Ask:
  What famous city is this? (Venice)
  Do you think big cruise ships are good or bad for this city?
- Students complete the text.
- Check answers as a class.

1 in 2 in 3 on 4 in 5 on 6 in 7 in 8 on 9 at

Exercise 9 page 113

- Go through the discussion points together. Ask students to think about different aspects of tourism in their country, e.g. its effect on nature and wildlife, culture and traditions, the economy.
- Circulate and monitor, helping with vocabulary and ideas.

Vocabulary bank: Types of holidays page 135	
1 1 beach holiday	7 cruise
2 guided tour	8 day trip
3 walking holiday	9 ski trip
4 activity holiday	10 farm holiday
5 camping holiday	11 sightseeing holiday
6 study holiday	12 summer camp
2 1 cruise	5 day trip
2 camping holiday	6 sightseeing holiday
3 farm holiday	7 beach holiday
4 guided tour	8 study holiday
3 Students' own answers	

DVD extra Venice at risk

Learning outcome

Ask students: *What have you learned today? What can you do now?* and elicit answers: *I can name difference places. I can understand a text about the pros and cons of tourism. I can use the prepositions of place 'in', 'on' and 'at'. I can discuss tourism in my own country.*

10B Grammar and listening

Adventure

Lesson summary
Topic: Extreme challenges
Grammar: Present perfect: affirmative and negative
Listening: A discussion about a long cycling trip
Reading: Adventurer rows the oceans
Speaking: Talking about life experiences
Communication worksheet 10A: Have you ever … ?

Lead-in

- Write *Adventure holiday* on the board and translate *adventure* if necessary. Then tell students to imagine they are planning an adventure holiday, e.g. a trip to climb Mount Everest, a cycling trip across Africa. Ask them to work in groups and make plans for their holiday.
- Write the following questions on the board to help them:
  Where are you planning to go?
  How are you going to get there?
  Who are you going to go with?
  Why is this holiday exciting / different?
  What do you want to achieve?
- Give students three minutes to discuss their ideas in groups. Whose holiday is the most exciting?

Exercise 1 page 114

- Focus attention on the photos and tell students to use them as visual clues to choose the correct words.
- Check answers as a class. Point to the *oars* in the main photo to explain what a *rowing boat* is.

1 rowing boat 2 flying squid

Exercise 2 page 114

- Give students two minutes to read the text and check their ideas.
- Divide the class into three teams and ask each team to look for the answer to one of the three questions.
- Check answers as a class.

She has rowed across the Atlantic, Pacific and Indian Oceans.
She was at sea for 500 days.
She travelled 24,000 km.

Exercise 3 page 114

- Ask students to vote on whether they would like to go on a journey like Roz's. Then divide the class into two groups – those who would like to go on a journey like Roz's, and those who would not.
- Each group brainstorms reasons for their preference, e.g. *It's very dangerous. It's difficult to be away from your family for a long time. It's an amazing achievement. You can see some interesting things.*
- When they have finished, ask a student from each group to share their group's ideas with the class.

Language note: Present perfect affirmative and negative: regular verbs

We use the present perfect to talk about experiences, but we use the past simple to give details about it. The present perfect focuses on the experience itself.
I've sailed across the Pacific Ocean.
I sailed across the Pacific Ocean in 2009.

We also use the present perfect to talk about a recent event, e.g. an event in the news.
A car has crashed into a house in Liverpool.
Three prisoners have escaped from Parkhurst Prison.

Exercise 4 page 114

- Students find the sentences and complete them.
- Ask different students to write the completed sentences on the board. You can use these to show the structure of the present perfect. Ask students to identify the two negative sentences (1 and 4). Then point to *She's* in sentence 2 and ask: *Does this mean 'She is' or 'She has'?* (She has)

1 hasn't rowed
2 's travelled
3 have rescued
4 haven't stopped

Exercise 5 page 114

- Students look at the sentences on the board again and complete the rules.
- Check answers as a class.

1 don't say   2 have   3 past simple

Reference and practice 10.1 Workbook page 129

1 2 haven't   3 posted   4 offered   5 haven't
   6 hasn't

2 2 's baked   6 hasn't visited
   3 's walked   7 've answered
   4 's finished   8 haven't tidied
   5 've talked

3 2 My parents have taught at different schools around the world.
   3 They haven't given any money to charity.
   4 I haven't heard this song before.
   5 Mike's run two marathons this year.
   6 You've made a terrible mistake.
   7 My sister's met several famous actors.
   8 We haven't had a reply from him.

4 2 've written   6 haven't won
   3 've known   7 's ridden
   4 hasn't been   8 hasn't met
   5 've broken

Exercise 6 page 115

- Encourage students to use the contracted form *'s* + past participle after *he, she* or *it* and explain that we only use the full form in very formal contexts.
- Students work individually to complete the sentences.
- They then compare answers in pairs.

1 haven't talked; have looked
2 's studied
3 's worked
4 have discovered
5 's competed; hasn't finished
6 's used; haven't lasted
7 hasn't rowed
8 has named

Exercise 7 page 115

- Students read the article again and focus on the highlighted irregular past participles. Remind them to record the irregular forms in their notebooks and revise them regularly. Point out the list of irregular verbs on page 126 of the Workbook.
- Ask students which past participle is the same for two verbs (*been* – *be* and *go*). Explain that we can also use *gone* but the meaning is different:
  I've gone there. = I went there and I'm still there.
  I've been there. = I went there and then I came back.

be been   **become** become   **break** broken   **do** done
go been   **see** seen   **swim** swum   **take** taken   **win** won

Irregular verb list Workbook page 126

Exercise 8 page 115

- Students complete the profile, using the verbs in exercise 8. With a **weaker class**, tell students the infinitive form of the correct verb for each gap.
- Check answers as a class.

1 hasn't taken
2 hasn't won
3 has done
4 has swum
5 have broken
6 has become
7 has been
8 have seen
9 has been / has swum

Exercise 9 2•34 page 115

- Warn students that the conversation they will hear is long, but they only have to find the answers to two questions.
- Play the recording.
- Check answers as a class.

Audio script

Sophie Hey, Paul. Let's go on a cycling trip.
Paul OK. Where do you want to go? A park or the countryside?
Sophie Why don't we cycle to South Africa?
Paul South Africa?! You're joking, Sophie!
Sophie No, I'm not. I've read about some really long cycling trips. People have cycled all round the world. There's a woman called Amaya Williams. She and her husband Eric Schambion have travelled 120,000 km by bike.

Unit 10 Explore 121

Paul 120,000 km! Their poor legs!
Sophie I know! They're amazing. They've been to ninety-three different countries on six different continents. But they haven't taken their bikes to Antarctica.
Paul Well, cycling in snow isn't easy.
Sophie But they've cycled from Europe to South Africa and back again, and they've crossed the USA. They've stayed in some campsites, but they've often camped at the side of the road. They've spent six years on their bikes, and they haven't stopped.
Paul But I'm sure it hasn't all been great. They've probably had some really bad days, too.
Sophie Yes. They've had terrible weather – snow storms and things like that. They've survived a difficult day in the desert without any water. But they've seen some beautiful places: the Andes mountains, the Amazon Rainforest, waterfalls … We should go on a cycling trip like theirs.
Paul Hmm. I don't know. Maybe next year …

Sophie wants to go on a cycling trip to South Africa. Paul doesn't want to do it.

Exercise 10 2·34 page 115

- Give students a minute to read the sentences before you play the recording again.
- With a **stronger class**, ask students to choose the correct words before listening. They then listen to check their answers.
- Check answers as a class.

1 read   2 120,000   3 ninety-three   4 haven't
5 South Africa   6 camping   7 years   8 weather
9 desert   10 seen

See exercise 9 for audio script

Exercise 11 page 115

- Ask two students to read out the example dialogue.
- Students then play the game in pairs, telling each other surprising true and false facts about their life experiences.

Learning outcome

Ask students: *What have you learned today? What can you do now?* and elicit answers: *I know about Roz Savage's ocean row. I can use the present perfect affirmative and negative. I can understand a conversation about a cycling trip. I can discuss my own life experiences.*

10C Culture, vocabulary and grammar

Travel USA

Lesson summary
Topic: The USA
Grammar: Present perfect: questions and short answers; *ever* and *never*
Reading: Staycations in the USA
Vocabulary: American English
Speaking: Asking and answering about experiences
Communication worksheet 10A: Have you ever … ?

Lead-in

- Divide the class into four or five teams. Tell them that they are going to play a game called: *Name four …* . Write the following categories on the board: *States in the USA*, *Cities in the USA*, *US presidents*, *Most popular US team sports*.
- The teams race to write four names or words for each category. The first team to finish is the winner. (Note: the four most popular sports in the USA are *American football*, *basketball*, *baseball* and *ice hockey*.)
- Then ask students to open their books and see if any of the states or cities they named are in the texts.

Exercise 1 page 116

- Give students two minutes, in pairs, to read the statements in the USA Quiz and decide if they are true or false.
- Read out each statement and ask students to vote *True* or *False*. Write the scores on the board, e.g. *1: True – 7 votes; False – 11 votes*. Do not tell students if the statements are correct or incorrect.

Exercise 2 page 116

- Students read the text and check their answers to the quiz.
- Check answers as a class. They can see which statement received the most incorrect votes.
- Ask: *Which answer is the most surprising?*

1 True   2 True   3 True   4 False   5 False   6 False

Exercise 3 page 116

- Explain that the eight sentences are all from different people who want to visit the USA. Students have to read them and find the best state for the people to visit.
- With a **weaker class**, point out that students need to read *all* the information in sentence 7 to find the correct state.
- Check answers as a class.

1 Florida   2 Alaska   3 California   4 Florida   5 Hawaii
6 Massachusetts   7 Wyoming   8 California

> **Additional vocabulary**
>
> The following words are from the blog post *Staycations in the USA*:
>
> - *geyser* /ˈɡiːzə(r)/ (n) a natural spring that sometimes sends hot water or steam up into the air
> - *pow-wow* /ˈpaʊwaʊ/ (n) a meeting of Native Americans
> - *alien* /ˈeɪliən/ (n) a person or an animal that comes from another planet
> - *mine* /maɪn/ (n) a very big hole in the ground where people work to get things like coal, gold or diamonds
> - *sled* /sled/ (n) a small vehicle with pieces of metal or wood instead of wheels that you sit on in order to move over snow

Culture notes: Holidaying at home
There are a number of reasons why North Americans do not travel abroad as much as Europeans do.
- The USA offers a rich diversity of landscapes, climates and cultural experiences.
- North Americans tend to have far fewer days of paid holiday than Europeans. On average, workers in Europe have between four to six weeks of paid holiday, whereas North Americans usually have two weeks of paid holiday.
- Travelling abroad can be very expensive for North Americans because of the distances involved.

Exercise 4 page 116
- Students discuss the questions in pairs.
- Ask a few students to share their ideas with the class.

Extra activity: Further discussion
Ask students to discuss these questions in groups:
Do you prefer to travel by train, plane, bus or boat? Why?
Imagine you are planning a six-month trip around the world. Agree on six important things (apart from clothes) that you must pack.
Do you think it's important to speak the language of the country you are visiting? Why / why not?

Exercise 5 2•35 page 117
- Go through the strategy with students. Ask: *Do people use different words for things in different parts of your country?*
- Students match the highlighted words in the blog with the British English words.
- Play the recording for students to check their answers. Point out the American spelling of *theater*.

autumn fall   cinema movie theater   flat apartment
holiday vacation

Exercise 6 2•36 page 117
- Give students three minutes to match the words.
- Play the recording for them to check their answers. Point out the following:
  Football is used in American English, but it refers to American football – a different game from *football* in British English.
  Sweet (British English) is a countable noun and has a plural form, but the American English equivalent, *candy*, is uncountable.

candy sweets   eraser rubber   fries chips
garbage rubbish   pants trousers   soccer football
sweater jumper

Exercise 7 page 117
- Students work individually to complete the sentences.
- They then compare answers in pairs.
- Check answers as a class.

1 sweater; pants   2 movie theater   3 fries   4 soccer
5 vacation; apartment   6 fall

Exercise 8 page 117
- Students complete the rules on their own or in pairs.
- Check answers as a class. Explain that we nearly always use the contracted form in negative short answers.

a Have / Has   b haven't / hasn't

Reference and practice 10.2 Workbook page 130
1 2 Has he read your book?
   3 Have you received my email?
   4 Where have you put your homework?
   5 Have you found your dog?
   6 Has the glass broken?
   7 What has she said?
   8 How many people have seen this film?

Exercise 9 page 117
- Go through the first item together. Elicit the correct verb (meet) and ask: *What is the past participle of 'meet'?* (met) Write the question on the board and ask a few students to answer it.
- Students complete the questions.
- Check answers as a class.
- Students ask and answer the questions in pairs.

1 Have you met
2 Have your parents had
3 Has your English teacher taught
4 Have you and your fiends been
5 Has your school organized

Exercise 10 page 117
- Students find the underlined sentences in the blog. Ask:
  Which sentences are questions? (1 and 3)
  Has the writer left the USA? (no)
  Has the writer seen polar bears? (no)
- Students complete the rules.
- Check answers as a class.

a questions   b negative   c before

Reference and practice 10.3 Workbook page 131
1 2 Has Sara ever taught English? Yes, she has.
   3 Have they ever visited the museum? Yes, they have.
   4 Have you ever climbed a mountain? No, I haven't.
   5 Has he ever sung in public? Yes, he has.
   6 Have the girls ever played basketball? No, they haven't.
   7 Have you and your friends ever been camping? Yes, we have.
   8 Has Dan ever won a competition? No, he hasn't.
2 3 's never walked   7 've swum
   4 's jumped   8 've walked
   5 's ridden   9 haven't jumped
   6 have never sailed   10 haven't ridden

Exercise 11 page 117
- Ask two students to read out the example dialogue.
- Students then ask and answer the questions in pairs. Circulate and monitor, noting any common errors.

Unit 10 Explore   123

Learning outcome

Ask students: *What have you learned today? What can you do now?* and elicit answers: *I know about some states in the USA. I can use British English and American English words. I can ask questions and give short answers using the present perfect. I can use the present perfect with 'ever' and 'never' to talk about experiences.*

10D Listening, speaking and vocabulary

Trans-Siberian

Lesson summary
Topic: Travel itineraries
Vocabulary: Travel collocations; Vocabulary bank: Holidays: phrasal verbs
Speaking: Talking about holidays; tourist information language
Listening: Trans-Siberian travel itinerary

Lead-in

- Write *Trans-Siberian Express* on the board. Explain that many people travel through Russia on this famous train.
- Write these numbers and words in a cloud on the left hand side of the board: *990, Vladivostok, 60 km/h, 1916, 9,288 km*.
- Write these words and phrases in a cloud on the right side of the board: *total distance, officially opened, number of stations, average speed, name of the final station*.
- Students work in pairs as fast as they can to match the numbers and words on the left with the words and phrases on the right.

990 number of stations **Vladivostok** name of final station
60 km/h average speed **1916** officially opened
9,388 km total distance

Exercise 1 page 118

- Brainstorm words for different forms of transport onto the board, e.g. *train*, *boat*, *bicycle*, *bus*, *car*, *plane*. Ask students to vote for their favourite form of transport.
- Then ask them to work in pairs and think of two advantages and two disadvantages of travelling by train. Give them two minutes to discuss their ideas.
- When they have finished, ask a few students to share their ideas with the class.

Exercise 2 2·37 page 118

- Focus attention on the travel itinerary and explain that an itinerary is a plan of a journey. Students look at the itinerary and think about what type of information is needed to complete it.
- Play the recording once for students to do the exercise.
- Check answers as a class.

Audio script

Girl Hi, Matt. Have you made any plans for your next holiday?
Matt Yes, I have. Well, it's more than a holiday. I'm going to be away for two months.
Girl Wow! Lucky you! Where are you going?
Matt To China.
Girl Have you booked your plane ticket?
Matt No, I haven't. I'm not going to go by plane.
Girl What do you mean? You can't walk there!
Matt No, but I'm going to take the train.
Girl It's a very long way! Why do you want to go by train?
Matt I'm going to go on the Trans-Siberian railway. I've always wanted to go on it, because it's really famous. It's the longest train route in the world! First, I'm going to catch the train in London. The journey from London to Moscow takes forty-eight hours. Then I'm going to spend two days in Moscow.
Girl What are you going to do there?
Matt I'm going to stay in a cheap hotel – it's called the Stravinsky Hotel, I think – and see the sights … and buy some Russian souvenirs, maybe. Then I'm going to get on the Trans-Siberian railway, and six days later I'll be in Beijing!
Girl Six days on a train! That'll be boring! When you pack your bag, remember some good books.
Matt Trains aren't boring. They're great! On a plane, you don't really see anything. I'll see a lot of amazing countryside on the train.
Girl Yes, that'll be nice …
Matt And I'll meet a lot of people, too. I can't wait!
Girl But you'll be very tired at the end of your journey.
Matt Oh, I'll have a bed on the train, so I'll be OK. It's better than sleeping on a plane. And the best thing about travelling there by train is, I can go to lots of new countries. I've been abroad before, but only to France and Spain. On this journey I'm going to go to six countries for the first time: Belgium, Germany, Poland, Belarus, Russia and China.
Girl Well, it'll be an amazing adventure. Don't miss the train! And send me a postcard!

1 London **2** Moscow **3** Hotel **4** Beijing **5** six

Culture note: Trans-Siberian Express
The Trans-Siberian Express is the longest railway in the world. It begins at Moscow and ends at Vladivostok in Siberia. Many tourists also use the Trans-Siberian Express as part of their journey to Beijing. They change to the Trans-Manchurian or the Trans-Mongolian line at Ulan Ude, in Siberia.

Exercise 3 2·37 page 118

- Go through the strategy together. Ask: *When do you take notes in your language?* (e.g. in lessons at school, when taking a phone message)
- Read out the question and emphasize that students need to identify five reasons.
- Play the recording again. With a **weaker class**, pause the recording after each reason to give students time to write notes, but make sure they do not write full sentences.
- Check answers as a class.

He's always wanted to go on it, because it's really famous.
It's the longest train route in the world.
He'll see a lot of amazing countryside on the train.
He'll meet a lot of people.
He can go to lots of new countries.

See exercise 2 for audio script

Exercise 4 2·38 page 118

- Remind students that *collocations* are words that often go together. Ask if they can remember any of the collocations with *take* which they learned in Unit 8, e.g. *take control*, *take a break*, *take part*, *take photos*, *take care*.
- Students work individually to make collocations. Then play the recording for them to check their answers and repeat the phrases.
- Check answers as a class.

1 e   2 a   3 f   4 g   5 b   6 d   7 c

Exercise 5 2·39 page 118

- Students use the travel collocations in exercise 4 to complete the travel advice.
- Play the recording for them to check their answers.
- Check answers as a class.

1 Book your holiday
2 pack your bag
3 miss your train
4 catch the train
5 Stay in a hotel
6 go abroad
7 buy souvenirs
8 Send postcards

Exercise 6 page 119

- Ask two students to read out the example dialogue. Remind students to use the present perfect with *ever* and *never*, and to try to use the travel collocations in exercise 5.
- Circulate and monitor, helping with vocabulary if necessary.

Vocabulary bank: Holidays: phrasal verbs page 135

1
1 take off
2 check into
3 check out of
4 queue up
5 set off
6 get back
7 chill out
8 get into
9 get out of
10 get away
11 drop off
12 pick up
13 look forward to
14 get off
15 get on

2
1 get away
2 set off
3 pick (us) up
4 got into
5 dropped (us) off
6 got out of
7 queue up
8 got on
9 took off
10 got off
11 checked into
12 chilled out
13 looking forward to
14 check out of
15 got back

3 Students' own answers

Exercise 7 page 119

- Focus attention on the photos and ask students to guess where the places are.
- Give students one minute to discuss their ideas in pairs.
- Check answers as a class.

A St Basil's Cathedral, Moscow
B The Kremlin, Moscow

Exercise 8 2·40 page 119

- Explain to students that they are going to hear a dialogue in a tourist office. They have to identify which of the two places the tourists are talking about.
- Play the recording.
- Check the answer as a class.

Audio script
Tourist officer Hello. Can I help you?
Matt Yes, please. I'd like some information about visits to St Basil's Cathedral. What time does it open?
Tourist officer The cathedral opens at ten o'clock, seven days a week.
Matt And what time does it close?
Tourist officer At seven o'clock.
Matt And how much do tickets cost, please?
Tourist officer Two hundred and fifty rubles for adults, and fifty rubles for people under the age of eighteen.
Matt Is there a discount for students?
Tourist officer Yes, there is. Students pay fifty rubles, and on the last Sunday of each month, visits are free for students and children.
Matt Oh, that's good. It's the last Sunday of the month tomorrow. And can we take photos in there?
Tourist officer Yes, of course. But you have to pay 160 rubles.
Matt Oh, OK. And is it possible to have a guided tour of the cathedral in English?
Tourist officer I'm afraid not. We usually have English-speaking guides, but there aren't any this week.

They are talking about Photo A: St Basil's Cathedral.

Exercise 9 2·40 page 119

- Play the recording for students to complete the phrases.
- To check answers, ask individual students to read out the phrases.

1 like   2 What   3 much   4 for   5 Can we   6 it   7 of   8 I'm

See exercise 8 for audio script

Exercise 10 2·41 page 119

- Read out the phrases. With a **weaker class**, help them to identify Matt's phrases and the tourist officer's phrases before they try to complete the dialogue.
- Students compare answers in pairs by reading the dialogue.
- Play the recording again for them to check their answers.

1 D   2 E   3 B   4 A   5 C

Exercise 11 page 119

- Students read the dialogue again and identify the phrases that ask for, give and refuse permission.
- Check answers as a class.

Asking permission Can we go up the tower? Is it possible to have lunch inside?
Giving permission Yes, of course.
Refusing permission Sorry, there isn't a café.
Tourist officer offers to help Can I help you?

Exercise 12 page 119

- Students use the information in the table to role-play two dialogues. Circulate and monitor, helping with vocabulary and ideas if necessary.
- When they have finished, ask a few pairs to act out a dialogue for the class.

Learning outcome

Ask students: *What have you learned today? What can you do now?* and elicit answers: *I know travel collocations. I can understand a conversation about a travel itinerary. I can talk about my holidays. I can ask for information and permission at a tourist office.*

10E Writing

A profile

Lesson summary
Topic: Profile of a hero
Vocabulary: Linking words: *so* and *because*
Reading: A profile of TV presenter Simon Reeve
Writing: A profile of your hero or heroine

Lead-in

- Write *My hero* on the board. Ask students to think about who could be a hero. Write these categories on the board: *sport*, *TV*, *ordinary life*, *family*, *politics*.
- In small groups, students think of one 'hero' for each of the categories. When they have finished, ask one student from each group to tell the class about their group's heroes. Did groups come up with any of the same names?

Exercise 1 page 120

- Write the following questions on the board:
  What's his job? (TV presenter)
  How many countries has he visited? (more than 110)
  Which charity does he work for? (World Wide Fund for Nature)
  Then give students one minute to read the profile and find answers to the questions.
- Ask students to vote on whether they would like to watch Simon Reeve's programme and elicit reasons.

Exercise 2 page 120

- Students work individually to list all the past participles in the text and identify the irregular forms (they are all irregular).
- Check answers as a class.

(born,) made, been, met, had, eaten, written

Exercise 3 page 120

- Tell students that we use linking words to join two shorter sentences. Linking words can help to make our writing more fluent and interesting.
- Give students two minutes to underline the sentences in the profile. Make sure that they understand *reason* and *result* and translate these words into the students' own language if necessary.

He's been to more than 110 countries, so he's met a lot of different people and animals.

I really admire Simon Reeve because his programmes show you amazing places and also teach you about the lives of ordinary people around the world.

A lot of people don't leave their hotel when they go abroad, so they don't learn much about where they are.

1 reason   2 result

Exercise 4 page 120

- Do the first item together. Students then work individually to complete the sentences.
- To check answers, ask different students to read out their sentences.

1 so   2 because   3 because   4 because   5 so
6 because   7 so   8 so

Exercise 5 page 120

- Go through the strategy together. Explain that it is important to use a range of tenses in a profile in order to describe past actions, achievements and present situations.
- Students read the profile again and find examples of the three tenses.
- Ask different students to read out the example sentences and check that the whole class agrees about the tense in each sentence.

present simple is, works, does, admire, show, teach, don't leave, go, don't learn, shows
past simple was (born), left, grew up, got, started, was
present perfect has made, has been, 's met, has had, (has) been, (has) eaten, has (also) written, has had

Exercise 6 page 120

- Remind students to refer to the strategy to help them choose the right tense for each sentence.
- Students work in pairs to complete the sentences.
- Check answers as a class.

1 ate; eats
2 went; visited
3 has climbed; has swum
4 loves; goes / has been
5 has never seen; has seen
6 took

Writing guide page 121

- Read the **task** together, making sure students are clear that they have to write a profile of their hero or heroine similar to the profile of Simon Reeve.
- Give students five to ten minutes to complete the **ideas** stage and **plan** their profile. Circulate and monitor, helping with language and ideas as necessary. Remind students to write notes, not full sentences.
- Circulate and monitor while students **write** their profiles, encouraging them to use the linking words *because* and *so* and a variety of tenses. Remind them to activate the language they learned earlier in the unit (holiday places, travel collocations, the present perfect, *ever* and *never*).
- When students have finished, they **check** their work. Refer them to the checklist to make sure they have completed the task as well as they can.

Extension: Fast finishers
Ask **fast finishers** to swap their profiles with another student to read and check for mistakes.

Additional writing activity
Write a profile of a person in your family who has been very important in your life. Include details of what they did in the past, what they have achieved and why they are important to you now.

Learning outcome
Ask students: *What have you learned today? What can you do now?* and elicit answers: *I can read and understand a profile of a hero. I can use the linking words 'so' and 'because'. I can use the right tense. I can write a profile of my hero.*

Review 10 page 121

1 1 in 2 on 3 in 4 on 5 at 6 at 7 in 8 on

2 1 flat 2 rubbish 3 chips 4 trousers 5 jumper 6 holiday 7 cinema 8 autumn

3 1 pack
2 missed
3 Have (you ever) booked
4 Do (you) send
5 have (never) stayed
6 Did (you) buy
7 goes
8 took

4 1 Have (you ever) heard
2 has walked
3 has sailed
4 had
5 hasn't stopped
6 has climbed
7 has run
8 has helped
9 have donated
10 hasn't crossed
11 has said
12 have planned
13 haven't forgotten

5 1 Have (you ever) been
2 have
3 have (you) done
4 've surfed
5 've dived
6 haven't tried
7 have fallen
8 has (he) done
9 has tried
10 hasn't had
11 Has (he ever) had
12 hasn't
13 has seen

Pronunciation insight 10 Workbook page 136
Answer key: Teacher's book page 155

Cumulative review Units 1–10

pages 122–123

1 2•42

Audio script

1
Woman This is an announcement for passengers on flight EZY3650 from Madrid to Bristol. There has been a change to the departure gate for this flight. The new gate is B7. Will passengers who are waiting at gate B28 please go to the new gate immediately. That's a gate change for flight EZY3650 from gate B28 to gate B7. Boarding will start in approximately ten minutes.

2
Girl Hi! You're back. How was your holiday?
Boy Cool! I had a great time.
Girl What did you do? Did you go and see all the sights?
Boy No, we went to the beach every day.
Girl Oh. Do you like sunbathing?
Boy No, I hate it. But there were some people playing volleyball, so I went and joined in.
Girl That sounds like fun.
Boy Yeah, it was.

3
Man Good morning. I have a reservation.
Receptionist Hello. Can you give me your name, please?
Man Yes, it's Williams. Anthony Williams.
Receptionist Thank you, Mr Williams. Yes, here we are. You're staying for two nights, is that right?
Man Well, actually, I'd like to stay for an extra night. Is that OK?
Receptionist Is that just one extra night, Mr Williams?
Man Yes, that's right.
Receptionist So, three nights in total. That's fine. Here's your key card, Mr Williams. You're in room 101 on the second floor.
Man Thanks a lot.

4
Tour guide Hello, everybody. Just to let you know the plan for this afternoon before our beach barbecue tonight. Our first stop will be the aquarium – we're going to spend an hour there, so you have time to see it all. I know you'll probably all want to see the sharks … Anyway, at about four o'clock we're going to drop you in town, so that you can go shopping. And then we'll pick you up at six to go to the beach for the barbecue tonight. How does that sound?

5
Taxi driver Where to, sir?
Man Um, can you take me to the Hilton Hotel, please?
Taxi driver Which one?
Man Um, hold on a minute. I'll have a look.
Taxi driver Is it the Hilton at Paddington Station?
Man No, it isn't that one. It's nearer the centre.
Taxi driver Perhaps it's the Hilton at Trafalgar Square?
Man No, I don't think so.
Taxi driver Then it's probably the Hilton Metropole.
Man No, that doesn't sound right, either. Here it is. You were right, it's the Hilton Trafalgar Square.

1 1 a   2 a   3 c   4 c   5 b
2 Students' own answers
3 c
4 1 D   2 F   3 A   4 C   5 B
5 1 b   2 a   3 c   4 b   5 a   6 b   7 c   8 a   9 b
   10 c
6 Students' own answers

Additional materials
Literature insight 5 Workbook page 100   Answer key: Teacher's book page 153
Exam insight 5 Workbook page 110   Answer key: See website

Workbook answer key

Welcome

Welcome A (page 4)

Hello

Exercise 1 3·01

Sport: football, baseball, karate
Music: hip hop, samba, rock
Country: Russia, Brazil

Audio script

1 j – a – p – a – n, Japan
2 r – u – s – s – i – a, Russia
3 f – o – o – t – b – a – l – l, football
4 b – a – s – e – b – a – l – l, baseball
5 h – i – p – h – o – p, hip hop
6 b – r – a – z – i – l, Brazil
7 s – a – m – b – a, samba
8 k – a – r – a – t – e, karate
9 r – o – c – k, rock

Exercise 2

2 Spain   3 Belgium   4 Polish   5 Turkish   6 Italian
7 Canada   8 the Netherlands   9 Thai   10 Egyptian
11 Luxembourg   12 Irish   13 Hungarian   14 Czech
15 Slovakia   16 Argentina   17 Mexican   18 Kenyan
19 New Zealand   20 Moroccan

Exercise 3

2 like   3 'm not into   4 don't like   5 'm into

Exercise 4

Students' own answers

Exercise 5

2 two   3 thirteen   4 twenty-one   5 ten
6 twenty-seven   7 twelve   8 three   9 thirty
10 fifteen   11 sixteen   12 eighteen   13 nine
14 eleven   15 fourteen

Exercise 6

2 Brazil; ten; love; music; computers
3 China; sixteen; 'm not into; into; don't like
4 Germany; fourteen; like; music; computers
5 India; twenty-seven; like; love; don't like

Exercise 7

Students' own answers

Welcome B (page 5)

Are you in a band?

Exercise 1

2 're   3 's   4 're   5 're   6 's   7 's   8 are

Exercise 2

2 'm   3 's   4 's   5 'm   6 're   7 's   8 's   9 're   10 're

Exercise 3

1 'm not   2 aren't   3 aren't   4 isn't   5 isn't   6 are not

Exercise 4

2 I'm not Russian.
3 My home isn't in Moscow.
4 My friends aren't at a concert.
5 We aren't into samba music.
6 You aren't in a samba band.

Exercise 5

2 Is he from Glasgow?
3 Are we at the same school?
4 Am I good at music?
5 Are they into baseball?
6 Are you fifteen?
7 Is Eva good at sport?

Exercise 6

2 d   3 e   4 f   5 a   6 b

Exercise 7

2 's   3 Are   4 'm not   5 'm   6 're   7 Are   8 'm not
9 'm   10 'm   11 'm   12 Is   13 isn't   14 's   15 Are
16 aren't   17 're

Exercise 8

Students' own answers

Welcome C (page 6)

Happy families

Exercise 1

2 parents   3 son   4 sister   5 cousins   6 grandmother
7 grandparents   8 nephew   9 uncle   10 granddaughter

Exercise 2

black, blue, green, orange, pink, purple, red, white, yellow

Exercise 3

2 their   3 your   4 our   5 his   6 my   7 its

Exercise 4

2 You're   3 They're   4 Its; It's   5 Your   6 their

Exercise 5

2 excited   3 bored   4 angry   5 sad   6 hot   7 tired
8 thirsty   9 cold   10 hungry

Exercise 6

2 People   3 brothers   4 countries   5 teams   6 men

Exercise 7
1 This   2 Those   3 These   4 That

Exercise 8
Students' own answers

Welcome D page 7

Friends

Exercise 1
2 haven't got   3 hasn't got   4 've got   5 hasn't got
6 've got   7 haven't got   8 've got

Exercise 2
2 Has Bethany got a cousin?; has
3 Have they got a cat?; haven't
4 Have I got your book?; haven't
5 Have we got a new teacher?; have
6 Have you got a mobile phone?; haven't
7 Has Jake got a guitar?; hasn't

Exercise 3
2 old   3 curly   4 short   5 dark   6 straight   7 fair
8 long   9 small   10 young   11 big

Exercise 4
2 them   3 her   4 us   5 her   6 him

Exercise 5
2 it   3 me   4 him   5 us

Exercise 6
2 the   3 a   4 an   5 a; The   6 an; the

Exercise 7
2 Has   3 short   4 hasn't   5 's   6 long   7 tall   8 it
9 me   10 Has   11 a   12 him   13 him   14 short
15 them

Exercise 8
Students' own answers

Welcome E page 8

The world is a village

Exercise 1
2 Monday   3 Tuesday   4 Wednesday   5 Thursday
6 Friday   7 Saturday

Exercise 2
Across:
5 October   6 May   7 July   10 September
Down:
2 August   3 February   4 April   5 June   8 November
9 December
Extra month: January

Exercise 3
1 winter   2 spring   3 summer   4 autumn

Exercise 4
2 g   3 e   4 h   5 j   6 a   7 c   8 b   9 i   10 d

Exercise 5
2 fifty-six   3 seventy-three   4 ninety-eight
5 three hundred   6 five thousand

Exercise 6
2 three o'clock   6 twenty-five to eleven
3 twenty past seven   7 quarter to four
4 ten to six   8 five to five
5 quarter to one

Exercise 7
1 twelfth   2 third   3 sixteenth   4 fourth   5 second
6 twentieth   7 twenty-fourth   8 thirty-second
9 thirteenth   10 eleventh

Exercise 8
1 2   2 5   3 4   4 3   5 1

Exercise 9
Students' own answers

Welcome E page 9

The world is a village

Exercise 1
2 What   3 Where   4 Have   5 Describe   6 Who
7 When   8 What

Exercise 2
b How old are you?
c When is your birthday?
d Who is your favourite singer?
e Describe your family.
f What is your favourite sport?
g Have you got a pet?

Exercise 3 3•02
See exercise 2

Audio script

Presenter Today we're with Ruby Ali! She's a raga singer. Raga is traditional Indian music. Where are you from?
Ruby I'm from Sheffield. It's a big city in the UK. My grandparents are from India and my family love Indian music!
Presenter How old are you?
Ruby I'm 23.
Presenter When is your birthday?
Ruby It's on the 21st April. It's in my favourite season, spring.
Presenter Who is your favourite singer?
Ruby My mum, Rabinda! She's into music, too. She's in a raga group with me and my dad – he plays the sitar.
Presenter Describe your family.
Ruby They're great! I've got my mum and dad, and I've got two brothers, Anil and Mirat. Mum is tall. She's got long, black hair.

Dad's got short, grey hair (and he hasn't got a lot of it!). He's tall, too. Anil is short. He's got straight hair. Mirat is tall. Mirat loves sport. He's in his school football team.
Presenter What's your favourite sport?
Ruby I'm not into sport! I don't like it. But I like my brother's team. So … the answer is football!
Presenter Have you got a pet?
Ruby No, I haven't. I love dogs, but I haven't got one. Mum and Dad have got three pets. They've got two cats and a dog. Their favourite is the dog. Her name is Mili. She's my favourite, too!
Presenter Thanks, Ruby!

Exercise 4 3•02

1 Sheffield   2 23   3 21st   4 dad   5 long   6 grey
7 dogs
See exercise 3 for audio script

Exercise 5

2 Ruby, Rabinda   3 Anil   4 Mirat   5 Dad

Exercise 6

2 Indian   3 spring   4 dad   5 her dad   6 Mirat

Exercise 7

Students' own answers

Welcome reading   page 10

Languages

Exercise 1

See Workbook page 10

Exercise 2

1 around
2 a over   b under

Exercise 3

1 Over   2 Approximately   3 About   4 Over

Exercise 4

Students' own answers

Welcome Progress check   page 11

A
1 Please refer to Student's Book page 5.
2 Please refer to Student's Book page 4.
3 a twenty-three   b twelve   c eighteen   d fourteen
   e thirty
B
4 1 am   2 are
5 1 aren't   2 'm not
6 1 Are you from the USA? Yes, I am.
   2 Is he good at sport? No, he isn't.
C
7 a grandfather   b uncle   c brother   d husband   e dad
8 a your   b her   c our   d their
9 Please refer to Student's Book page 9.
10 a children   b men   c nationalities   d women

D
11 a He's got a guitar.   b They haven't got a dog.
    c Have you got a brother?
12 a old   b fair   c big   d short   e straight
13 Please refer to Student's Book page 11.
14 a; the
E
15 a thirty-one
    b three thousand, six hundred and twenty-one
    c six hundred and forty-seven
    d two thousand, one hundred and ten
16 a the twenty-fifth of December
    b the thirty-first of October   c the first of January

Unit 1 That's life

Vocabulary   page 12

Breakfast in space

Exercise 1

2 f   3 g   4 a   5 e   6 h   7 b   8 c

Exercise 2

2 have   3 get   4 start   5 do; get   6 use   7 chat
8 meet

Exercise 3

2 have a shower   3 get dressed   4 have breakfast
5 start school   6 have dinner   7 get home   8 go to bed
9 do homework   10 meet my friends

Exercise 4

2 before   3 In   4 on   5 In   6 at   7 At   8 in

Exercise 5

2 get   3 before   4 –   5 breakfast   6 start   7 at
8 On   9 in   10 home   11 do   12 watch   13 in   14 in

Exercise 6

Students' own answers

Grammar   page 13

Bright and early

Exercise 1

2 You talk a lot in class.
3 Jenny likes pizza.
4 My brother studies English and Spanish.
5 My parents use the internet at work.
6 Ana does exercise every afternoon.

Exercise 2

2 has   3 starts   4 teaches   5 go   6 does   7 likes
8 feel

Exercise 3

2 doesn't use   3 don't have   4 don't meet   5 doesn't take   6 don't chat   7 don't watch   8 doesn't sleep

Exercise 4

2 Dad doesn't use the internet at work.
3 My friends and I don't meet at the cinema.
4 My cousins don't live in London.
5 My sister doesn't sleep a lot.
6 I don't like swimming.

Exercise 5

2 doesn't work   3 start   4 have   5 don't have   6 gets
7 watch   8 finishes   9 gets   10 don't meet

Exercise 6

Students' own answers

Vocabulary and grammar page 14

British schools

Exercise 1

2 science   3 ICT   4 maths   5 history   6 religious education   7 geography   8 modern languages

Exercise 2

2 C   3 C   4 B   5 C   6 B   7 B   8 C   9 B   10 C
11 C   12 B   13 C   14 C   15 B   16 B   17 C   18 B

Exercise 3

2 Does your dad start work early?
3 Do you use the internet in class?
4 Does your friend like maths?
5 Do your friends have PE on Wednesday?
6 Does your school finish at 4.00?
Students' own answers

Exercise 4

2 When   3 Who   4 What   5 How many   6 How old
Students' own answers

Exercise 5

2 Who's   3 Do you have   4 Do you read   5 Where is
6 Do you want

Exercise 6

Students' own answers

Listening, speaking and vocabulary page 15

Journeys to school

Exercise 1

2 cycle   3 by car   4 fly   5 by train   6 drive   7 walk
8 cycle

Exercise 2

Students' own answers

Exercise 3

1 Answer   2 Look   3 Don't eat   4 Sit   5 Work
6 Don't use

Exercise 4 3·03

Correct order: 4, 2, 1, 6, 5, 3

Audio script

Teacher Good morning. Sit down, please. OK, please look at the board. What does the diagram show?
Clara Excuse me, Mr Lake. What does 'diagram' mean?
Teacher Diagram – this is a diagram. It's a picture that helps us understand something.
Clara Oh, OK. It's a diagram of a human skeleton.
Teacher Yes, good. OK. Open your books on page 122.
Clara Can you say that again, please?
Teacher Page 122. Look at the diagram and answer the questions. Yes, Clara?
Clara Sorry, I don't understand. Where is the diagram?
Teacher Page 122 – that's the wrong book. Open your textbook. And Clara, please don't use your mobile phone in class!
Clara Sorry, Mr Lake.
Teacher OK. You can work in pairs to answer the questions. Andrew! It's not lunchtime yet. Don't eat in class!

Exercise 5 3·03

a, b, d, e, g, h, j, k
See exercise 4 for audio script

Exercise 6 3·03

1 Sit down, please.
2 look at the board
3 What does 'diagram' mean?
4 Open your books on page 122.
5 Can you say that again, please?
6 Sorry, I don't understand.
7 don't use your mobile phone in class
8 Don't eat in class!
See exercise 4 for audio script

Exercise 7

Students' own answers

Reading pages 16–17

On the road

Exercise 1

1 b   2 a   3 c

Exercise 2

2

Exercise 3

2 He is on tour with Coldplay.
3 He likes watching concerts every night and working with great people.
4 Science helps Matt in his job.
5 Matt is in Paris tonight.
6 After a concert, Matt puts everything in the tour bus.

7 Matt doesn't like missing his family, only seeing the theatres in the cities they go to, and the boring journeys.

Exercise 4
1 T 2 T 3 F 4 F 5 F 6 T

Exercise 5
2 visit 3 stage 4 typical 5 concert 6 job
7 operate 8 boring

Exercise 6
2 typical 3 operates 4 boring 5 miss 6 stage
7 concert 8 job

Exercise 7
Students' own answers

Writing page 18

A questionnaire

Exercise 1
1 I've got science, English and maths today.
2 My birthday is in July. My brother's birthday is in October.
3 Have I got homework today?
4 My friend's name is Jessica Smith and she is great.
5 My favourite film is Twilight.
6 I play football on Wednesday.
7 ✓
8 My cousin is French.

Exercise 2
1 D 2 E 3 B 4 A 5 C

Exercise 3
A I love Diary of a Wimpy Kid, because it very funny and I like the drawings. I read it at night before I go to sleep. I also really like the films.
B Spring! I also love summer, because we have a long summer hoilday. I meet my friends_ swim in the sea and go on holiday with my family. Perfect!
C Tintin! He's an old cartoon caracter, but I think he's great! He's very clever. My parents love him, too! Jake, my brother, has got all the tintin books. Tintin is belgian – that's great!
D I love swimming. I meets my friends Holly and Cameron and we walk to the swimming pool. We are in a swimming team_ On Saturday, we swim in the morning from nine to twelve o'clock. Sometimes we has a swimming competition in the afternoon.
E It's April, because my birthday is in april. I also like April because I love spring. I usually cycle a lot in spring because the weather is nice.

Exercise 4
A … it very funny … G
  I also really like the films P
B hoilday S
  I meet my friends swim in the sea … P
C caracter S   tintin C   belgian C

D swimming S   I meets my friends … G
  We are in a swimming team On Saturday … P
  Sometimes we has a swimming competition … G
E april C

Exercise 5
A … it very funny …   … it's very funny …
  I also really like the films   I also really like the films.
B hoilday   holiday
  I meet my friends swim in the sea …   I meet my friends, swim in the sea …
C caracter   character
  tintin   Tintin
  belgian   Belgian
D swiming   swimming
  I meets my friends …   I meet my friends …
  We are in a swimming team On Saturday …   We are in a swimming team. On Saturday …
  Sometimes we has a swimming competition …   Sometimes we have a swimming competition …
E april   April

Unit 1 Progress check page 19

A
1 Please refer to Student's Book pages 14 and 15.
2 Please refer to Student's Book page 14.
3 Please refer to Student's Book page 15.
B
4 Please refer to Student's Book page 16.
5 We use the present simple to talk about routines and true situations.
6 1 They don't watch films at the weekend.
  2 She doesn't like pizza.
C
7 At a day school students go to school in the morning and they go home in the afternoon. At a boarding school students sleep at the school during term time.
8 a maths b Spanish / modern languages c geography
9 1 Do you study history?
  2 Does your friend like homework?
  Students' own answers
10 a What b When c Who d How many / How old
D
11 1 I go to school on foot.
   2 I go to my friend's house by bike.
12 Please refer to Student's Book page 21.
E
13 place names, months, days of the week, nationalities
14 Please refer to Student's Book page 22.
15 Please refer to Student's Book page 22.

Unit 2 Time out

Vocabulary page 20

Cycling in the desert

Exercise 1
2 playing the drums 3 playing computer games 4 rock climbing 5 painting 6 acting

Exercise 2

2 singing 3 cooking 4 playing tennis 5 dancing
6 skateboarding 7 painting

Exercise 3

2 into 3 likes 4 hates 5 interested in 6 likes
7 interested in 8 loves 9 into 10 loves

Exercise 4

2 I hate dancing.
3 They are interested in cooking.
4 Dad likes my music.
5 Kelly isn't into sport.
6 I enjoy playing computer games.
7 We aren't interested in photography.
8 I dislike playing tennis.

Exercise 5

Ball sports: cricket, hockey, rugby, volleyball
Team sports: basketball, cricket, hockey, rugby
Individual sports: aerobics, archery, athletics, badminton, canoeing, gymnastics, karate, running, skiing

Exercise 6

Students' own answers

Vocabulary and grammar page 21

Healthy living

Exercise 1

2 We don't often watch TV.
3 Jade always does aerobics on Tuesday.
4 I never do homework at the weekend.
5 Tom is usually hungry after training.
6 He usually meets Kelly after school.
7 My dad sometimes plays the guitar.
8 I am often bored on Sunday.

Exercise 2

2 She never goes to the gym on Sunday.
3 She doesn't often go swimming in the afternoon.
4 She sometimes goes to the gym in the afternoon.
5 She always relaxes on Sunday.

Exercise 3

2 do 3 play 4 play 5 play 6 go 7 play 8 do
9 go 10 go 11 play 12 do 13 do 14 do 15 go

Exercise 4

2 canoeing 3 hockey 4 rugby 5 basketball

Exercise 5

Students' own answers

Vocabulary and grammar

Making music

Exercise 1

2 keyboards 3 flute 4 guitar

Exercise 2

2 saxophone 3 keyboards
4 cello, drums, guitar, keyboards, piano, violin
5 clarinet, flute, saxophone, trumpet

Exercise 3

1 quiet 2 unusual 3 bad 4 different 5 an old
6 difficult

Exercise 4

2 sing 3 can 4 can't 5 you dance 6 can't
7 swim 8 drive

Exercise 5

2 Ryan can sing, but Abbie can't sing.
3 Abbie and Ryan can't cook.
4 Abbie can dance, but Ryan can't dance.
5 Ryan can draw, but Abbie can't draw.

Exercise 6

2 can't speak 3 can sing 4 can read 5 can play
6 violin 7 drums 8 can't play 9 can dance

Exercise 7

Students' own answers

Listening, speaking and vocabulary page 23

Superheroes

Exercise 1

2 a 3 e 4 b 5 c 6 d

Exercise 2

2 well 3 quickly 4 badly 5 hard 6 quietly

Exercise 3

2 I speak quickly.
3 Do you play your violin quietly?
4 I can't play the keyboards well.
5 Athletes train hard every day.
6 You run slowly.
7 Can you learn new dances easily?

Exercise 4 3·04

1 B 2 D 3 A 4 C

Audio script

1
Teacher Could you help me, please?
Student Yes, of course! Where's your car?
Teacher It's over here. Thank you.

2
Boy Can you get me a drink from the kitchen?
Mum No, sorry. I can't. I want to work. You can get a drink.
Boy Oh. OK, then.

3
Woman Excuse me. Can you get me a pizza, please?
Man Yes, of course! Here you are.
Woman Thank you.

4
Woman Could you open the window, please?
Guard No, sorry. I can't. It doesn't open.
Woman Oh! It's very hot in here.

Exercise 5

A, B

Exercise 6   3•04

1 Could you help me, please?; c
2 Can you get me a drink from the kitchen?; d
3 Can you get me a pizza, please?; a
4 Could you open the window, please?; b
See exercise 4 for audio script

Exercise 7

Students' own answers

Reading   pages 24–25

Free time = screen time?

Exercise 1

Students' own answers

Exercise 2

2 B   3 A   4 D   5 C

Exercise 3

2 c   3 b   4 d   5 b   6 c

Exercise 4

2 as well as   3 in fact   4 a quarter   5 going online
6 such as

Exercise 5

2 The children play football as well as hockey.
3 Liam loves art. However, he can't paint.
4 He spends a quarter of his time playing computer games.
5 I go online every evening.
6 I love modern languages, such as French.

Exercise 6

Students' own answers

Writing   page 26

An informal letter

Exercise 1

1 12 Manchester Drive   5 Dear Charlie
2 Westcliff   6 Best wishes
3 SS0 9YH   7 Gemma
4 24 October 2013

Exercise 2

a and   b but   c and / but   d and   e and / or   f but

Exercise 3

1 but   2 and   3 or   4 or   5 but   6 and

Unit 2 Progress check   page 27

A
1 Please refer to Student's Book page 24.
2 Please refer to Student's Book page 25.
B
3 Please refer to Student's Book pages 26 and 27.
4 a play rugby   b do aerobics   c go running
5 usually, often, not often, never
C
6 a Mia can ride a bike.   b Adam can't dance.
   c Can Alice swim?
7 a quiet   b unusual   c bad   d the same   e old
   f difficult
D
8 a French   b Russian   c Chinese   d Polish   e Italian
9 a badly   b quickly   c quietly   d easily   e hard
   f well
Students' own answers
10 Please refer to Student's Book page 31.
E
11 1 in the top right hand corner
    2 with Dear + the person's name
    3 with Best wishes or All the best
12 1 and   2 but   3 or
13 Please refer to Student's Book page 32.

Unit 3 Home and away

Vocabulary   page 28

House of the future

Exercise 1

2 kitchen   3 bathroom   4 living room   5 garden

Exercise 2

Inside: ceiling
Outside: roof
Inside and outside: door, wall, window

Exercise 3

2 freezer   3 fridge   4 stairs

Exercise 4
2 Behind   3 next to   4 front of   5 between
6 opposite   7 In   8 near

Exercise 5
2 flowers and a newspaper   3 sink   4 cooker   5 chair
6 wardrobe   7 rug   8 washbasin

Exercise 6
Students' own answers

Grammar page 29

Enjoy the view

Exercise 1
2 e   3 f   4 a   5 d   6 b

Exercise 2
2 any   3 a   4 some   5 a   6 any   7 any   8 an

Exercise 3
2 Is there a swimming pool? No, there isn't.
3 Are there toilets in the bedrooms? No, there aren't.
4 Is there a restaurant? No, there isn't.
5 Are there any shelves in the bedrooms? Yes, there are.
6 Are there any activities? Yes, there are.
7 Is there a fireplace? No, there isn't.
8 Is there a bed in each bedroom? Yes, there is.

Exercise 4
2 Is there a   3 There's a   4 there isn't a
5 there are some   6 Is there a   7 Are there any
8 Are there any   9 There's a   10 There's a
11 there are some

Exercise 5
Students' own answers

Vocabulary and grammar page 30

Underground city

Exercise 1
2 shopping centre   3 museum; theatre   4 bank
5 train station   6 leisure centre   7 café   8 restaurant

Exercise 2
2 Clara's library ticket   5 my sister's friend
3 men's clothes   6 the children's pictures
4 my grandmother's house

Exercise 3
1 yours   2 mine   3 hers   4 his   5 theirs   6 ours
7 ours   8 theirs   9 yours   10 ours

Exercise 4
2 yours   3 's   4 ours   5 whose   6 yours   7 mine
8 's   9 yours

Exercise 5
Students' own answers

Listening, speaking and vocabulary page 31

Around town

Exercise 1
2 town   3 village   4 countryside   5 suburb
6 city centre

Exercise 2
2 city   3 city centre   4 suburb   5 countryside   6 town

Exercise 3 3•05
1 b   2 b

Audio script
Ben Excuse me. Is this Green Street?
Woman Oh. No, it isn't. This is the High Street. Where do you want to go?
Ben I want to go to the museum.
Woman The Science Museum or the Art Museum?
Ben The Science Museum. How do you get to the Science Museum, please?
Woman Oh, OK. Let's see. Cross the road and then turn right down the High Street – towards the hospital. You can see it at the end of the street.
Ben Yes, I see it.
Woman Take the first road on the left, between the police station and the cinema. That's Summer Street, it's opposite the restaurant. Go straight up Summer Street to the university.
Ben Summer Street to the university. OK.
Woman At the end of the street, turn left onto University Street. Stay on University Street, go past the park on your right, and the Science Museum is in front of you, next to the stadium.
Ben Thanks.

Exercise 4 3•05

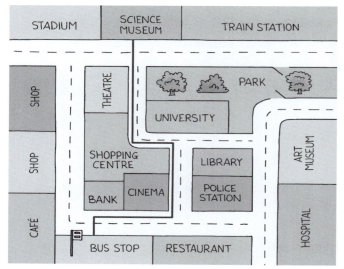

See exercise 3 for audio script

Exercise 5 3·05
Correct order: 4, 5, 7, 2, 1, 3, 8, 6
See exercise 3 for audio script

Exercise 6
Students' own answers

Reading page 32

Going down!

Exercise 1
Students' own answers

Exercise 2
1 B   2 D   3 A   4 E

Exercise 3
1 d   2 c   3 d   4 c   5 d   6 b

Exercise 4
2 damp   3 peaceful   4 create   5 cramped   6 convert

Exercise 5
2 share   3 damp   4 creates   5 converts   6 cramped

Exercise 6
Students' own answers

Writing page 34

A tourist guide

Exercise 1
1 B   2 C   3 F   4 E   5 A   6 D

Exercise 2
1 First   2 After that / Next / Then   3 After that / Next / Then   4 After that / Next / Then   5 Finally

Exercise 3
go; Have; walk; Take; Look; find; have; visit; explore

Unit 3 Progress check page 35

A
1 You build an Earthship in front of a hill.
2 kitchen
3 Please refer to Student's Book page 37.
B
4 Please refer to Student's Book page 38.
5 a Are there any shutters?   b There's a TV.   c There aren't any shelves.
6 Please refer to Student's Book pages 38 and 39.
C
7 1 It's my brother's bedroom.
   2 They are the children's toys.
8 1 It's her bag.   2 This is our house.

D
9 Please refer to Student's Book page 42.
10 Please refer to Student's Book page 43.
E
11 Please refer to Student's Book page 44.
12 Please refer to Student's Book page 44.

Unit 4 The natural world

Vocabulary page 36

It's wild!

Exercise 1
Across:
6 cloud   7 flower   9 cactus   10 plant
Down:
2 sand   3 tree   4 snow   5 mountain

Exercise 2
2 giraffe   3 tiger   4 whale   5 monkey   6 spider
7 eagle   8 elephant   9 pig   10 chicken   11 horse
12 cow

Exercise 3
2 run away   3 carry   4 bite   5 dig   6 follow
7 look for

Exercise 4
2 sand   3 cactus   4 clouds   5 flowers   6 digs
7 look for

Exercise 5
Students' own answers

Vocabulary and grammar page 37

What are you watching?

Exercise 1
1 parrot   2 tortoise   3 hamster; mouse
4 guinea pig; rabbit   5 cat; dog   6 fish   7 lizard; snake

Exercise 2
2 Are you doing   3 'm not studying   4 'm watching
5 'm learning   6 's following   7 isn't making
8 Is the tiger chasing   9 isn't running away   10 's biting

Exercise 3
2 Are the bears eating a lot? No, they aren't.
3 Are the cubs playing? Yes, they are.
4 Are the females eating? Yes, they are.

Exercise 4
2 're doing   3 're staying   4 aren't walking
5 'm looking   6 's playing   7 're carrying   8 's talking
9 're cooking   10 'm learning   11 isn't watching

Exercise 5
Students' own answers

Workbook answer key   137

Vocabulary and grammar

What's the weather like?

Exercise 1

1 hot   2 cold   3 cool   4 warm

Exercise 2

2 stormy   3 snowy   4 cloudy   5 windy   6 rainy

Exercise 3

2 snow in Prague
3 windy in the desert
4 rain in the UK
5 storm in California at the moment
6 sunny

Exercise 4

2 ✓
3 It snows every winter in Russia.
4 ✓
5 It's raining today in London.
6 Kim and Dan are doing their homework now.
7 We start school at 9.00 every day.
8 Mum is visiting my aunt this week.

Exercise 5

2 The lions are sleeping at the moment.
3 Paul is having lunch now.
4 My mum works in a zoo every Monday and Thursday.
5 Are you doing your homework now?
6 I'm not enjoying this film.
7 Have you got a pet?
8 Zoe is travelling in India this month.

Exercise 6

2 don't know   3 aren't   4 tells   5 have got
6 's coming   7 are staying   8 don't live   9 covers
10 are your grandparents doing   11 're playing
12 's buying

Exercise 7

Students' own answers

Listening, speaking and vocabulary page 39

Get active

Exercise 1

2 surfing   3 caving   4 bungee jumping
5 snowboarding

Exercise 2

2 bungee jumping   3 bouldering   4 mountain biking
5 horse riding   6 zorbing   7 canoeing   8 surfing
9 snowboarding   10 diving

Exercise 3

2 mountain biking; he doesn't like cycling
3 horse riding; she likes animals and being outdoors
4 surfing; she doesn't like going to the beach or swimming
5 snowboarding; he likes the mountains and winter
6 caving; he doesn't like the dark

Exercise 4 3·06

They decide to go to tennis club.

Audio script

Josh Oh, look. Basketball practice is cancelled today.
Anna Oh no! I can call my mum and ask her to come and pick us up.
Josh No, look, there are lots of other clubs today. Let's do something else.
Anna Good idea. What about going mountain biking?
Josh That sounds great, but I haven't got my helmet with me.
Anna OK, then. Let's go to running club! Look, they are training for a half-marathon! That's cool!
Josh I'd prefer to do something inside. Look out of the window! It's raining!
Anna Right, inside. Well, what about chess club? Can you play chess?
Josh I can, but I'd prefer to do a sport.
Anna Oh look – there's tennis in the sports hall.
Josh Fine, I love tennis. Let's go!

Exercise 5 3·06

2 mountain biking   3 running club   4 chess club
5 tennis booster
See exercise 4 for audio script.

Exercise 6

a R   b S   c R   d S   e S

Exercise 7 3·06

1 What about going mountain biking?
2 That sounds great,
3 Let's go to running club!
4 I'd prefer to do something inside.
5 what about chess club?
See exercise 4 for audio script.

Exercise 8

Students' own answers

Reading pages 40–41

Storm chasing

Exercise 1

1 c   2 b

Exercise 2

2 A   3 E   4 D   5 F

Exercise 3

1 F   2 F   3 F   4 T   5 T   6 T

Exercise 4
2 hail   3 fed up   4 shelter   5 huge   6 flooded
7 incredible

Exercise 5
2 huge   3 instruments   4 hail   5 fed up   6 incredible
7 flooded

Exercise 6
Students' own answers

Writing page 42

Describing a photo

Exercise 1
1 I think   2 probably   3 Perhaps   4 I think / Perhaps
5 probably   6 Perhaps   7 probably   8 probably

Exercise 2
(Possible answers)
1 beach, penguins
2 clouds, snow, water, mountains
3 a penguin
4 three scientists, wear jackets, push a boat into the water
5 three scientists, wear jackets, push a boat into the water
6 clouds, penguin

Exercise 3
1 (some) penguins   2 two   3 middle   4 right   5 left
6 left   7 mountains

Exercise 4
Students' own answers

Unit 4 Progress check page 43

A
1 Please refer to Student's Book page 46.
2 Please refer to Student's Book pages 46 and 47.
3 1 runs away   2 digs
4 Please refer to Student's Book page 47.

B
5 Please refer to Student's Book pages 48 and 49.
6 Please refer to Student's Book page 48.

C
7 Please refer to Student's Book page 50.
8 a snowy   b windy   c rainy
9 Sentence a describes a routine (present simple) and sentence b describes an activity that is happening now (present continuous).

D
10 Please refer to Student's Book page 52.
11 a bungee jumping, rock climbing
   b snowboarding, zorbing   c bouldering
   d caving, horse riding, rock climbing
12 Please refer to Student's Book page 53.
13 Please refer to Student's Book page 53.

E
14 Please refer to Student's Book page 54.
15 Please refer to Student's Book page 54.

Unit 5 Food, glorious food

Vocabulary page 44

Food matters

Exercise 1
2 a   3 i   4 g   5 h   6 j   7 d   8 c   9 l   10 b
11 e   12 k

Exercise 2
Across:
2 sweets   3 peach   4 rice   7 cream   8 crisps
10 sugar   11 potatoes   13 salmon   15 steak   16 grapes
Down:
2 spinach   5 ketchup   6 pepper   9 pasta   11 peas
12 salt   14 onions

Exercise 3
2 sandwich   3 pizza   4 cream   5 cake   6 salad
7 oil   8 juice

Exercise 4
Students' own answers

Grammar page 45

School food with a difference

Exercise 1
2 C   3 UC   4 C   5 UC   6 UC   7 C   8 UC   9 UC   10 C

Exercise 2
2 d   3 h   4 b   5 g   6 c   7 a   8 e

Exercise 3
2 any   3 any   4 any   5 some   6 any   7 some
8 some   9 any   10 any

Exercise 4
2 I haven't got much pasta for dinner.
3 How many potatoes do you want?
4 We have got a lot of food.
5 How much fruit is there?
6 The shop has got a lot of sweets.
7 Kia hasn't got many vegetables for her lunch.

Exercise 5
2 many   3 a lot of   4 a lot of   5 much   6 much
7 much   8 a lot of   9 many   10 a lot of   11 a lot of
12 much

Exercise 6
2 any   3 any   4 much   5 some / a lot of   6 a lot of
7 many   8 some   9 some   10 much   11 some

Exercise 7
Students' own answers

Vocabulary and grammar page 46

Traditional food

Exercise 1

2 glass 3 cup; mug 4 plate 5 bowl 6 fork; knife

Exercise 2

1 ✓ 2 ✓ 3 a packet of pasta 4 a slice of cake
5 a packet of crisps 6 ✓ 7 a jar of coffee
8 a carton of orange juice 9 ✓ 10 ✓

Exercise 2

Students' own answers

Exercise 3

2 little 3 little 4 few 5 little 6 few 7 little 8 few

xercise 4

2 There are a few tomatoes.
3 There's a little milk in the fridge.
4 I've got a few oranges.
5 There's a little bread.
6 I've got a little pasta.

Exercise 5

2 packets 3 loaf 4 little 5 carton 6 litre 7 knife
8 forks 9 glasses

Exercise 6

Students' own answers

Listening, speaking and vocabulary page 47

Delicious or disgusting?

Exercise 1

2 delicious 3 strange 4 boring 5 interesting
6 disgusting 7 scary 8 lovely

Exercise 3

1 Starters 2 Main courses 3 Drinks 4 Desserts

Exercise 4 3•07

Lisa doesn't eat meat or fish.

Audio script

Joe Mmmm! I'm hungry! Let's see … Ooh, chicken curry – that's my favourite!
Lisa Oh. I'm vegetarian. Is there anything without meat or fish?
Joe Let's see … Yes, look. Some of the starters are OK – and you can have pasta.
Lisa And all the desserts are vegetarian! Great! I'm starving!
Waiter Hello. Are you ready to order?
Joe Yes, thank you.
Waiter Would you like a starter?
Lisa Yes, please. I'd like a green salad.
Waiter OK. And what would you like for your starter?
Joe I'd like some pea and ham soup.
Waiter What would you like for your main course?
Lisa Can I have the pasta with pesto and tomato sauce, please?
Joe And I'd like the chicken curry and rice.
Waiter Would you like anything to drink?
Joe I'd like a glass of apple juice.
Lisa Can I have a sparkling water, please?
Waiter Of course. Do you want to order dessert now?
Lisa Hmmm. I love trifle! Can I have some trifle, please?
Joe No, I'm fine, thanks.
Waiter OK. Thank you.

Exercise 5 3•07

1 green salad 2 pea and ham soup 3 pasta with pesto and tomato sauce 4 chicken curry and rice
5 apple juice 6 sparkling water 7 trifle
See exercise 4 for audio script

Exercise 6

a W b J c W d J e W f L

Exercise 7 3•07

1 a 2 c 3 b 4 e 5 f 6 d
See exercise 4 for audio script

Exercise 8

Students' own answers

Reading pages 48–49

London restaurants

Exercise 1

1 Archipelago 2 Circus 3 LMNT

Exercise 2

1 a 2 c 3 c 4 b 5 a 6 c

Exercise 3

1 Circus 2 Circus 3 Archipelago 4 LMNT 5 Circus
6 Circus

Exercise 4

2 lively 3 original 4 simple 5 ancient 6 entertaining

Exercise 5

2 entertaining 3 ancient 4 original 5 tasty 6 lively

Exercise 6

Students' own answers

Writing page 50

A description of a festival

Exercise 1

1 Yes, because he starts the email with 'Hi'.
2 informal

Exercise 2

1 Chinese New Year
2 first month of spring

140 Workbook answer key

3 It's the start of a new year.
4 clean houses to clean away all the bad things; have a special meal of traditional food; have fireworks; wear red clothes; give money and sweets; have a lantern festival; have a dragon dance
5 They eat traditional food.
6 They wear red clothes.
7 His favourite part is the dragon dance.

Exercise 3

2 I also like ~~also~~ buying the presents.
3 The children in my family ~~also~~ are also very excited!
4 We ~~too~~ are busy, too.
5 My mum also sings ~~also~~.
6 My family give ~~too~~ cards, too.

Exercise 4

1 I give them presents, too.
2 We also eat chocolate eggs!
3 We are also happy.
4 We also buy them.
5 The girls send the boys cards, too.

Unit 5 Progress check page 51

A
1 Please refer to Student's Book page 58.
2 Please refer to Student's Book page 59.
3 Please refer to Student's Book page 58.
4 Fruitarians don't kill living things for food.
B
5 a uncountable b countable c uncountable d countable
6 some; any
7 1 a lot of 2 many 3 many
C
8 Please refer to Student's Book pages 62 and 63.
9 Please refer to Student's Book pages 62 and 63.
10 a a packet of b a bottle of / a carton of / a litre of c a bag of / a kilo of
11 a little; a few
D
12 Please refer to Student's Book page 64.
13 Please refer to Student's Book page 65.
E
14 1 too 2 also
15 Please refer to Student's Book page 66.

Unit 6 Material world

Vocabulary page 52

Nearly new

Exercise 1

2 shirt 3 scarf 4 cardigan 5 jacket 6 necklace
7 hat 8 rucksack 9 jumper 10 shorts 11 dress
12 sandals 13 boots 14 tights 15 shirt 16 socks
17 trainers 18 trousers

Exercise 2

2 e 3 b 4 f 5 a 6 c 7 d

Exercise 3

2 greengrocer's 3 butcher's 4 baker's 5 newsagent's
6 sandwich shop 7 department store

Exercise 4

2 unhappy 3 unfriendly 4 unlucky 5 informal
6 incomplete 7 intolerant 8 unkind

Exercise 5

Students' own answers

Grammar page 53

Cyber Monday

Exercise 1

1 Jacob 2 Helen 3 Tom 4 Jane 5 Adam

Exercise 2

2 quicker, cheaper, (bigger)
3 noisier, (better) busier
4 (easier) more unusual, more interesting
5 worse, further, (wetter)
6 safer, (bigger) larger

Exercise 3

2 My shoes are smaller than your shoes.
3 Shopping online is more convenient than going to the shops.
4 Your rucksack is better than mine.
5 George is busier than Helen.
6 Nik's clothes are more unusual than Gemma's clothes.

Exercise 4

2 bigger 3 worse 4 quieter 5 more fashionable

Exercise 5

2 better 3 cheaper 4 lower 5 more important
6 better 7 more difficult 8 more interested 9 easier
10 better

Exercise 6

Students' own answers

Vocabulary and grammar page 54

Black Friday

Exercise 1

Across:
3 dollars 6 consumer 8 credit card 10 discount
Down:
2 half price 4 wallet 5 sales 7 bargain 9 debt

Exercise 2

2 sales; discount 3 consumers; purchases
4 a credit card; debt 5 bargain; half price

Workbook answer key 141

Exercise 3

2 the busiest   3 The worst   4 The most important
5 The cheapest; the best   6 the furthest

Exercise 4

2 The most unusual thing I've got is …
3 The best shop in our town is …
4 The worst TV programme is …
5 The easiest subject at school is …
Students' own answers

Exercise 5

2 most unusual   3 most expensive   4 biggest
5 most convenient   6 best

Exercise 6

Students' own answers

Listening, speaking and vocabulary   page 55

Can't live without it

Exercise 1

2 e-reader   3 games console   4 camera   5 tablet
6 laptop   7 MP3 player

Exercise 2

2 take back   3 unzip   4 look for   5 do up   6 undo
7 put on   8 take off   9 put away   10 hang up
11 take out   12 zip up

Exercise 3   3·08

1 T
2 F: The trainers are too big.
3 T
4 T
5 F: The pink jacket isn't in the sale.
6 F: She doesn't buy anything.

Audio script

1
Assistant Hello. Do you need any help?
Boy Oh, hi. Yes, I'm looking for some new trainers.
Assistant What size are you?
Boy Size forty-two.
Assistant Well, we've got these ones here.
Boy They're cool. Do they come in different colours?
Assistant Yes, they do. We have them in black, brown or yellow.
Boy OK, can I try the yellow ones on, please?
Assistant Yes, of course … Size forty-two … here you are.
Boy Thanks.
Assistant How are they?
Boy They're too big. Have you got a smaller size?
Assistant One moment. Here. These are size forty-one.
Boy They fit perfectly. Thanks, I'll take them.
2
Assistant Hello, can I help you?
Girl Yes, please. I'm looking for a new jacket.
Assistant OK, we've got these ones here. Pink, black or red.
Girl Could I see the pink one, please?

Assistant Here you are. The changing rooms are over there.
Girl Thank you. It's lovely. How much does it cost?
Assistant Well, let's see. The pink jacket is £200.
Girl £200! Oh. Isn't it in the sale?
Assistant I'm afraid not.
Girl Oh, well, never mind then.

Exercise 4   3·08

1 C ✓   2 S ✓   3 C ✓   4 C ✓   5 C   6 S ✓   7 C ✓
8 C   9 C ✓   10 S ✓
See exercise 3 for audio script

Exercise 5

1 b   2 c   3 b   4 a

Exercise 6

Students' own answers

Reading   pages 56–57

The teen pound

Exercise 1

3

Exercise 2

1 D   2 F   3 A   4 B

Exercise 3

1 T
2 T
3 F – They buy the most popular computer games.
4 T
5 F – Some teenagers have weekend jobs.
6 T
7 F – They are too young to have credit cards.
8 F – They treat their parents like a bank.

Exercise 4

2 keep in touch   3 allowance   4 brand   5 account
6 invite   7 make-up   8 companies   9 waste

Exercise 5

2 invite   3 account   4 allowance   5 save   6 company
7 wastes   8 keep in touch   9 brands

Exercise 6

Students' own answers

Exercise 7

Students' own answers

Writing   page 58

A review of a gadget

Exercise 1

1 Dancing Feet shoe collection
2 Inside the shoes is an MP3 player that you control with your feet.

3 around £100
4 Students' own answers

Exercise 2

1 positive 2 negative 3 positive 4 positive
5 positive 6 positive

Exercise 3

1 unique 2 stylish 3 practical 4 irritating
5 reliable 6 favourite

Exercise 4

Students' own answers

Exercise 5

Students' own answers

Unit 6 Progress check page 59

A
1 Please refer to Student's Book page 68.
2 a baker's b butcher's c greengrocer's
   d fishmonger's
3 a unfair b inaccurate c unimportant d incorrect
B
4 a cheaper b bigger c busier d more exciting
   e better
5 1 Your dress is prettier than my skirt.
   2 Football is more popular than rugby.
C
6 1 discount 2 credit card 3 bargain
7 1 Ryan is the best guitar player.
   2 This jacket is the smartest in the shop.
   3 You listen to the most unusual music.
D
8 Please refer to Student's Book page 74.
9 a take off b undo c take out d unzip
10 Please refer to Student's Book page 75.
E
11 Please refer to Student's Book page 76.
12 Please refer to Student's Book page 76.

Unit 7 It's tough!

Vocabulary page 60

Different shapes

Exercise 1

1 face, neck
2 elbow, finger, shoulder, wrist
3 ankle, knee, toe
4 chest, stomach

Exercise 2

2 fingers 3 face 4 wrist 5 legs 6 ankles 7 hip
8 hand 9 head; neck 10 elbows; knees 11 arms
12 toes

Exercise 3

2 skater 3 player 4 competitor 5 visitor 6 driver
7 fighter 8 jogger

Exercise 4

2 legs 3 swimmer 4 shoulders 5 director
6 reporter 7 runner 8 stomach

Exercise 5

Students' own answers

Vocabulary and grammar page 61

Keep it clean!

Exercise 1

2 f 3 g 4 a 5 h 6 c 7 b 8 e

Exercise 2

2 do the shopping   5 walk the dog
3 load the dishwasher 4 6 hang out / bring in
   do the washing up   the washing

Exercise 3

2 should 3 has to 4 don't have to 5 have to
6 shouldn't

Exercise 4

2 I have to / don't have to wash the car on Saturday.
3 I have to / don't have to load and unload the
  dishwasher in the morning.
4 I have to / don't have to study French.
5 I have to / don't have to get up early on Sunday.
6 I have to / don't have to walk to school.
7 I have to / don't have to help my parents at home.

Exercise 5

(Possible answers)
2 You should prepare your own dinner.
3 You shouldn't go to the party at Jake's house.
4 You should tell her.
5 You shouldn't buy it.

Exercise 6

2 have to tidy 3 should do 4 have to go
5 should try to sleep 6 should read 7 shouldn't get up
8 shouldn't be 9 don't have to do 10 should clear

Exercise 7

Students' own answers

Vocabulary and grammar page 62

The first Thanksgiving

Exercise 1

1 ill 2 rich 3 happy 4 hard-working 5 dangerous

Exercise 2

2 poor 3 happy 4 hard-working 5 well

Workbook answer key 143

Exercise 3
Students' own answers

Exercise 4
2 wasn't 3 were 4 was 5 wasn't 6 was 7 were
8 were 9 were 10 was

Exercise 5
1 T
2 F – People could travel across the Atlantic by ship in 1838.
3 T
4 T
5 T
6 F – Engineers made the first telephone call across the Atlantic in 1926.

Exercise 6
2 weren't 3 was 4 could 5 was 6 couldn't
7 were 8 wasn't 9 could 10 were 11 wasn't
12 was 13 couldn't 14 was 15 were 16 could

Exercise 7
Students' own answers

Listening, speaking and vocabulary page 63

What's wrong?

Exercise 1
2 sneeze 3 dizzy 4 headache 5 sore throat; antibiotics 6 medicine; cough 7 injections 8 burn; bandage 9 a cut; a plaster 10 The flu; cold; painkillers

Exercise 2
2 plaster 3 injection 4 medicine 5 antibiotics
6 bandage

Exercise 3
1 ill; shivery; sick; unwell; weak
2 a bruise; a blocked nose; a nosebleed; a stomach ache; a temperature; a sprained ankle; hay fever; toothache

Exercise 4
2 feel weak 4 've got (a) nosebleed
3 's got hay fever 5 feel shivery

Exercise 5 3·09
2

Audio script
Dylan Hi, Helen! Are you OK?
Helen No, I'm not. I don't feel very well.
Dylan What's the problem?
Helen I've got a headache and I've got a really sore throat.
Dylan I can hear you've got a sore throat. Your voice sounds strange. Do you feel sick?
Helen No, I don't feel sick, but I've got a bad cough and I feel really cold.
Dylan Have you got a fever?
Helen I don't know.
Dylan Maybe you've got the flu. I think you should see a doctor.
Helen I'm not sure. I don't think there's any medicine for the flu. You can't take antibiotics.
Dylan Oh, yes, you're right. Well, you can take a painkiller. I've got some in my bag.
Helen Thanks. Have you got any water?
Dylan Yes, here you are. I think you should go home and go to bed.
Helen Yes, maybe you're right.

Exercise 6 3·09
4, 3, 6, 1, 5, 2
See exercise 5 for audio script

Exercise 7 3·09
1 don't feel very well 4 don't know
2 headache; I've got 5 maybe you're right
3 I don't feel sick
See exercise 5 for audio script

Exercise 8
Students' own answers

Reading pages 64–65

Medieval medicine

Exercise 1
Students' own answers

Exercise 2
1 E 2 A 3 D 4 B

Exercise 3
2 leeches
3 antibiotics
4 cutting open the swellings, cleaning the road outside the ill person's house
5 plants

Exercise 4
2 connections 3 useless 4 limited 5 – 6 common
7 fees 8 fancy 9 – 10 nonsense

Exercise 5
2 fees 3 fancy 4 limited 5 useless 6 connections
7 common 8 horrific

Exercise 6

Who do doctors treat?	doctors treat rich people
What do doctors make medicines from?	plants and animals
Are there special doctors who do operations?	No. Barbers and blacksmiths use their tools to do operations.
Are operations successful?	No. Death is common.
Do people suffer with infections?	Yes. There are often infections.

Students' own answers

Writing page 66

A letter of advice

Exercise 1

2 You could arrange a meeting with your teacher.
3 Perhaps you can ask your mother to help.
4 You should try to talk to him.
5 You shouldn't be unkind to her.

Exercise 2

Alisha isn't doing her own work.
Alisha doesn't think she can do her school work well this year.
Ruth doesn't want the teachers to know what Alisha is doing.

Exercise 3

1 Why don't you talk   4 should say
2 could   5 Perhaps
3 shouldn't copy

Unit 7 Progress check page 67

A
1 Please refer to Student's Book page 80.
2 a jogger   b designer   c competitor   d director
  e visitor

B
3 Please refer to Student's Book pages 82 and 83.
4 Please refer to Student's Book page 82.
5 (Possible answers)
  1 I shouldn't go to my swimming lesson.
  2 I should study for my maths exam.

C
6 Please refer to Student's Book page 84.
7 a safe   b ill   c lazy   d rich
8 1 I was tired.   2 They were on a boat.
  3 It wasn't cold.
9 1 Billy could swim.   2 We couldn't sing very well.

D
10 Please refer to Student's Book pages 86 and 87.
11 a broken   b feel   c have
12 1 I've got a sore throat.   2 I don't feel well.
   3 I can't sleep.
   Students' own answers

E
13 Please refer to Student's Book page 88.
14 Please refer to Student's Book page 88.

Unit 8 Life story

Vocabulary page 68

Life's ups and downs

Exercise 1

2 get divorced   3 be born   4 have a baby   5 go to university   6 fall in love   7 get a job   8 retire   9 die

Exercise 2

2 vet   3 accountant   4 scientist   5 electrician
6 teacher   7 engineer   8 plumber

Exercise 3

2 wonderful   3 natural   4 successful   5 beautiful
6 professional   7 peaceful   8 political

Exercise 4

2 successful   3 beautiful   4 powerful   5 wonderful
6 natural

Exercise 5

2 married   3 a baby   4 university   5 lawyer
6 political   7 peaceful   8 successful

Exercise 6

Students' own answers

Grammar page 69

The human story

Exercise 1

2 a   3 b   4 f   5 c   6 d

Exercise 2

2 In the twentieth century
3 in the past
4 in the 80s
5 In the late 1990s
6 when I was little

Exercise 3

1 played, walked
2 decided, retired
3 carried, tried
4 chatted, stopped

Exercise 4

2 disappeared   3 replied   4 survived   5 danced

Exercise 5

2 left   3 went   4 wore   5 sang   6 came

Exercise 6

1 saw; c   2 wrote; b   3 thought; e   4 became; d
5 made; a

Exercise 7

2 wanted   3 started   4 connected   5 wrote   6 arrived
7 appeared   8 came   9 thought   10 became

Exercise 8

Students' own answers

Vocabulary and grammar

Great writers

Exercise 1

2 fiction 3 poem 4 script 5 non-fiction 6 play
7 short story 8 article

Exercise 2

Students' own answers

Exercise 3

2 You didn't study a lot last weekend.
3 Jennie didn't visit Edinburgh last summer.
4 You didn't make the beds on Saturday.
5 The children didn't write these poems.

Exercise 4

2 Did grandma wear mini-skirts in the 1960s?
3 Did you cycle to school yesterday?
4 Who did you visit in the holidays?
5 When did Kelly arrive?
6 Where did you buy that coat?

Exercise 5

1 Yes, he did.
2 Hercule Poirot and Miss Marple.
3 Yes, we did.
4 No, I didn't.
5 They lived in Yorkshire.
6 We read *Wuthering Heights*.

Exercise 6

2 didn't know 3 read 4 Did you 5 I did 6 didn't write 7 did she do 8 want 9 didn't leave 10 didn't kill 11 did it 12 didn't stop

Exercise 7

Students' own answers

Listening, speaking and vocabulary page 71

Moments to remember

Exercise 1

2 control 3 break 4 a photo 5 a test 6 place
7 part 8 turns

Exercise 2

2 care 3 control 4 part 5 a break 6 a test
7 place 8 a photo

Exercise 3 3·10

saw someone get married, danced, listened to a band

Audio script

George Hi, Eden! Did you have a good weekend?
Eden Yes, I did. It was fantastic. My cousin, Ben, got married!
George That sounds fun.
Eden Yes, it was. We went to a big hotel in Scotland – the whole family. My grandparents, all my aunts and uncles and lots of cousins were there.
George How was the wedding?
Eden It was nice. My cousin's wife looked amazing.
George Was there a big party after your cousin got married? Was there some good music?
Eden No! It was a disaster!
George Oh no! Why?
Eden The band was terrible!
George Really?
Eden Yes, the singer was awful. He couldn't sing and we were all trying not to laugh.
George Poor man!
Eden Well, he didn't see us laughing! But in the end it was OK. We all danced and had a good time. And my cousin and his wife didn't care. They were very happy.
George Well, that's the most important thing.

Exercise 4 3·10

1 Did 2 was 3 sounds 4 How 5 disaster 6 Why
See exercise 3 for audio script

Exercise 5 3·10

1 Did you have a good weekend?
2 How was the wedding?
3 Was there some good music?
4 Why?
5 Really?
See exercise 3 for audio script

Exercise 6

1 b 2 b 3 a 4 b 5 a

Exercise 7

(Possible answers)
2 it was a disaster 3 Really 4 Bad luck 5 Poor you
6 Did you have a good weekend 7 It was fantastic
8 sounds good

Exercise 8

Students' own answers

Reading pages 72–73

The world of Roald Dahl

Exercise 1

Students' own answers

Exercise 2

1 D 2 C 3 F 4 B

Exercise 3

1 T
2 F – They are films and musicals.
3 F – They make people laugh.
4 T
5 F – She was the cruel teacher in *Matilda*.
6 T

Exercise 4

1 *James and the Giant Peach* and *Charlie and the Chocolate Factory*.
2 *Fantastic Mr Fox* and *Charlie and the Chocolate Factory*.
3 He died in 1990.
4 They can see the musical versions of *Matilda* and *The Witches*.
5 No, he hated going to boarding school because some of the teachers were unkind.

Exercise 5

2 adaptations   3 worldwide   4 scared   5 childhood
6 shows   7 cruel   8 popular   9 discover
10 comments   11 memory   12 characters

Exercise 6

2 shows   3 scared   4 cruel   5 worldwide
6 adaptation   7 delights   8 memory   9 comments
10 characters   11 discover   12 popular

Exercise 7

2 make   3 know   4 begin   5 eat   6 send   7 find

Exercise 8

Students' own answers

Writing page 74

A narrative

Exercise 1

1 at first   2 immediately   3 at last   4 soon   5 Suddenly

Exercise 2

1 immediately   2 At first   3 soon   4 at last   5 Suddenly

Exercise 3

1 They went to see a TV talent competition at a TV studio.
2 They met outside the TV centre.
3 They saw the film crew, lights and cameras.
4 They watched ten different singers.
5 They were on TV.

Exercise 4

1 because   2 wonderful   3 soon   4 stormy   5 Why?

Unit 8 Progress check page 75

A
1 Please refer to Student's Book page 90.
2 Please refer to Student's Book pages 90 and 91.
3 a natural   b wonderful   c powerful   d beautiful

B
4 1 yesterday   2 two months ago   3 six months ago
   4 the twentieth century
5 a I liked you.   b He watched TV.   c We played football.
6 1 Jess went to New York.   2 They sang together.

C
7 Mary Shelley wrote short stories and novels, such as *Frankenstein*. Emily Dickinson wrote poems.
8 Please refer to Student's Book page 95.

9 1 We didn't see the film.   2 I didn't study German.
10 1 Who wrote *Jane Eyre*?   2 What dress did you buy?
11 a didn't   b did

D
12 Please refer to Student's Book page 96.
13 Please refer to Student's Book page 97.

E
14 Please refer to Student's Book page 98.
15 Please refer to Student's Book page 98.

Unit 9 Changes

Vocabulary page 76

A new model

Exercise 1

2 a   3 g   4 c   5 h   6 b   7 d   8 e

Exercise 2

2 tanned   3 glasses   4 freckles

Exercise 3

1 are like   2 aren't like   3 doesn't look like   4 like
5 likes; doesn't like

Exercise 4

2 marble   3 metal   4 plastic   5 leather   6 wood

Exercise 5

2 looks like   3 freckles   4 bald   5 wax   6 look like

Exercise 6

Students' own answers

Grammar page 77

A new life

Exercise 1

2 aren't going to go   5 are going to write
3 'm not going to buy   6 isn't going to play
4 're going to tidy

Exercise 2

2 'm not going to spend   7 are going to join
3 'm going to walk   8 is going to organize
4 'm not going to get   9 are going to help
5 'm going to work   10 're going to do
6 'm not going to work

Exercise 4

2 Are you going to visit your grandfather?
3 Where are we going to go on holiday?
4 What film are you going to watch?
5 How are you going to travel to Italy?

Exercise 5

2 a   3 c   4 c   5 a   6 b   7 b   8 c

Workbook answer key   147

Exercise 6
Students' own answers

Vocabulary and grammar page 78

A new year

Exercise 1
2 amusement   3 attraction   4 celebration
5 decoration   6 disappointment   7 donation
8 education   9 enjoyment   10 entertainment
11 government   12 information   13 payment
14 prediction

Exercise 2
2 amusement   3 government   4 donation
5 information   6 payment

Exercise 3
2 I will / won't travel around Europe.
3 I will / won't buy a house.
4 I will / won't get a good job.
5 I will / won't get married.
6 I will / won't have children.

Exercise 4
1 ✓
2 ✗ Cara will pass her exams.
3 ✓
4 ✓
5 ✗ I won't see you for a long time.
6 ✗ The weather will be awful tomorrow!

Exercise 5
2 predictions   3 will   4 will   5 achievement
6 will find   7 won't   8 will   9 won't be   10 will work

Exercise 6
Students' own answers

Listening, speaking and vocabulary page 79

A new business

Exercise 1
2 Put together   3 look for   4 give up   5 set up
6 go ahead

Exercise 2
b put together   c look for   d go ahead   e give up
f come up with

Exercise 3
2 cut   3 look   4 pick   5 get; call   6 put; hold

Exercise 4   3•11
1 T
2 T
3 F – The course is next month.
4 F – She wants to study sculpture.
5 T

Audio script
Man Hello.
Megan Hello. Is that Dan?
Man No, this is his dad! Who's calling, please?
Megan It's Megan. Can I speak to Dan, please?
Man Hi, Megan. I'm sorry, he's not here at the moment. He's out cycling. He'll be back later this afternoon. Do you want to leave a message?
Megan Yes, can you tell him there's a sculpture course next month at the East-West Arts Centre. I'm going to do it. I think Dan would like it, too.
Man That's sounds good. What kind of sculpture?
Megan All sorts. They're going to show people how to work with metal, wood, paper – lots of things.
Man Sounds great. I'll tell him you called.
Megan Thanks. I'm going to call the Centre now.
Man OK.
Megan Bye.
Man Bye.

Exercise 5 3•11
1 It's   2 Can   3 sorry   4 Do you want   5 tell
See exercise 4 for audio script

Exercise 6 3•12
1 Could you put me   2 Who's calling   3 This is   4 I'm afraid   5 Can I take   6 I'll give him

Audio script
Receptionist Hello, East-West Arts Centre. Can I help you?
Megan Hello. Could you put me through to Jed Matthews in the sculpture studio, please?
Receptionist Yes, of course. Who's calling, please?
Megan This is Megan Yates.
Receptionist Just a moment, Ms Yates. I'm afraid Mr Matthews isn't there. Can I take a message?
Megan Yes, please. Could you ask him to call me on 0782 224 224 to give me some information about the course, please?
Receptionist 0782 224 224. Yes, no problem. I'll give him the message.
Megan Thank you. Goodbye.
Receptionist Goodbye.

Exercise 7
a Could you put me
b I'm afraid
c Can I take
d I'll give him

Exercise 8
Students' own answers

Reading pages 80–81

Youth in Action

Exercise 1
1 B   2 G   3 A   4 C   5 E   6 D

Exercise 2
1 a   2 c   3 b   4 b   5 a   6 c

Exercise 3
Introduction a   Paragraph 1 a   Paragraph 2 b   Paragraph 3 a
Paragraph 4 a   Paragraph 5 a   Paragraph 6 b

Exercise 4
2 backgrounds   3 employers   4 encourage
5 inclusion   6 runs   7 grant   8 finances

Exercise 5
2 backgrounds   3 apply   4 runs   5 Employers
6 grant   7 inclusion   8 encourage

Exercise 6
Students' own answers

Writing   page 82

An informal email

Exercise 1
1 e   2 a   3 c   4 b   5 h   6 f

Exercise 2
1 He took a music exam.
2 She went to a concert.
3 He's going to take the exam again.
4 He's going to Prague.
5 Students' own answers
6 She's going to Spain.
7 She's going to visit the Alhambra in Granada and take lots of photos.
8 She's going to work at a restaurant near the beach where she lives.

Unit 9 Progress check   page 83

A
1 Please refer to Student's Book page 102.
2 Please refer to Student's Book pages 102 and 103.
3 1 look like   2 like   3 'm like

B
4 1 Tim is going to study French next year.
   2 I'm not going to go to the cinema.
   3 Are you going to see Jack later?

C
5 Please refer to Student's Book page 106.
6 a achievement   b celebration   c disappointment
   d prediction
7 1 We'll be happy after our exams.
   2 They won't move house.

D
8 a come up with   b look up   c work out
9 Please refer to Student's Book page 109.
10 Please refer to Student's Book page 109.

E
11 a can't   b Lots   c Write
12 Please refer to Student's Book page 110.

Unit 10 Explore

Vocabulary   page 84

Tourists … Who wants them?

Exercise 1
2 lake   3 volcano   4 island   5 campsite   6 coast
7 ski resort   8 temple

Exercise 2
1 island   2 campsite   3 coast   4 volcano   5 harbour
6 temples   7 beaches   8 tower   9 lakes   10 ski resort

Exercise 3
2 in; a   3 at; e   4 in; d   5 on; c

Exercise 4
2 cruise   3 farm   4 activity   5 summer camp
6 guided tour   7 study   8 sightseeing

Exercise 5
2 a   3 c   4 b   5 a   6 a   7 b   8 d

Exercise 6
Students' own answers

Grammar   page 85

Adventure

Exercise 1
2 haven't worked   3 has rowed   4 hasn't used
5 have competed   6 haven't studied

Exercise 2
2 have travelled   3 have / has helped   4 have rescued
5 've climbed   6 've swum   7 haven't tried   8 've carried

Exercise 3
2 's done   3 's had   4 haven't swum   5 hasn't won
6 haven't been

Exercise 4
2 's swum with dolphins.
3 hasn't seen the Egyptian pyramids.
4 's taken lots of photos.
5 hasn't spent a lot of money
6 hasn't been bored

Exercise 5
2 's studied   3 's taken   4 hasn't spent   5 's travelled
6 hasn't been   7 's done   8 hasn't had
9 's slept   10 has sailed   11 's stayed   12 's been
13 hasn't been   14 hasn't finished

Exercise 6
Students' own answers

Workbook answer key   149

Vocabulary and grammar page 86

Travel USA

Exercise 1

2 an apartment 3 garbage 4 soccer 5 pants
6 sweater 7 vacation 8 eraser

Exercise 2

2 vacation 3 apartment 4 yard 5 sweater
6 movie theater 7 soccer 8 fries 9 candy

Exercise 3

2 Has Jack visited; b
3 Have your friends lived; d
4 Has Mum been; e
5 Has David tried; a
6 Have you and Dan eaten; c

Exercise 4

2 Have the children swum in a lake?
3 Has Lily studied Italian?
4 Have your friends tried these candies?
5 Has Harry competed in a marathon?
6 Have you and your brother visited the USA?

Exercise 5

2 never 3 never 4 ever 5 never 6 ever

Exercise 6

2 vacation 3 have 4 never 5 an apartment
6 never 7 ever 8 have 9 never 10 have
11 you brought 12 pants 13 candy

Exercise 7

Students' own answers

Listening, speaking and vocabulary page 87

Trans-Siberian

Exercise 1

2 a 3 e 4 f 5 d 6 c

Exercise 2

2 abroad 3 hotel 4 bus 5 bag 6 plane

Exercise 3

2 chill out 3 look forward to 4 take off 5 get on
6 get back 7 queue up

Exercise 4

2 Get into 3 get off 4 get out of 5 pick up 6 set off

Exercise 5 3·13

1 I'd like some information about Lindisfarne.
2 Is it possible to go there today?
3 So, what time is the road open tomorrow?
4 And what time does it close?
5 How much do the tickets cost, please?
6 Is there a discount for students?

Audio script

Assistant Hello. Can I help you?
Alex Yes, please. I'd like some information about Lindisfarne. Is it true that it's an island sometimes?
Assistant Yes, that's right. When the sea is at its highest level, the road is covered with water. Lindisfarne becomes an island.
Alex Wow! Is it possible to go there today?
Assistant I'm afraid not. It's too late today.
Alex So, what time is the road open tomorrow?
Assistant Tomorrow the road is open from 7.15.
Alex And what time does it close?
Assistant It closes at 14.10, but it opens again in the evening at 19.35. Do you want to visit the Lindisfarne castle?
Alex How much do the tickets cost, please?
Assistant They're £5.
Alex Is there a discount for students?
Assistant Yes, there is. It's £4.50 for students.
Alex Thank you.
Assistant You're welcome. Goodbye.

Exercise 6

1 b 2 c 3 a 4 d 5 f 6 e

Exercise 7

Students' own answers

Reading pages 88–89

Go for it!

Exercise 1

2

Exercise 2

See exercise 1

Exercise 3

1 B 2 H 3 G 4 E 5 D 6 A

Exercise 4

1 T
2 F – He has travelled to many places.
3 T
4 T
5 T
6 F – He challenged people to enter any race or competition.
7 F – He has never won a race in his life.
8 T
9 T
10 T

Exercise 5

2 river 3 volcanoes 4 home 5 taking part

Exercise 6

2 source 3 excuses 4 impressive 5 suggestion
6 crave 7 micro 8 challenges

Exercise 7

2 fortune 3 micro 4 source 5 excuses 6 challenge
7 craves 8 impressive

Exercise 8

Students' own answers

Writing page 90

A profile

Exercise 1

1 so 2 because 3 so 4 because 5 so 6 because
7 so

Exercise 2

1 She's sailed around the world. She's ridden a horse across South America. She's competed in marathons all over the world. She's run 27 marathons in 27 days.
2 Because she appeared in newspapers and on TV.
3 Her husband died of cancer.
4 She decided to run around the world.
5 Because she has big ideas for big adventures.

Exercise 3

1 – 2 so 3 because 4 – 5 because 6 –
7 because 8 – ; so

Unit 10 Progress check page 91

A
1 Please refer to Student's Book page 112.
2 a in b at c on

B
3 1 She has travelled around the world.
  2 We haven't visited Italy.
4 a hasn't been b have broken

C
5 Please refer to Student's Book page 116.
6 a garbage b pants c yard d fries
7 a Has your teacher taught; Yes, he / she has.
  b Have you been; No, I haven't.
8 a ever b never

D
9 a buy b pack c go
10 a check into b chill out c get off
11 1 What time does it open / close?
   2 How much do tickets cost, please? Is there a discount for students?

E
12 a because b so
13 Please refer to Student's Book page 120.

Literature insight 1 pages 92–93

The Adventures of Tom Sawyer – Mark Twain

Before you read

1 He was twelve when he left school. His first job was as a printer.
2 Tom lives with his Aunt Polly and his half-brother Sid.

Exercise 1

He is going down to the river.

Exercise 2

1 B 2 D 3 E 4 G 5 F 6 A 7 C

Exercise 3

(Possible answers)
1 He is painting the fence because his aunt wants him to, and because he is good at painting.
2 Because Tom makes painting the fence sound interesting and exciting.
3 Students' own answers

Exercise 4

They decide to run away.

Exercise 5 3.14

swimming and fishing

Audio script

After breakfast they walked through the island, swam some more, talked, fished, and swam again. They came back to their fire in the afternoon. Suddenly, Tom looked up and said, 'Listen. Can you hear boats?'
There were twenty or more boats on the water. Every boat in St Petersburg was out.
'What are they doing?' asked Joe.
'They're looking for a dead body, I think,' said Huck. 'They did that last summer when Bill Turner fell in the river and drowned.'
'Who's dead, do you think?' asked Joe.
The boys watched the boats. Suddenly, Tom cried, 'I know who's dead! It's us! They're looking for us!'
Tom looked at his friends. 'We're famous!' he said. 'Everybody in St Petersburg is talking about us. And they all feel sorry for us!'
Night came, and the boys went to sleep. But Tom did not sleep, and when morning came, he wasn't there!
'Huck, where's Tom?' cried Joe.
'I don't know,' Huck began, 'but—Look! There he is. He's swimming across to the island now. Hey, Tom!'
At breakfast Tom told his story.

Exercise 6 3.14

1 F – He can hear boats.
2 T
3 F – He fell in the river last summer.
4 F – Tom can't sleep.
5 F – Tom isn't there.
6 F – He tells his story at breakfast.
See exercise 5 for audio script

Exercise 7

(Possible answers)
1 Because they want to do something exciting.
2 They swim, fish and talk.
3 They see the boats after breakfast. Twenty or more boats are looking for them – every boat in St Petersburg.
4 Tom goes home.

Exercise 8

Students' own answers

Literature insight 2 (pages 94–95)

The Wizard of Oz – L. Frank Baum

Before you read
1 His father built him a theatre.
2 To a country called Oz.

Exercise 1
A big lion.

Exercise 2
2 a   3 g   4 e   5 b   6 h   7 d   8 c

Exercise 3
1 Students' own answers
2 Students' own answers
3 Dorothy wants to go back to Kansas, the Scarecrow wants some brains and the Tin Man wants a heart.

Exercise 4
They take the straw out of the Scarecrow, they break the Tin Man, they put the Lion in the cellar and they carry Dorothy and Toto to the Witch's house.

Exercise 5 3•15
She wants the red shoes.

Audio script
Now Dorothy did not know this, but the red shoes were magic. The Witch wanted those shoes very much, but Dorothy never took them off. She took them off when she washed, of course, but the Witch never went near water. She was very, very afraid of water.
Then, one morning, Dorothy's left shoe fell off.
The Witch picked up the shoe at once. 'This is my shoe now!' she shouted.
Dorothy loved her red shoes, and she was very angry. There was a bucket of water near the door. Dorothy picked up the bucket and threw the water at the Witch.
The water hit her in the face, and she cried out, 'Help! Help! The water is killing me! The – water – is …'
And then she disappeared! There was only her tall black hat and a long black dress.
Dorothy picked up her red shoe and put it on.
'Now, how can I help my friends?' she said. 'Can I call the Magic Monkeys?' She picked up the Witch's black hat and looked at it. 'Perhaps I must wear this magic hat when I speak.' So she put the hat on and called, 'Magic Monkeys – come!'

Exercise 6 3•15
1 A   2 A   3 B   4 A   5 B   6 A   7 A   8 B   9 A   10 A
See exercise 5 for audio script

Exercises 7 and 8
Students' own answers

Literature insight 3 (pages 96–97)

Macbeth – William Shakespeare

Before you read
1 He was eighteen.
2 They tell him that he is the father of kings.

Exercise 1
Banquo's ghost.

Exercise 2
1 F – They are in the dining room.
2 T
3 T
4 F – The ghost looks at him, but doesn't speak.
5 F – They can't see the ghost.
6 F – She tells them that her husband isn't well.
7 T
8 F – He does appear again.

Exercise 3
1 He says he is late.
2 He is sitting in Macbeth's chair. Macbeth is afraid.
3 No, he isn't. Students' own answers

Exercise 4
He is afraid of Macduff.

Exercise 5 3•16
She talks and walks in her sleep.

Audio script
It was late at night. One of Lady Macbeth's servants was with the doctor. 'I'm worried about the queen,' said the servant. 'At night, when she's sleeping, she sometimes gets up and walks out of her room. She talks, and does strange things.'
'When she talks in her sleep, what does she say?' asked the doctor.
'I'm sorry, sir, but I don't want to tell anyone. Look, here she comes now!'
Lady Macbeth's door opened, and she walked out. She carried a candle in her hand.
'Her eyes are open, but she's sleeping,' said the doctor. 'Where did she find the candle?'
'She always has a candle by her bed, sir. She's afraid of the night, and doesn't like it when it's dark.'
Lady Macbeth put down the candle and began to speak. 'We must wash our hands. Are you a man or are you afraid? No one is going to know the truth. What's this? Blood!'
In her sleep, she looked at her hands and cried, 'There's blood on my hands! He was an old man but he had a lot of blood in him. Macduff's wife, and their children! Where are they now?'

Exercise 6 3•16
1 a   2 a   3 c   4 b   5 c   6 c
See exercise 5 for audio script

Exercises 7 and 8
Students' own answers

Literature insight 4 — pages 98–99

The Withered Arm – Thomas Hardy

Before you read

1 Yes, it is a very old place name for the south-western part of England.
2 He brings his new wife (Gertrude) home.

Exercise 1

Her wedding-ring.

Exercise 2

1 c 2 b 3 b 4 a 5 a 6 a

Exercise 3

1 The phantom of Gertrude Lodge.
2 No, she doesn't sleep again. She feels ill in the morning.

Exercise 4

Gertrude Lodge has a withered arm.

Exercise 5 3•17

She sees it in the reflection in a glass of water.

Audio script

They found Mr Trendle's house outside the village. He was at home when they arrived. He was an old man with grey hair, and he looked long and hard at Rhoda when he saw her. Mrs Lodge told him about her arm, and he looked at it carefully.
'No, doctors can't do anything for this,' he said. 'This is the work of an enemy.'
'An enemy? What enemy?' asked Mrs Lodge.
'I don't know,' said the Wise Man, looking at her. 'But perhaps you do. I can show the person to you. Do you want me to do that?'
'Yes,' said Gertrude. 'Yes, please show me.'
Mr Trendle took Gertrude into another room, but the door was open, and Rhoda could see into the room.
The Wise Man took an egg, and did something to it. Then he put a glass of water on the table, and carefully broke the egg open. The white of the egg went down into the water, changing to a milky white colour, and moving slowly round and round.
'Look down into the water,' he said. 'Look for a face.'
Gertrude stared down into the water.
'Do you see a face?'
Gertrude whispered something, but Rhoda could not hear. When Mrs Lodge came out, her face was pale. Mr Trendle closed the door behind her, and the two women began to walk home. But things were not the same between them.

Exercise 6 3•17

1 C 2 C 3 B 4 A 5 B 6 A 7 B
See exercise 5 for audio script

Exercise 7

1 He's an old man with grey hair.
2 She sees Rhoda's face.
3 Students' own answers

Exercise 8

Students' own answers

Literature insight 5 — pages 100–101

Sherlock Holmes and the Duke's Son – Conan Doyle

Before you read

1 One of his teachers, Dr Joseph Bell.
2 He went out of his bedroom window and climbed down the ivy.

Exercise 1

He received a letter.

Exercise 2

1 He writes things in his notebook.
2 The school asked his father and he is afraid for his son.
3 Dr Huxtable is the unhappiest man in England.
4 The Duke doesn't like people talking about his life.
5 The police found a man and a boy at the station in Liverpool.
6 He doesn't learn German.
7 He caught the first train to London.
8 The German teacher owns a bicycle.

Exercise 3

Students' own answers

Exercise 4

He finds cow tracks, bicycle tracks and blood.

Exercise 5 3•18

He runs quickly down the hill to the school.

Audio script

'Shall I run back to the school?' I said.
'No, I need you with me. Look!' he said. 'There's a workman over there. He can go back to the school for us.'
I went and got the workman, and Holmes wrote a note for Dr Huxtable. The poor workman took one look at the body, and began to run quickly down the hill to Ragged Shaw.
'Now,' said Holmes, 'before we go on, let's think carefully for a minute. What do we know so far? First, the boy left freely. He was dressed, he did not leave suddenly, he wanted to go – perhaps with someone, perhaps not. But the German teacher left without his socks and without his shirt, so he left very suddenly. And why did Heidegger go? Because, from his bedroom window, he saw the boy. But why doesn't Heidegger just run after the boy? A man can easily run faster than a boy – but Heidegger doesn't do this. He gets his bicycle. Why?'
'Ah,' I said, 'because the boy has a bicycle.'
'Not so fast, Watson. Think about it. Heidegger dies eight kilometres from the school. So the boy is moving very fast, because it is eight kilometres before a man on a bicycle can get near him. And Heidegger dies because someone hits him very hard on the head.'

Exercise 6 3•18

1 school 2 note 3 hill 4 thinks 5 socks and shirt
6 died 7 very fast 8 head
See exercise 5 for audio script

Exercises 7 and 8

Students' own answers

Pronunciation insight answer key

Pronunciation insight 1 page 132

Exercises 1 and 2 3•24

/ɪz/ finishes, watches
/z/ does, goes, loves
/s/ eats, likes, talks

Exercises 3 and 4 3•25, 3•26

/ɪz/ washes, uses
/z/ has, feels, lives
/s/ gets, takes, walks

Exercise 5 3•27

1 /z/   2 /s/   3 /ɪz/

Exercise 6 3•28

2 watches; /ɪz/   3 has; /z/   4 gets; /s/   5 starts; /s/
6 uses; /ɪz/   7 chats; /s/   8 studies; /ɪz/

Pronunciation insight 2 page 132

Exercise 1 3•29

1 I can't act.   2 Carl can swim.   3 Can Sally sing?
4 I can't ride a bike.   5 Can they speak French?
6 Lisa can play football.

Exercise 2 3•30

1 a   2 a   3 b   4 a   5 b   6 b

Exercise 3 3•31

	Bethany	Leo
play football	✓	✓
play basketball		✓
do karate	✓	
draw	✓	
act		✓
sing	✓	✓
dance		
speak Spanish	✓	
speak German	✓	✓

Audio script

Bethany Hi, Leo! Look! I've got the new list of after school activities. Let's choose some.
Leo OK. Let's see. Great, there are different sports clubs on Mondays. I love sport. I can play football and basketball.
Bethany I can play football, but I can't play basketball. But I can do karate – there's karate, too.
Leo I can't do karate! I don't like it. What's on Tuesday … art … that's no good for me. I can't draw, but you can draw.
Bethany It's true. I like drawing. Hey, look, on Wednesdays there's theatre club. That's good for you. You can act and you can sing.
Leo Yes, maybe. But I can't dance. Can you dance?
Bethany No! I can't dance or act, but I can sing.
Leo What about languages on Friday? They do Spanish and German. I can't speak Spanish, but I can speak German.
Bethany I don't know. I'm not very good at languages.

Leo Yes, you are! You can speak Spanish and German!
Bethany Yes, but I can't speak them very well.

Exercises 4 3•32

1 Harry can run fast.   2 We can't sing.   3 Mum and Dad can't dance.   4 Can you speak English?   5 You can play tennis.   6 Can Carla cook?

Pronunciation insight 3 page 133

Exercise 1 3•33

1 /z/   2 /z/   3 /s/   4 /z/   5 /s/   6 /s/

Exercise 2 3•34

1 /z/   2 /z/   3 /z/   4 /s/   5 /z/   6 /z/   7 /z/   8 /z/   9 /s/

Exercises 3 and 4 3•35

1 b   2 b   3 a   4 a   5 b

Pronunciation insight 4 page 133

Exercise 1 3•36

2 chicken
3 eagle
4 desert
5 monkey
6 cactus
7 tiger
8 rabbit
9 flower
10 pigeon

Exercises 3 and 4 3•38, 3•39

1 /ɪ/   2 /ɑː/   3 /æ/   4 /iː/   5 /ɑː/   6 /æ/   7 /ɒ/   8 /ɪ/
9 /ɒ/   10 /ə/

Exercise 5 3•40

2 cactus   3 butterfly   4 water   5 tortoise   6 lizard
7 desert   8 hamster   9 polar bear   10 kangaroo

Exercise 6 3•40

1 flower
2 cactus
3 butterfly
4 water
5 tortoise
6 lizard
7 desert
8 hamster
9 polar bear
10 kangaroo

Pronunciation insight 5 page 134

Exercise 1 3•41

1 b   2 a   3 g   4 c   5 f   6 e   7 h   8 d

Exercise 2 3•42

1 bathroom, bedroom   2 train station, bus station
3 text book, book   4 football, volleyball

Exercise 3 3•43

1 bread   2 milk   3 milk   4 pizza   5 cola
6 tomatoes   7 coffee   8 crisps   9 apples   10 milk

Pronunciation insight 6   page 134

Exercise 1   3·44

	/ə/	/ɪ/
bigger	✓	
biggest		✓
oldest		✓
better	✓	
easier	✓	
furthest		✓

Exercise 2   3·45

1 My cat is thinner than your cat.
2 Berlin is the most exciting city I know.
3 Rosa is better at dancing than me.
4 This dress is the cheapest in the shop.
5 Jasmine's skirt is prettier than Claire's.
6 My bedroom is the smallest room in the house.

Exercise 3   3·46

2 e   3 d   4 f   5 a   6 c

Exercise 4   3·47

1 /ɔː/   2 /ʊ/   3 /ɔː/   4 /ʌ/   5 /ɜː/   6 /e/   7 /ɜː/   8 /ʌ/

Pronunciation insight 7   page 135

Exercise 2   3·49

1 ✓   2 ✓; ✗   3 ✗; ✓   4 ✓; ✓   5 ✓; ✓   6 ✗; ✓   7 ✗; ✗
8 ✗; ✗

Exercise 3   3·49

1 I wasn't at school today. I was at home.
2 I could dance when I was younger, but I couldn't sing.
3 We weren't safe. The road was dangerous.
4 You were popular because you could play football really well.
5 Josh could cycle to school because it was near his house.
6 You weren't happy last night. I was worried about you.
7 Kelly and I weren't well. We weren't at the cinema.
8 They couldn't go to the concert because they couldn't get tickets.

Exercise 4   3·50

1 There were two women next to the window.
2 Are you going to wear that coat for the whole winter?
3 Where were you when I was at my swimming lesson?
4 I want to write on this white paper.
5 Who is with you?
6 Are we walking in the wrong direction?

Pronunciation insight 8   page 135

Exercises 1 and 2   3·51

/t/ liked, stopped, talked
/d/ listened, loved, changed
/ɪd/ chatted, invented, visited

Exercise 3   3·52

1 started; /ɪd/   2 finished; /t/   3 watched; /t/
4 wanted; /ɪd/   5 opened; /d/   6 lived; /d/

Exercise 4   3·53

1 like; present simple   4 works; present simple
2 chatted; past simple   5 studies; present simple
3 arrived; past simple   6 loved; past simple

Exercise 5   3·54

2, 3 and 5

Pronunciation insight 9   page 136

Exercise 1   3·55

1 (01729) 752 456   3 0798 250 9461
2 0789 538 0485   4 (0208) 725 198

Exercise 2   3·56

double seven, triple eight

Exercise 4   3·57

1 look up   2 put together   3 come up with
4 find out about   5 set up   6 go ahead

Exercise 5   3·58

1 a   2 a   3 b   4 b   5 b

Pronunciation insight 10   page 136

Exercise 1   3·59

1 a   2 a   3 b   4 a   5 b   6 b

Exercise 2   3·60

1 Have you swum in a lake? Yes, I have.
2 Has she visited Thailand? No, she hasn't.
3 Have you ever been to Egypt? Yes, we have.
4 Have your parents seen the Eiffel Tower? No, they haven't.
5 Has David won the match? Yes, he has!

Exercise 3

Students' own answers

Exercise 4   3·61

1 c   2 e   3 a   4 f   5 b   6 d

Exercise 5   3·61

1 Have you ever been to the USA? Yes, I have. I went to New York last year.
2 Has David ever worked abroad? No, he hasn't. He's never had a job outside this country.
3 Have they ever cycled in France? Yes, they have. They took their bikes there last June.
4 Has Maria ever visited Canada? Yes, she has. She stayed with her friend in Toronto.
5 Have you ever seen the Parthenon? No, we haven't. We've never been to Greece!
6 Have we ever met him before? No, we haven't. We've never seen him before.

Teacher's Resource Disk

The **Teacher's resource disk** contains:
- Communication worksheets
- Documentary video clips and DVD worksheets
- How to guides
- Functional language bank
- Writing bank

Communication worksheets

Fun, communicative practice for pairs and groups

There are twenty communication activity worksheets (two per unit) and two project worksheets for Pre-Intermediate *insight*. Intended for classroom use, they offer further practice of the grammar, vocabulary, functions and skills taught in the Student's Book.
Procedural notes accompany each activity worksheet.

Unit 1 Worksheet A: Do you … ?
Activity: Categorizing, gapfill and asking questions
Language point: Prepositions of time; present simple questions and short answers (Unit 1, Sections A and C)
Time: 15–20 minutes
Materials: One handout for each pair of students, cut in half.

Unit 1 Worksheet B: In the classroom
Activity: Dialogue gapfill; remembering phrases
Language point: To practise classroom language; instructions and asking for help (Unit 1, Section D)
Time: 15 minutes
Materials: One handout for each pair of students, cut along the lines.

Unit 2 Worksheet A: How often … ?
Activity: Board game
Language point: Adverbs of frequency (Unit 2, Section B)
Time: 15–20 minutes
Materials: One handout for each group of students, counters and dice.

Unit 2 Worksheet B: Do you like … ?
Activity: Questionnaire
Language focus: Abilities, likes and dislikes; free-time activities (Unit 2, Sections A and C)
Time: 15–20 minutes
Materials: One handout for each pair of students, cut along the dotted lines and folded.

Unit 3 Worksheet A: What's in the room?
Activity: Describing and asking questions about photos
Language point: Vocabulary for rooms and furniture; *there is / are* (Unit 3, Sections A and B; Vocabulary bank 3)
Time: 15 minutes
Materials: One handout for each pair of students, cut along the line.

Unit 3 Worksheet B: Where's the bank?
Activity: Error correction; dialogue gapfill
Language point: Asking for and giving directions (Unit 3, Section D)
Time: 15 minutes
Materials: One handout for each pair of students, cut in half.

Unit 4 Worksheet A: Find someone who …
Activity: Gapfill; asking and answering questions
Language point: Present simple and present continuous tenses (Unit 4, Section Sections B and C)
Time: 15 minutes
Materials: One handout for each student.

Unit 4 Worksheet B: What's the weather like?
Activity: Three-card pelmanism
Language point: Weather nouns and adjectives (suffix *-y*) (Unit 4, Section C)
Time: 15 minutes
Materials: One handout for each group of students, cut along the dotted lines.

Unit 5 Worksheet A: Party time!
Activity: Categorizing; gapfill
Language point: Countable and uncountable nouns; *much*, *many*, *a lot of*, *a little*, *a few* (Unit 5, Sections B and C)
Time: 15 minutes
Materials: One handout for each pair of students, cut along the dotted lines.

Unit 5 Worksheet B: What's your opinion?
Activity: Anagrams; asking opinions
Language point: Opinion adjectives (Unit 5, Section D)
Time: 15 minutes
Materials: One handout for each pair of students, cut along the dotted lines.

Unit 6 Worksheet A: The more the better!
Activity: Card game (Old Maid)
Language point: Comparative and superlative adjectives (Unit 6, Sections B and C)
Time: 15–20 minutes
Materials: One handout and scissors for each pair of students.

Unit 6 Worksheet B: Find the mistakes
Activity: Error correction
Language point: Vocabulary for shopping, clothes and accessories; adjectives / negative prefixes (Unit 6, Sections A, C and D)
Time: 15 minutes
Materials: One handout for each pair of students.

Unit 7 Worksheet A: Who does what?
Activity: Wordsearch; gapfill
Language point: Noun suffixes *-er* and *-or* (Unit 7, Section A)
Time: 15 minutes
Materials: One handout for each pair of students.

Unit 7 Worksheet B: What should I do?
Activity: Asking for advice
Language point: *Should* and *have to*; making suggestions and giving advice (Unit 7, Sections B and E)
Time: 15 minutes
Materials: One set of cards per 12 students, cut along the dotted lines.

Unit 8 Worksheet A: Good weekend, bad weekend
Activity: Half dialogues
Language point: Talking about the weekend, responding, expressing interest and expressing sympathy (Unit 8, Section D)
Time: 15–20 minutes
Materials: One handout for each pair of students, cut along the dotted lines.

Unit 8 Worksheet B: That's life!
Activity: Reading and checking facts
Language point: Past simple questions (Unit 8, Sections B and C)
Time: 15–20 minutes
Materials: One handout for each pair of students, cut in half and folded where indicated.

Unit 9 Worksheet A: Tell me about your …
Activity: Asking about people's character, appearance and likes
Language focus: Different uses of *like* (Unit 9, Section A)
Time: 15 minutes
Materials: Dice and one set of cards for each group of students, cut along the dotted lines.

Unit 9 Worksheet B: What are you going to do?
Activity: Question and answer formation
Language point: *going to* for plans and intentions (Unit 9, Section B)
Time: 15 minutes
Materials: One handout for each pair of students, cut in half (vertically) and folded where indicated (to make double sided cards).

Unit 10 Worksheet A: Have you ever … ?
Activity: Gapfill; questionnaire (Find someone who …)
Language point: Present perfect and past simple (Unit 10, Sections B and C)
Time: 15 minutes
Materials: One handout for each student.

Unit 10 Worksheet B: Have a nice holiday!
Activity: Defining words and solving anagrams
Language point: Vocabulary for holidays and transport (Unit 10, Section A)
Time: 15 minutes
Materials: One handout for each pair of students.

Project 1: Free time survey report
Aims: To give students the opportunity to work on a group project to conduct a class survey. To enable students to use sources of information in English with the help of ICT
Time: 15–20 minutes + extra time for the students to interview each other (and write their reports)
Materials: One handout for each pair of students.

Project 2: Famous writer profile
Aims: To give students the opportunity to work on a project to create a mini biography (including past simple and present perfect tenses). To enable students to use sources of information in English with the help of ICT
Time: 15 minutes + extra time for the students to research and write their biographies
Materials: One handout for each pair of students.

DVD extra

There are ten documentary video clips with ready-to-use worksheets and teacher's notes to support the Elementary level of *insight*. The clips, worksheets and teacher's notes can be accessed from the Teacher's Resource Disk and also the iTools disk. Each clip has optional subtitles and has been selected to relate to, and build on, the theme of the unit. Grammar and vocabulary from the unit are recycled, but the primary function of these varied clips is to offer further cultural information via an easily-accessible medium.

The purpose of the worksheets is to help students to understand the content of the clip, and to provide ideas for discussion and project work around the content and the general topic. Each worksheet has been carefully designed for flexible use in the classroom and comprises:

- Start thinking – an activity to activate students' schemata.
- Comprehension check – a series of activities which check students' understanding of the clip and encourage them to react to it.
- Vocabulary and Extension, which can both be done without the need to see the clip again – a series of activities which exploit the clip for useful vocabulary. The extension activity allows students to work in groups and personalize the topic of the clip. Useful functional language is fed in where needed.
- Teacher's notes – these explain how to get the most out of the worksheets, provide useful background information to the clip and include a full answer key.
- Video scripts – the script for the clip is provided in full to allow further analysis of the language.

Unit 1 (1C): School life

Subject: different types of British secondary schools

Grammar: present simple affirmative and negative; present simple questions and short answers; question words

Vocabulary: attend   blazer   boarding school   dormitory   drama   finish   packed lunch   PE   private school   pupil   school canteen   school uniform   secondary school   start   state school

Extension activity: debate 'The best school timetable is from 7.30 in the morning to 1.30 in the afternoon'

Unit 2 (2C): A famous music school

Subject: Chetham's School of Music

Grammar: adverbs of frequency; *can / can't* for ability

Vocabulary: beautiful(ly)   become   brilliant(ly)   gain (experience)   hard(ly)   have (lessons)   ideal(ly)   intense(ly)   miss   perfect(ly)   play (the violin)   read (music)   spend (time)   successful(ly)   win

Extension activity: make a poster about a famous musician

Unit 3 (3C): A room with a view?

Subject: the Malmaison Oxford hotel

Grammar: *there is / there are* with *some / any*; possessive *'s*; possessive pronouns and *whose*

Vocabulary: beautiful   delicious   fascinating   fashionable   front door   heavy   high   hotel room   internet access   open   prison cell   room service   satellite TV   tiny

Extension activity: give a tour of an old building

Unit 4 (4C): Measuring the weather

Subject: the weather

Grammar: present continuous; present simple or present continuous

Vocabulary: average   blow   crops   device   direction   drop   fall   grow   level   measure   monitor   sleet   speed   temperature

Extension activity: give a presentation about a country's weather

Unit 5 (5C): Borough Market
Subject: a London food market
Grammar: countable and uncountable nouns; *much, many, a lot of, a little, a few*
Vocabulary: butcher delicious enormous famous fishmonger healthy ingredients oyster parsnip railway reasonable snack stall sweet traditional unusual
Extension activity: prepare a dinner menu and write a shopping list

Unit 6 (6B): Shopping in London
Subject: shopping
Grammar: comparative adjectives
Vocabulary: brand clothes shop designer clothes fashion designer Ferris wheel high street make-up perfume roof toys tourist destination
Extension activity: make an advert for a new shopping centre

Unit 7 (7B): Cleaning beaches
Subject: beach cleaning
Grammar: *should / shouldn't, have to, don't have to, want to*
Vocabulary: conserve difficult environmental importance international leaders manufacturer natural operations organization relaxing rewarding stunning unfortunately
Extension activity: give a presentation about a volunteer project

Unit 8 (8C): The magic of Roald Dahl
Subject: a popular children's author
Grammar: past simple affirmative: regular and irregular verbs; past simple negative, questions and short answers
Vocabulary: accident adventure army boarding school cheerful dramatic homesick hut inspiration lonely magical naughty replica report successful
Extension activity: make a poster about a famous English-language writer

Unit 9 (9D): i-mag: 'zine for teens
Subject: an online magazine for teenagers
Grammar: plans and intentions: *going to*: plans and intensions; *will*: predictions
Vocabulary: beginning contact discuss improve issue oversee range reporter reviewer role run teenager view
Extension activity: make a page for a magazine

Unit 10 (10A): Venice at risk
Subject: the risks of sinking water levels in Venice
Grammar: present perfect; present perfect with *ever* and *never*
Vocabulary: canal deal (with) defend drop flood foundations lagoon mainland refugee resident sink solve threaten tide trade
Extension activity: give a presentation about a well-known city